STANHOPE FORBES
AND THE NEWLYN SCHOOL

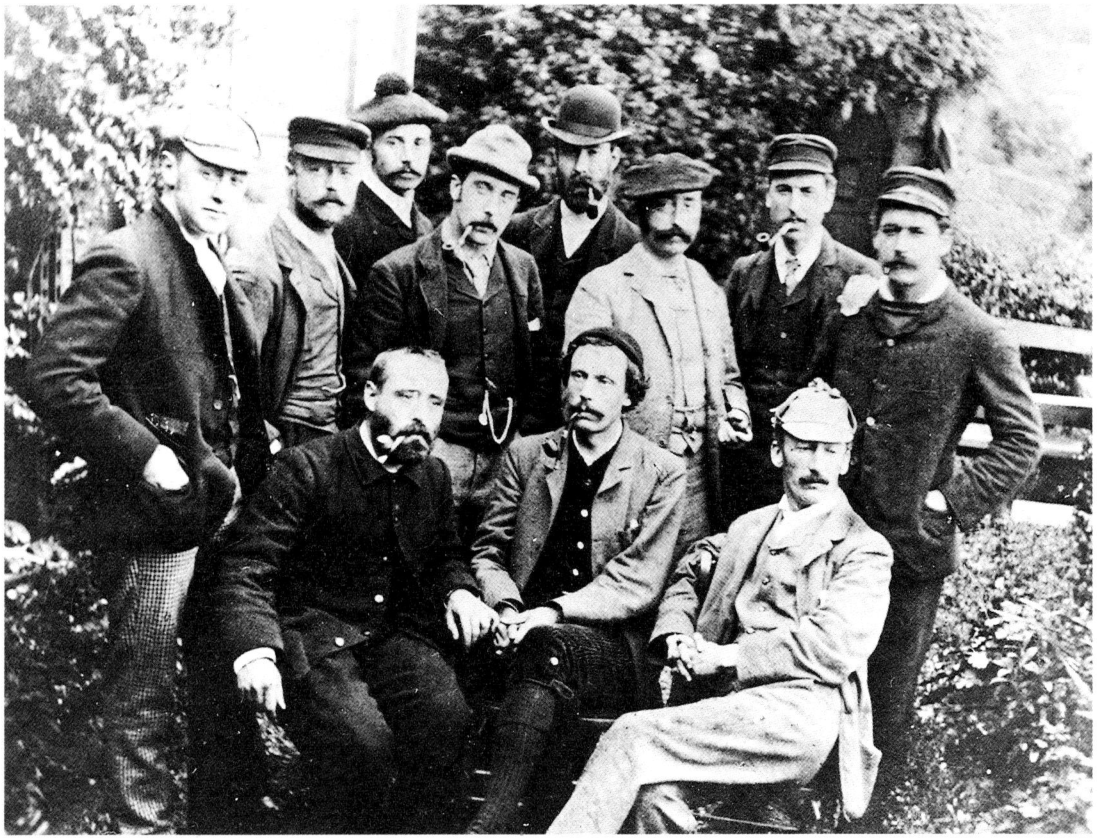

Artists in Newlyn, probably Autumn 1884.
Left to right standing: Frank Bodilly, Fred Millard, Frank Bramley, William Blandford Fletcher, William Breakspeare, Ralph Todd. Left to right seated: William Wainwright, Edwin Harris, Stanhope Forbes.

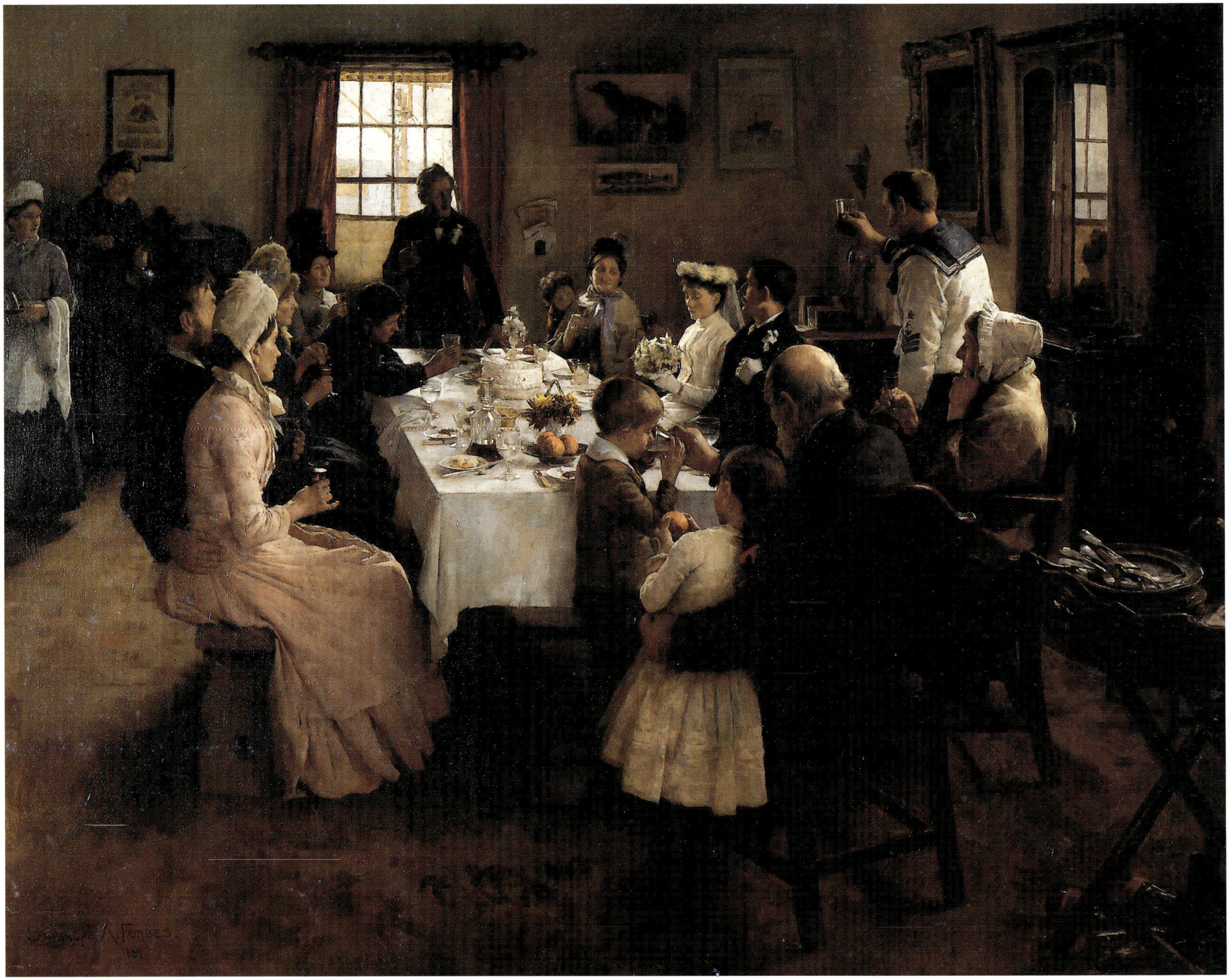

THE HEALTH OF THE BRIDE (1889)
Stanhope Alexander Forbes
Oil on canvas, 60 x 78¾in (152.5 x 200cm)
Tate Gallery, London

CAROLINE FOX

STANHOPE FORBES AND THE NEWLYN SCHOOL

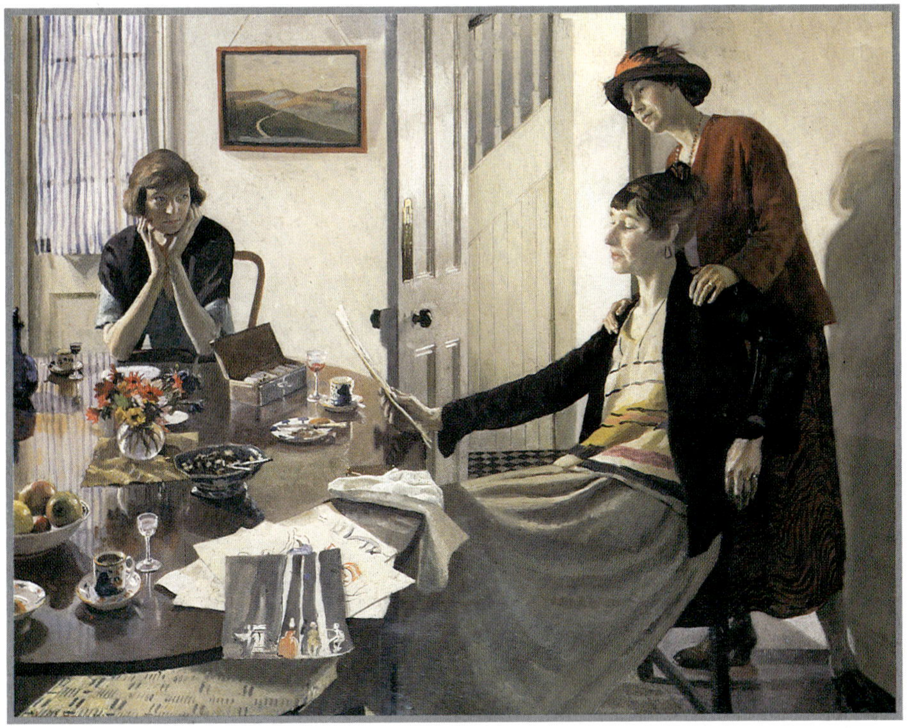

THE CRITICS (see page 77)

David & Charles

ACKNOWLEDGEMENTS

The people and organisations who contributed information, lent paintings and in any way helped with the research and organisation of the 1979 and 1985 Newlyn School Exhibitions, are too numerous to mention individually, but I would like nevertheless to express my great debt to them all. I am also most grateful to all owners of paintings, both private and public, which are illustrated in this book, and in particular to the Richard Green Gallery, Christie's, and the David Messum Gallery. I am especially grateful to Edward Morris of the Walker Art Gallery, Liverpool, who most generously made available his research on the three paintings by Forbes in the Walker Art Gallery's Collection. Thanks also go to Wendy Sheridan of the Science Museum for additional information on Forbes' *Munition Girls*.

Thanks to George Greenfield, literary executor of the Dame Laura Knight Estate, for permission to quote from *The Magic of a Line*.

The following publications have been a great help in writing the book and may also serve as further reading for those interested:

Mrs Lionel Birch, *Stanhope A. Forbes ARA and Elizabeth Stanhope Forbes ARWS* (1906).

Caroline Fox and Francis Greenacre, *Painting in Newlyn 1880–1930* (Barbican Art Gallery Exhibition catalogue 1985). (For further detail see: Caroline Fox and Francis Greenacre: *Artists of the Newlyn School 1880–1900* (1979) and Caroline Fox: *Painting in Newlyn 1900–1930* (1985). Both exhibition catalogues produced by the Newlyn Orion Galleries, Newlyn, Cornwall).

Betsy Coggar-Rezelmann, *The Newlyn Artists and their place in late-Victorian Art* (Thesis for Doctorate of Philosophy, Indiana University, 1984).

Laura Wortley: *British Impressionism – A Garden of Bright Images* (The Studio Fine Art Publications, 1987).

Kenneth McConkey, *British Impressionism* (Phaidon Press, 1989).

Jacket illustrations. (Front) Stanhope Forbes, *Gala Day at Newlyn* (1907), oil on canvas, 41¾×53¾in, Gray Art Gallery and Museum, Hartlepool. (Back, clockwise from top left) Elizabeth Forbes, *A Game of 'Old Maid'* (1891), oil on canvas, 40×25in (101.5×63.5cm), private collection; Laura Knight, *The Beach* (1909), oil on canvas, 50¼×60¼in (127.5×153cm), Laing Art Gallery, Newcastle upon Tyne; Harold Harvey, *The Close of a Summer's Day* (1909), oil on canvas, 50×40in (127×101.5cm) private collection; Harold Knight, *In the Spring* (1908–9), oil on canvas, 52×62¼in (132×158cm), Laing Art Gallery, Newcastle upon Tyne.

A DAVID & CHARLES BOOK

First published 1993
Reprinted 1994, 1997
First paperback edition 1997

British Library Cataloguing in Publication Data
A catalogue record for this book is available from the British Library.

Hardback ISBN 0 7153 9911 X
Paperback ISBN 0 7153 0693 6

Typeset by ABM Typographics Ltd, Hull
and printed in Singapore by CS Graphics Pte Ltd
for David & Charles
Brunel House Newton Abbot Devon

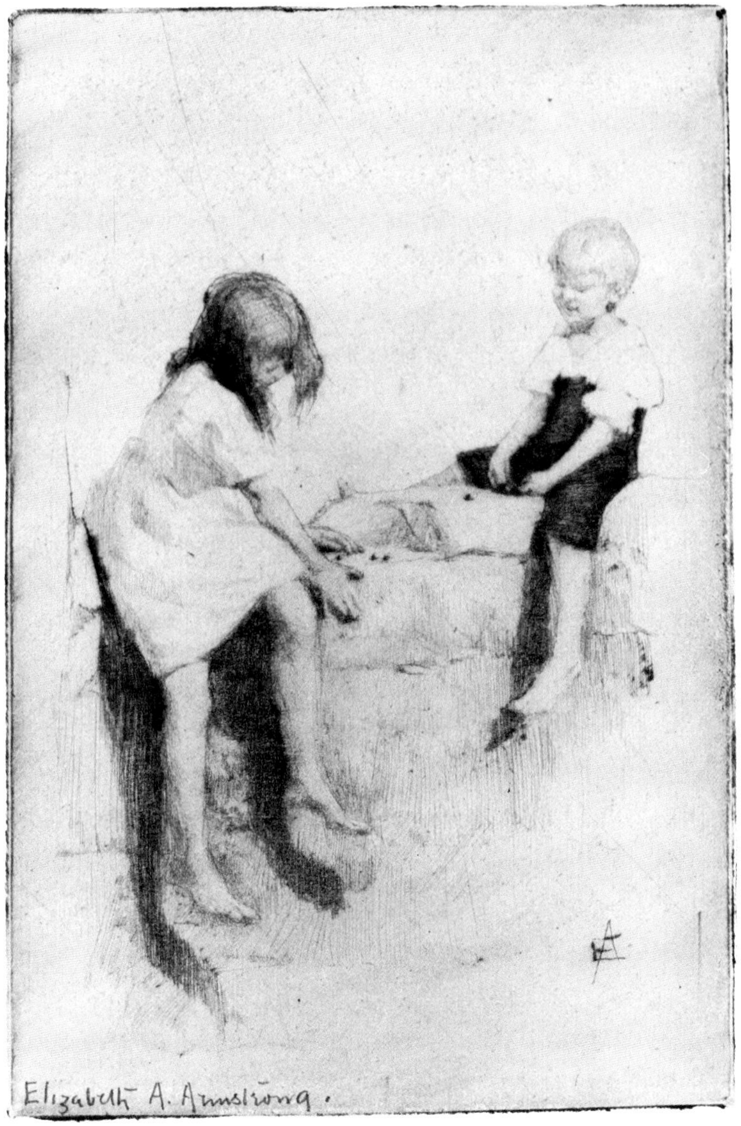

CONTENTS

TWO CHILDREN ON A WALL (n.d.)
Elizabeth Forbes

Dry point print, 6 x 6in (15.5 x 15.5cm)
Victoria and Albert Museum, London

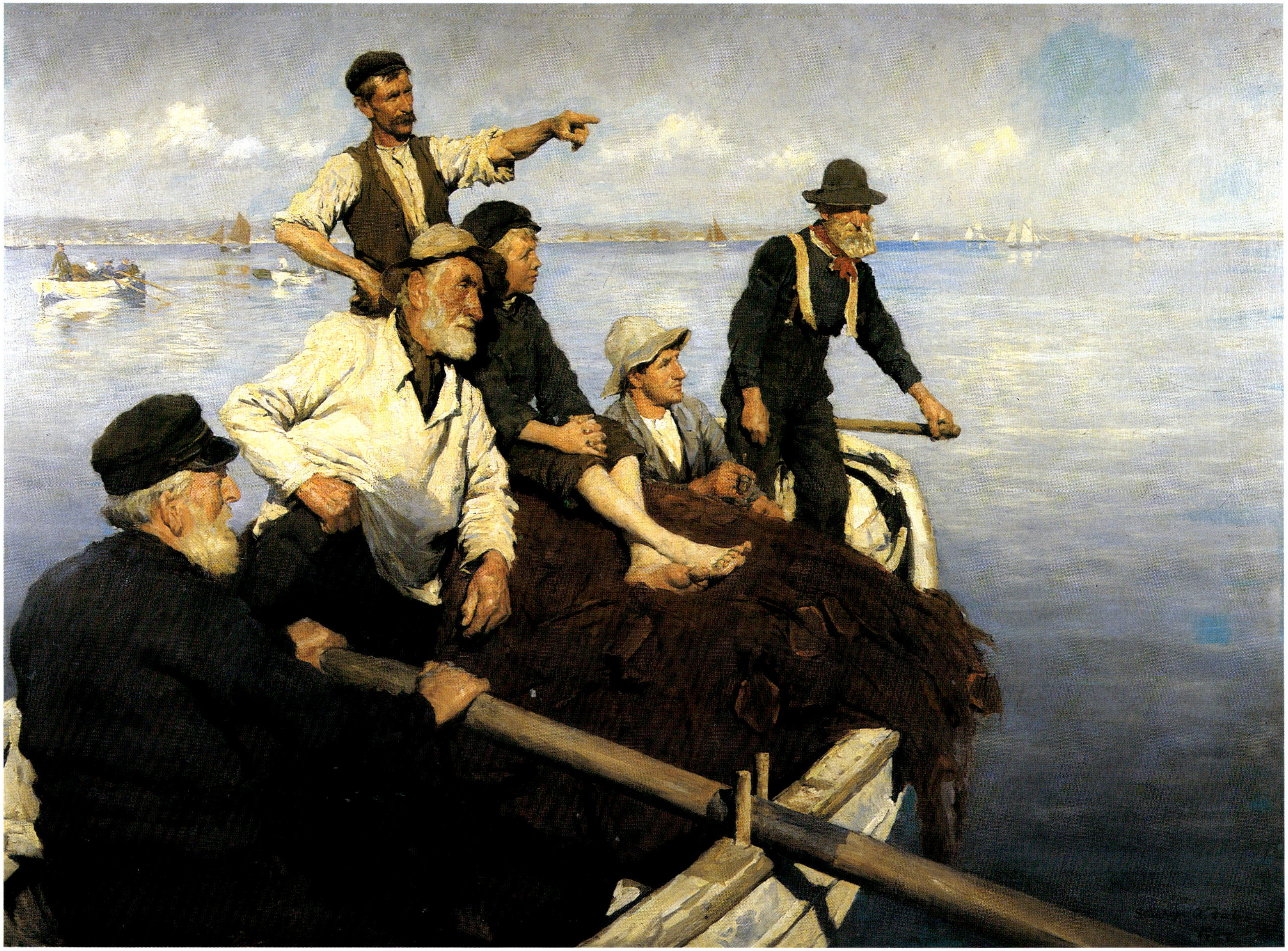

THE SEINE BOAT (1904)
Stanhope Alexander Forbes

Oil on canvas
By courtesy of David Messum, London

CHAPTER ONE

THE HISTORICAL CONTEXT

Stanhope Forbes lived at a time of great artistic change and upheaval. The variety and complexity of late Victorian painting, with its multiple strands and influences, must have appeared quite bewildering to young artists growing up in the 1870s and 1880s. On the one hand there was the lingering Pre-Raphaelite dream of artists such as Rossetti and Burne-Jones, the classicising tendencies of Lord Leighton and G. F. Watts and eastern influences of J. F. Lewis and others. On the other hand, there was a welter of artists painting genre and landscape scenes in a more straightforward manner, sometimes idealised, sometimes with a story to tell and sometimes with a definite social realist message such as can be found in some of the work of Holl, Herkomer and Fildes.

On the whole, the artists of Forbes' generation felt a need to reject the excesses of the classicising and Pre-Raphaelite influences and to choose their own form of realism without too many disturbing allusions to poverty or illness. Onto this they grafted a knowledge of French painting techniques learnt during their period of study in the Parisian *ateliers*. Foremost among these was the need to paint *en plein air*, which gave their work a freshness and immediacy of execution not previously shown in British painting.

They were nonetheless careful not to go too far in their exploration of foreign technique, and it is probable that few of them had ever seen the work of the French Impressionists when studying in Paris during the early 1880s. While they were prepared to take on board certain aspects of their painting techniques, gleaned second hand from artists such as Bastien Lepage, they would probably have been horrified to be considered 'Impressionist' themselves. Their need for artistic companionship, coupled with a strong desire to live near their subject matter, encouraged some of these artists to move to rural areas in Britain and thus we find the formation of groups, such as that at Newlyn, during the early 1880s.

The Newlyn artists produced their most popular work during the 1880s and early 1890s, and many of these paintings found their way into major public and private collections. These works, which were highly realistic portrayals of life in a Cornish fishing village, were drawn with attention to detail and composition and painted with a real understanding of tonal values.

But who were the antecedents of the Newlyn School? The rapid spread of urbanisation resulting from the Industrial Revolution of the late eighteenth century brought with it a nostalgia for country life and ways. Rural life was idealised by some who regarded it as the solution to all the ills of modern civilisation, and it was felt necessary to record fast-vanishing ways of traditional rural life for posterity. Others were only too aware of the social implications and sought to bring the harsh conditions endured by the poor to the notice of a wider public with a view to social justice. The latter group were known as social realists, although the degree of realism varied greatly according to whether the artist wished to rouse the public to righteous indignation or just to satisfy the requirements of his would-be purchasers.

In France there was already a tradition of artists who went to live in the country in order to paint nature at first hand. From the 1830s onwards, a group of artists made their home in the tiny hamlet of Barbizon in the Forest of Fontainebleau in order to paint the landscape and the local people in their environment. Théodore Rousseau (1812–67), Diaz de la Peña (1807–76) and Charles Daubigny (1817–78) were landscape artists who chose to convey the freshness and vibrance of the surrounding countryside by working out of doors. The beauty and immediacy of their work challenged the more prosaic paintings then on view at the Salon in Paris, but they were initially felt to be too revolutionary. Only later did those artists achieve honours.

J. F. Millet (1814–75) chose to depict the local peasants performing their daily tasks – subjects previously considered unworthy of the brush. Some of his paintings demonstrate the extreme harshness of peasant life at that time, such as the *Man with a Hoe* (1859–69, private collection, USA). Others are gentler and more harmonious, pervaded with religio-classical overtones, such as *The Angelus* (1858, Louvre, Paris). Millet's paintings were felt to have political overtones and became increasingly popular after the revolution of 1848. However, Millet did not deliberately set out to shock his public, unlike Gustave Courbet (1819–77), a determined realist whose overt renderings of peasant life were particularly disturbing (for example, *The Stonebreaker*, 1849, formerly Dresden Museum, destroyed in World War II).

Paintings by members of the Barbizon School were especially well received in Britain where the works of Constable and the Pre-Raphaelites had already encouraged an interest in landscape and figure in a landscape subjects, and they found their way into many British collections.

The British also admired the work of a group of Dutch artists, known as the Hague School. These artists, who included Joseph Israels (1824–1911), Jacob, Matthys and Willem Maris, and Anton Mauve, settled in the area around The Hague where they painted the landscape and the local people. The best-known of the group was Joseph Israels who produced monochrome studies of peasant life such as *The Frugal Meal* (1876, Glasgow Museum and Art Gallery) and *Fisherman Carrying a Drowned Man* (1861, National Gallery, London). This latter was greatly admired at the International Exhibition of 1862 in London, and the artist, who came to Britain on several occasions, was honoured at a gala banquet the following year.

It should be noted that before 1830 painting out-of-doors was an extremely laborious process. Not only did the artist have to carry his easel and stool, but also his paints, pots and solvents, which had to be mixed out-of-doors. With the introduction of paint in tubes after that date, outdoor painting became feasible and the colours themselves were richer and more vivid. Interest in the French realist movement spread to Britain in the 1860s through books, periodicals and exhibitions. The work of Millet was especially popular, and in 1881 *Twenty Etchings and Woodcuts of Millet* was published by the Fine Art Society. The same year, a biography of Millet by A. Sensier (*J. F. Millet, Poet and Painter*) was published. The biography presented Millet as the hero of the realist movement, so that he soon became the example *par excellence* for all young artists to follow. Other French realists, such as Legros and L'Hermitte, exhibited

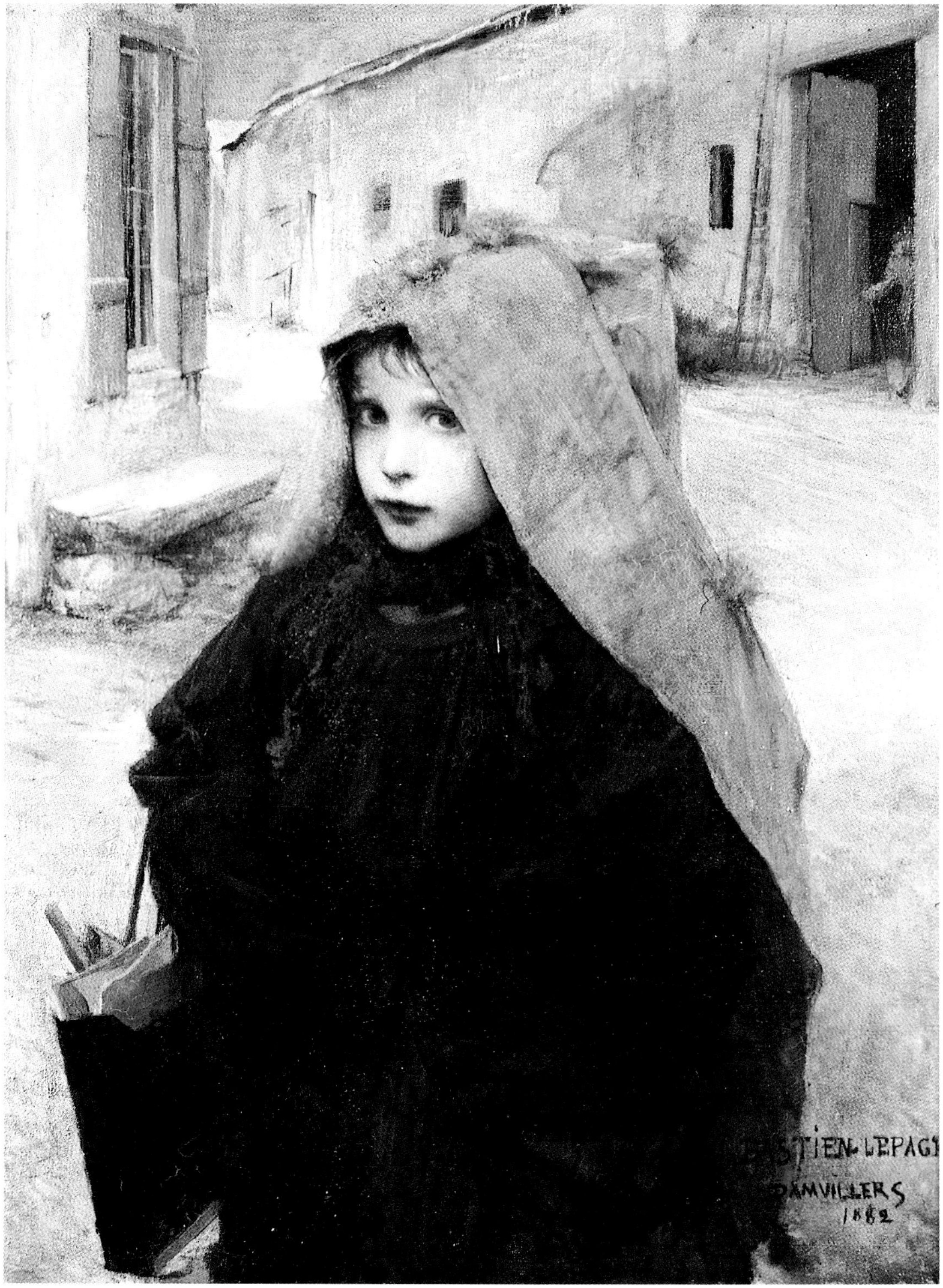

GOING TO SCHOOL (1882)
Jules Bastien Lepage

Oil on canvas, 32 x 23¾in (81 x 60cm)
City of Aberdeen Art Gallery and Museums Collections

Lepage's fascination with the inhabitants of his home village of Damvilliers in the Meuse region of France is similar to that of Forbes in his adoption of Newlyn. This work not only indicates Lepage's interest in painting children but also his concern to show poverty – for the child in the painting is obviously a beggar child. He painted other pictures of beggars and Pas Mêche *(1882, Glasgow Museum and Art Gallery) shows typically raggedly-dressed young boys. In these works Lepage is more concerned with the appealing expression of the child than with the harsher realities of poverty. This painting was originally bought for the collection of Forbes' uncle, James Staats Forbes, before being purchased by Aberdeen Art Gallery in 1927.*

in England from the 1860s, and Jules Bastien Lepage (1848–84) visited London in the 1870s.

Lepage was an extremely important influence on a whole generation of British artists for whom he served as a figurehead, while for others he acted as a controversial catalyst. He succeeded in combining a devotion to realism and the importance of living among his subjects in order to paint where possible *en plein air*, with a style more acceptable to a middle-of-the-road audience, who appreciated the mixture of academic and impressionist sources contained in his work. Although paintings such as *Les Foins* (1879, The Louvre, Paris), exhibited at the Grosvenor Gallery in 1882, shocked the British public with its clear depiction of poverty and the brutalisation of labour, his work was widely exhibited in London and he visited Britain on three occasions over the period 1879–82. An article in *The Spectator* of 1880 stated that Lepage had taken the position usually held by Burne-Jones and Holman Hunt, and that around his work there gathered 'a little knot of worshippers or scoffers, admiring or condemning in the most vehement manner'. An article in the *Magazine of Art* of 1883 commented: 'M. Bastien Lepage is not perhaps the greatest of living French painters, but he is at the present moment, considerably the most interesting. It is for this reason of course, that he is most discussed.'

The 'worshippers' consisted mainly of those British artists who had studied abroad – the members of the Newlyn and Glasgow groups, as well as individuals such as George Clausen, Henry La Thangue, Walter Osborne, and William and Edward Stott. They were contemporaries of Lepage and admired his combination of realism with a hint of impressionism. Norman Garstin confirmed his impact on British painting in the 1880s: 'the greatest of our day – almost all his contemporaries have felt his power; many imitated him, no one surpassed him . . . His men and women breathe air, not linseed oil'.

Some British artists painted realist subjects, but not necessarily in the style of Lepage. Examples include Frank Holl's *Hard Times* (1885, Royal Holloway College, University of London); Hubert von Herkomer, *On Strike* (1891, Royal Academy); and Sir Luke Fildes (1843–1927) *Application for Admission to a Casual Ward* (1874, Royal Holloway College, University of London), which parallels in paint Mrs Gaskell's descriptions of Manchester's urban poor in her novel *Mary Barton* (1848). Miles Birket Foster (1825–1905) and Helen Allingham (1848–1926) painted idealised country cottages with gardens and girls in pretty clothes, contrasting with Thomas Hardy's stark and often bleak accounts of Dorset's rural poor.

The formation of the Newlyn art colony in the early 1880s was part of an international movement in which artists settled in rural areas throughout Europe, Scandinavia and even in Russia and the USA. They were mostly rebelling against conventional academic painting, preferring to live among rural subjects and paint direct from life. Most of them had studied abroad in the Parisian *ateliers* and hoped to prolong their carefree student life, finding that continued living among their fellows provided constructive criticism and support which could be very helpful to their life and work. Colonies arose where there was a sympathetic landlord or landlady, and where accommodation could be provided at a reasonable price. They were also facilitated by the spread of the railway network into inaccessible areas.

The artist and critic R. A. M. Stevenson, who with his brother Robert had spent some time at the French colony of Grèz sur Loing, described colonies as places 'where more than half the ideals of the nineteenth century have been hatched'. Nevertheless, the psychological implications of living in isolated groups took their toll. He went on, 'Any writer could tell you that they found those colonies more suited for the study of the human heart than for that of trees or rocks. You saw the very bones and muscles of the passions laid bare.' Colonies tended to attract hangers-on or 'snoozers and dozers', as they were called, who lived among their fellows but soon gave up doing any real work. Sometimes, however, colonies gave lesser artists just the right supportive environment in which to produce work they could not otherwise have done on their own. Many experimental communities were founded in the late nineteenth century as alternatives to urban life. These included Tolstoy's community on his own estate in Russia, and the William Morris-inspired Arts and Crafts communities in Britain. They all came to an end, often through internal difficulties, lack of finance, or the need for change. Usually by then, however, the original ideas that held the group together had been absorbed into the wider community.

During the 1880s several art colonies arose in Britain, while other artists such as George Clausen and Henry La Thangue worked individually to explore the depiction of rural life. The most directly comparable group to Newlyn was the Glasgow Boys, a group of Scottish artists who were based and worked in Glasgow. However, they also painted rural scenes, in the area around Cockburnspath. Initially they painted realist subjects in the manner of Lepage, but their work differs from that of the Newlyn group because of its greater emphasis on colour. Strong colour and vigorous handling were features of the work of William Macgregor (1888–1923) – for example *The Vegetable Stall* (1884, National Gallery of Scotland, Edinburgh).

Two works by another leading member of the Glasgow Boys, James Guthrie (1859–1930) *To Pastures New* (1885, Aberdeen Art Gallery), and *Schoolmates* (1884, Museum of Fine Arts, Ghent) derive from the more sentimental paintings of Lepage, such as his *Pas Mèche* (1881, Glasgow Museum and Art Gallery) and *Pauvre Fauvette* (1881, National Gallery of Scotland, Edinburgh), where Lepage's emphasis is more decorative and sentimental. James Lavery (1856–1941) adopted a similar approach; *Under the Cherry Tree* (1884, Ulster Museum, Belfast) is an evocative painting of a riverside idyll showing a washerwoman chatting to a boy on a punt; the game of lawn tennis was the subject of Lavery's *The Tennis Party* (1885, Aberdeen Museum and Art Gallery).

Later works by the Glasgow Boys showed an even stronger tendency towards decoration – in particular the work of George Henry (c.1858–1943) and Edward Atkinson Hornel (1864–1933), who were both strongly influenced by a visit to Japan in 1893. The work of Hornel displays a rich impasto technique, while that of Henry is more subtle, at times coming near to the discoveries of Gauguin – see *Galway Landscape* (1889, Glasgow Museum and Art Gallery). At other times Henry displayed an unmistakable Japanese influence – as in *Japanese Lady with a Fan* (1894, Glasgow Museum and Art Gallery).

As with the Newlyn Group, the Glasgow Boys gradually dispersed during the 1890s when several members moved away from Glasgow to live in London or farther afield. Both Lavery and Guthrie became successful society portrait painters.

The other major art colony in Britain during the late nineteenth century was at St Ives, about ten miles across the peninsula from Newlyn. Unlike Newlyn, St Ives was quite cosmopolitan. There was a strong American community there, and it also contained Finnish and Swedish artists such as Helen Schjerfbeck and Anders Zorn. Zorn was to acquire an international reputation in his own right. The St Ives artists were more nomadic than their Newlyn contemporaries and used to 'come and go and come again'. It was the presence of professional women artists which made Elizabeth Armstrong feel more at home in St Ives than in Newlyn. St Ives generally attracted artists who were more interested in painting landscape. Forbes observed after a visit there in 1884, 'I am delighted with it but I doubt whether it would be as good as Newlyn for figure painting. Too much going on to work comfortably.'

There was some contact between the groups of artists, and Forbes recorded his interest in meeting Zorn on one occasion. The main contact, however, was at the annual cricket match. Forbes explained:

> There was one time, I regret to say, a rather bitter rivalry between the painters of Newlyn and the neighbouring colony of St Ives. Oh it was nothing to do with painting, or art of any kind: it was much more serious for it concerned cricket.

BEACH SCENE ST IVES (1886)
Stanhope Alexander Forbes
Oil on canvas, 7½ x 11in (19 x 28cm)
City of Bristol Museum and Art Gallery

The large expanse of empty sand in the foreground recalls the work of Whistler, while the small group of figures in the distance is reminiscent of Boudin. The unusually high horizon line is typical of the work of a follower of Lepage and the use of square-ended brushes is very evident in the surface texture.

He went on to describe how the watercolourist Henry Meynell Rheam was 'imported' from Polperro by the Newlyners especially to counter two notable St Ives batsmen!

The movement of which Forbes and his fellows were a part is perhaps best summed up by Forbes himself, writing in 1900:

> It was one of those distinct waves of feeling which occur occasionally in Art, as in Literature, and the tide had set strongly in favour of out-of-door work, and a very thorough study of all its changing effects. It was a breath of fresh air in the tired atmosphere of the studios, and painters began to see that it needed more than an occasional visit to the country to get at the heart of its mysteries; that he who wished to solve them must live amongst the scenes he sought to render, and become thoroughly familiarised with every aspect of nature. Not only for the landscape painter, who had perforce always made the country the scene of his labours; but equally for him who desired to study humanity in relation to its surroundings, was it essential that he should closely study every changing mood of outdoor life. In France, the movement had made great headway, if, indeed, it did not wholly originate there, fostered by the great school of painters who made famous the little village of Barbizon in the Forest of Fontainebleau. Under the spell of the genius Jean François Millet, and the most recent, and then living, Bastien Lepage, most of us young students were turning our backs on the great cities, forsaking the studios with their unvarying north light, to set up our easels in country districts, where we could pose our models, and attack our work, in sunshine or in shadow under the open sky.

CHAPTER TWO

FORBES IN FRANCE

Stanhope Forbes was born in Dublin in 1857, the son of William Forbes who was then the manager of the Midland Great Western Railway of Ireland. William Forbes was a man of cultivated literary tastes, being an enthusiastic admirer of Dickens and Thackeray, but more especially of Carlyle. One can only assume that his son inherited these interests, for in a letter to his mother from Brittany, Stanhope asks her to send him books by both Dickens and Thackeray, and in another letter he mentioned that he has just finished a book by Thomas Hardy. It appears, too, that William Forbes had a great interest in folk tales, which he gathered from the peasantry of western Ireland and Belgium, and this may have encouraged his son's later interest in depicting the local fisherfolk of Brittany and Newlyn.

William Forbes also seems to have been a sympathetic and kindly man with a great fondness for children and animals. His generosity and humour, evident during his many visits to Newlyn, were remembered by the local people, and it may have been from his father that Stanhope inherited his warm interest in and concern for ordinary people.

Forbes' uncle, James Staats Forbes, also a railway manager, possessed an extremely distinguished collection of paintings. The young Stanhope was very familiar with his uncle's collection, which included works by the French Barbizon and the Dutch Hague Schools of artists – both of which were, as we have seen, forerunners of the Newlyn and Glasgow Schools. Staats Forbes was a close friend of Joseph Israels, the leading artist of The Hague School Group, and his enthusiasm for all these artists undoubtedly fired the interest and imagination of his young nephew, encouraging his lifelong devotion to realism and the depiction of rural life. Staats Forbes used to purchase the works of another Newlyner, Walter Langley, whose work at times comes close to that of Israels. See, for example, Israels *Growing Old* (*c.*1878, The Hague, Haags Gemeentemuseum); and Langley *When One Is Old* (*c.*1891, Plymouth City Museum).

Stanhope's own brother, William, followed his father into railway management and was later knighted for his running of the London Underground. His cousin, William Alexander Forbes, was a brilliant scientist who died young, but not before he had won a distinguished position at the University of London and as Prosector to the Royal Zoological Society. Norman Garstin has described the Forbes as a stock 'which is essentially of the nineteenth century, full of its movement and restless activity'. It is certain that his inherited tenacity and drive helped Forbes in his struggles to succeed as an artist.

Forbes' mother, Juliette de Guise, a Frenchwoman, was a dominant force in the life of her son. The many hundreds of letters Forbes wrote to her while he was away in Brittany and Newlyn cover the events of his life in such detail that it would seem there was very little he did not tell her. This degree of intimacy and dependence might seem unusual for a young man in his twenties, and may partly stem from his delicate constitution, said to have been the result of his falling into the sea when aged about six years. Indeed, Forbes sometimes refers to bilious attacks and colds in his letters home, as well as a liver complaint, from which it appears his mother also suffered. His mother worried about his diet, complained if a letter was a day or two late, and visited him frequently both in Brittany and Newlyn. She was also extremely ambitious for her son and could be relied on for advice. She organised practical details concerned with his work, such as materials, framing, and, on occasion, even entertaining dealers.

Forbes and his brother were initially taught by a governess, Sophie Moran, who used to take them on lengthy visits to her home in Galway. Her father was the vicar of Killolgen and a very keen fisherman who, despite suffering from gout which confined him to a Bath chair, managed to teach Forbes to fish. Fishing was one of several interests besides painting which was to absorb Forbes both in Brittany and Newlyn.

During a holiday in the Ardennes, the family met the Harrison sisters, who were on a sketching tour. They took a great interest in Stanhope, then aged 11 and encouraged him to join their sketching expeditions. On the family's return to London the two sisters, who lived nearby, continued to provide support and encouragement, and Forbes would take his drawings to them for inspection and criticism. Later, they invited him to join them on a sketching tour in Scotland, and their opinion was still being sought by Forbes as late as 1881 when he painted his first major Breton works.

When the family moved to London, Forbes was sent to Dulwich College where he learnt to draw under the art teacher John Sparkes. Sparkes was an exceptional teacher who later became the head of the South Kensington Schools. He taught Forbes to draw from casts and models, which was a great improvement on the more usual practice at that time of copying drawings by other artists.

Drawing was always very important to Forbes, and he was particularly grateful for this training, employing similar methods with his own students in Newlyn during the early 1900s.

Not long after the move to London Forbes' father was appointed manager of the Great Luxembourg Railway and went to live in Brussels with his wife. The two boys then boarded at Dulwich in the term, spending their holidays with their parents. After a while his parents decided that, for health reasons, Forbes should study with a tutor in Brussels. This enabled him to give much more time to drawing than if he had been at school. Following the end of the Franco–Prussian War in 1871, the railway was purchased by the State of Luxembourg, and the family returned to London.

Forbes was particularly fortunate in that his father sympathised with his desire to be an artist and, although family friends suggested that he could pursue a business career while keeping art as a hobby, William Forbes realised that this was not a satisfactory solution for his son. He applied to Forbes' old tutor, John Sparkes, for the final word and the latter advised that Forbes should be allowed to follow his vocation.

He briefly attended the Lambeth School of Art before enrolling at the Royal Academy Schools, where he came under the influence of several major Victorian artists – in particular Millais, Leighton and Alma Tadema. The Royal Academy Schools was described in an article in *The Magazine of Art* of 1885 as follows:

> as an educational institution . . . it has little or nothing to teach; its students, as soon as they have passed the curriculum it imposes on them then make haste to betake themselves to France to learn, not only how to paint and draw, but to forget as much as they can of the practice and theory acquired at its schools.

Forbes initially took himself off to Galway in the summer and autumn of 1877 where he stayed with an old friend of his father's, Dr Andrew Melville. Dr Melville, a professor at Queen's College, Dublin, had a wide knowledge of the arts. There Forbes painted the Irish landscape and made his first attempts at outdoor figure subjects which he described as: 'a little picture of a Connemara child walking along with a milk-can in her hand and a basket of strawberries on her head, entitled *Strawberries and Cream.*' He went on:

> she is an extremely pretty child and if I can get her I will paint her often. Unfortunately there is a savage old grandmother who speaks no English and insists on staying in the room while the child is painted. I have tried to think of every kind of excuse to get rid of her, for she emits an unpleasant odour.

Forbes also began to paint his first portrait commissions at this time and was extremely anxious to prevent the news reaching his fellow Royal Academy students Goodall, Fisher, La Thangue and Miller, 'as the provincial portrait painter always comes in for a large share of chaff'. For financial reasons, he decided to continue with these commissions rather than put in for a medal at the Royal Academy. On his return to London he continued painting portraits through family contacts, one of which, depicting the daughter of a Harley Street specialist, was exhibited at the Royal Academy of 1878. The following year he exhibited three more portraits, and then two in 1880. Forbes painted portraits throughout his life and also employed his skills in portraiture when including models in his *plein air* compositions.

In the nineteenth century, Paris was the art capital of the world and consequently attracted students from many countries. After a period of introspection, Britain was going through a more expansive mood and British artists flocked to study in Paris or Antwerp, the other main centre at this period. Antwerp was visited by several future Newlyners, who would have attended the *atelier* of Charles Verlat. Verlat, a realist in the manner of Courbet, favoured the study of the natural world to that of the antique. Other Newlyners went to Paris to study under J. P. Laurens, Julian, or Léon Bonnat.

The companionship of the Parisian *ateliers* was particularly important to British artists, who were used to a much greater degree of isolation in the British art schools. New students had to go through an initiation test which could include having 'paint tubes, stools, cigar butts and oaths' hurled at them, and derogatory comments made upon their appearance and clothing. Once through this, however, the student was part of a group which met together in and out of working hours. In fact the evening hours spent together with fellow students in cafés discussing art were just as valuable as their daily work. Norman Garstin wrote: 'I seem to live in a world where people paint, paint, talk, paint and think. I know of nothing else and my days have nothing else in them.'

There was much frivolity in the *ateliers*, and working conditions were extremely noisy – the students often sang, whistled and talked while they worked. Gotch complained of 'the noise, the heat, the smoke and the students who depress me beyond measure' at Laurens; and the conscientious Bourdillon eschewed the evening visits to Parisian cafés because 'the noise is disagreeable, the drinks one is supposed to care for, distasteful, and the atmosphere of bad French tobacco absolutely poisonous'.

Nevertheless, the working day was a long one and students were expected to work very hard indeed. Bourdillon described his monotonous daily routine: 'Out to work at 8, stick to it till 12.30. Breakfast (a pretty square meal) till 1.30 and then work again till it gets dark in these short winter days.'

On the whole, British students kept together and did not mix with their foreign counterparts. It seems that few British students spoke French and therefore they did not go out of their way to make contact with more advanced French artists such as the Impressionists. Moreover, the *ateliers* they attended were chosen for their middle-of-the-road approach, so there was no encouragement to venture beyond the paths chosen by their teachers. It is significant that Norman Garstin, who was the most cosmopolitan and gregarious with foreigners, should have been the most open-minded in his tastes. His work demonstrates his admiration for Japanese art, Whistler, and the Impressionists, and his writings on art also reflect his more advanced views.

Forbes went to Paris in February of 1880 and enrolled at the studio of Léon Bonnat in the Place Vintimille below the foot of Montmartre. The studio was at the top of the house and was described by a former American student, E. H. Blashfield, as being 'fairly free and easy'. Students were of all nationalities, and Forbes was disappointed by the number of Americans in his group because he wished to practise his French. Bonnat used to visit the studio once a week on a Saturday and Forbes found him helpful, though he wished he would give more time to each individual. He added that Bonnat was 'no flatterer but strikes the nail on the head at once. With my particular faults in painting he is just the man.'

Bonnat himself was a vigorous artist who used a broad stroke, loaded pigment and deep, strong colours. He painted directly from nature and was particularly influenced by the work of Rembrandt and Ribera. Advising his students on how a figure could be best indicated and rubbed in he wrote, 'Make it as much like nature as possible in the first painting and in your second painting make it still more like.' These sentiments were repeated by Forbes to his own students many years later. Bonnat painted fairly traditional subject matter such as portraits, classical and religious subjects, however and was by no means in sympathy with the *plein air* ideals of Forbes and his fellow Newlynites.

Students worked long hours in Bonnat's studio – in the winter from 8am to 5.30pm, starting at 7.30am in the summer. There were 50 men in the studio working amidst terrific noise which included singing and whistling. When Forbes arrived in February, the students were busy organising a ball to be held in April. This was to be funded by forfeits from those who whistled, at a sou a time. Models were provided at the studio and Forbes recounted that he was painting a very unsuccessful study of a negro in the mornings and 'a more promising head of a little girl in the afternoons'. Both were pronounced '*pas mal*' by Bonnat. By April, Forbes and his friend Hacker had found a studio in the Rue Veron and Forbes worked there when he didn't like the model at Bonnat's. He employed a 'charming old woman' to model for him, dressed in 'black fichu, blue apron and white cap'.

By mid-May he was finding the model studies no easier and told his mother that he was beginning to realise how little he knew about painting. To his great consternation, Bonnat's visits were becoming less and less frequent because the latter was occupied with selecting work for the Salon. Forbes did feel, however, that the Salon was opening his eyes to a great deal, and that he was getting to know the work there very well.

It is hard to assess how much Forbes learnt from attending Bonnat's *Atelier*. References to Bonnat in the letters gradually dwindle away, and while Forbes was painting in Brittany he had little or no contact with the master. He told his mother in December 1881 that he would send his works to Bonnat in Paris 'although I don't quite see what he can tell me now that I don't know myself'. Other references show him still anxious for Bonnat's opinion of his work, despite the fact that the latter was not always readily available. While he probably learnt a great deal academically during the early days in Bonnat's studio, as their interests diverged and Forbes became increasingly absorbed in *plein air* work, he was to look to others for support and approval.

Forbes undoubtedly learnt most from the months spent during three consecutive years in Brittany (1881–83). It was his old friend Henry La Thangue (1859–1929), studying at the Ecole des Beaux Arts in Paris, who first encouraged him to go to Brittany and to paint out-of-doors. In July 1881 they visited St Briac but, finding it unsuitable, they quickly moved on to Cancale where Forbes remained, staying at the Hôtel de l'Europe until the end of October. Here he painted his first outdoor works and began to discover the difficulties involved. From the start he chose to work on two paintings simultaneously. One was an interior (whereabouts unknown) which he could work on when it was wet, and the other was *A Street in Brittany*: 'In the afternoon I am painting another little girl, in the shade fortunately, with an old street for a background and people working.' He realised that he would spend most of his time on these two works but added, 'It will repay I am sure.'

The street scene was not painted without difficulties such as changing light conditions and absenteeism among his models. He told his mother in October 1881, 'The street scene will I think please you. The sun's path is now so different from what it was when we came down that our effects have greatly changed.' The model for the girl in the foreground was almost certainly Desirée, of whom Forbes wrote, 'Always the same beautiful girl, she grows more perfect every day and seems to be as charming as she looks, but I fear this is not the case.' It transpired that Desirée had been dismissed for stealing from the hotel in which Forbes was staying:

> Consequently they all detest her . . . It took a good deal of persuasion to get her to sit for us in our room and I fear we have incurred the wrath of the family Perdrix by doing so, but she is too good a model for us to mind that and I won't believe half they say against her.

The situation was further complicated by the fact that Desirée herself had threatened to leave, and Forbes' attempts to ensure her constant attendance by keeping back some of her pay until the painting was completed were foiled by her refusal to sit at all until she was paid in full.

The composition of *A Street in Brittany* is extremely simple, relying for its interest on the juxtaposition between the foreground figure and the perspective of the buildings of the little street with the women sitting on their doorsteps knitting. Forbes wrote, 'the peasants do not wear the regular Breton costume for that is quite rare now, but

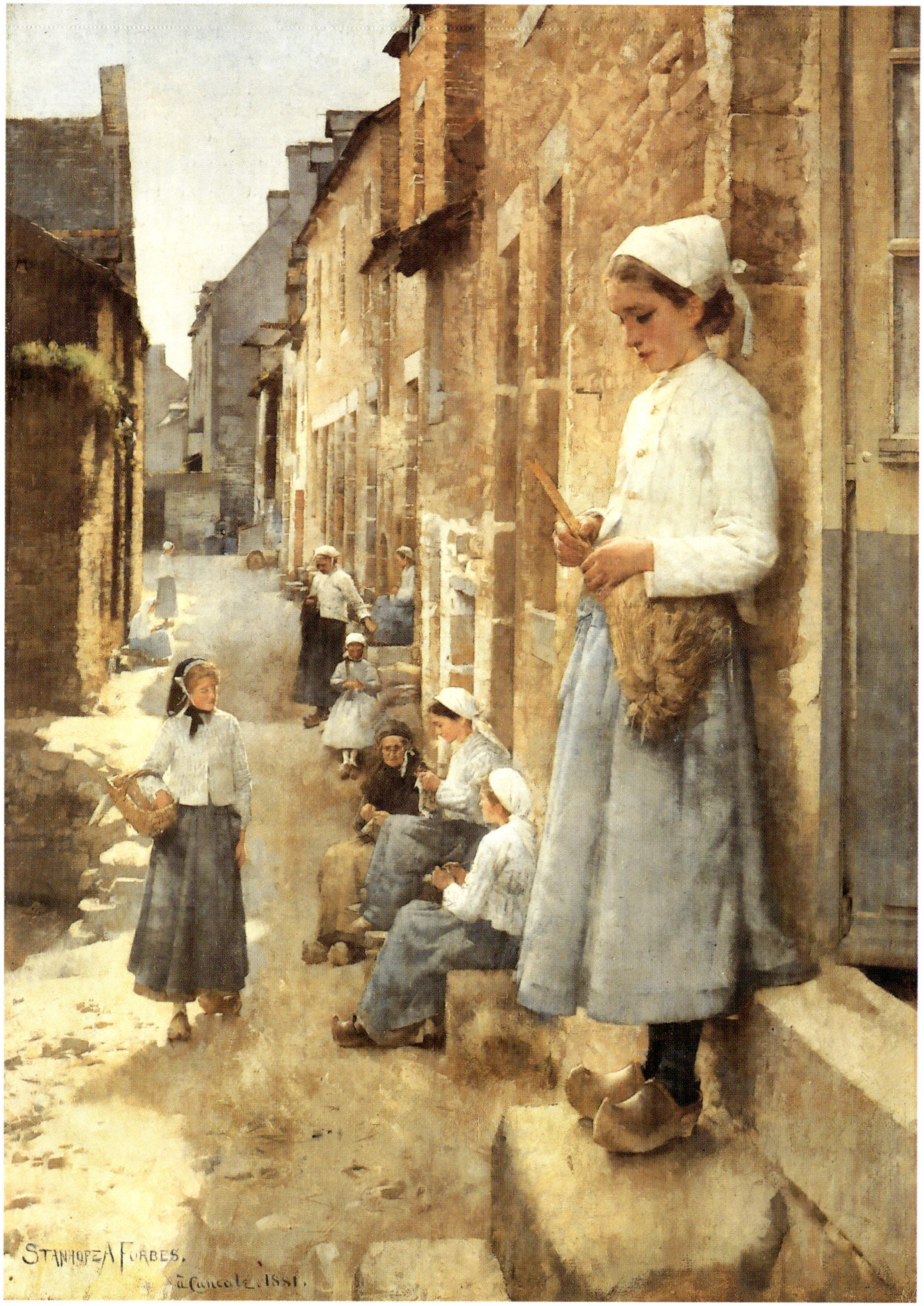

have a very pretty tasteful dress which I think even better.' In the foreground, Desirée holds the large needle traditionally used to repair nets, and may be working on netting attached to her belt.

A Street in Brittany and *The Interior* were on view in Forbes' Parisian studio in December 1881, and most visitors preferred the latter. Bonnat, however, although not over-enthusiastic about either, had a preference for the street scene. Forbes feared 'from certain peculiarities it won't go down at all with the British public'. Later he was more specific, asking his mother when it was to be on exhibition at the Royal Academy in London: 'I am most anxious to know if any of the critics noticed the disparity in the size of the figure in the foreground and those further off and was it found too blue?' He need not have feared, for the freshness and immediacy of observation in this painting do in fact surmount any awkwardness of perspective.

The painting was purchased for the Walker Art Gallery in Liverpool when on view at the Autumn Exhibition of 1882. Forbes told his mother in October: 'The collection seems a good one and I ought to be happy at being in such good company.' Later, he informed the curator at the Walker Art Gallery that it was their purchase of this painting which encouraged him to establish himself as an outdoor painter rather than settle for the more secure career of a portrait painter. It was an important step in his career, and one which was to set the pattern for the rest of his life.

In June of 1882, Forbes joined La Thangue at the Hôtel Metayer, Quimperlé. He immediately

◁ *A Street in Brittany* (1881)
Stanhope Alexander Forbes

Oil on canvas, 41 x 30in (104 x 76cm)
Trustees of the National Museums and Galleries on Merseyside (Walker Art Gallery)

Preparations for the Market, Quimperlé (1883) ▷
Stanhope Alexander Forbes

Oil on canvas, 66¾ x 52¾in (169 x 134cm)
Dunedin Public Art Gallery, New Zealand

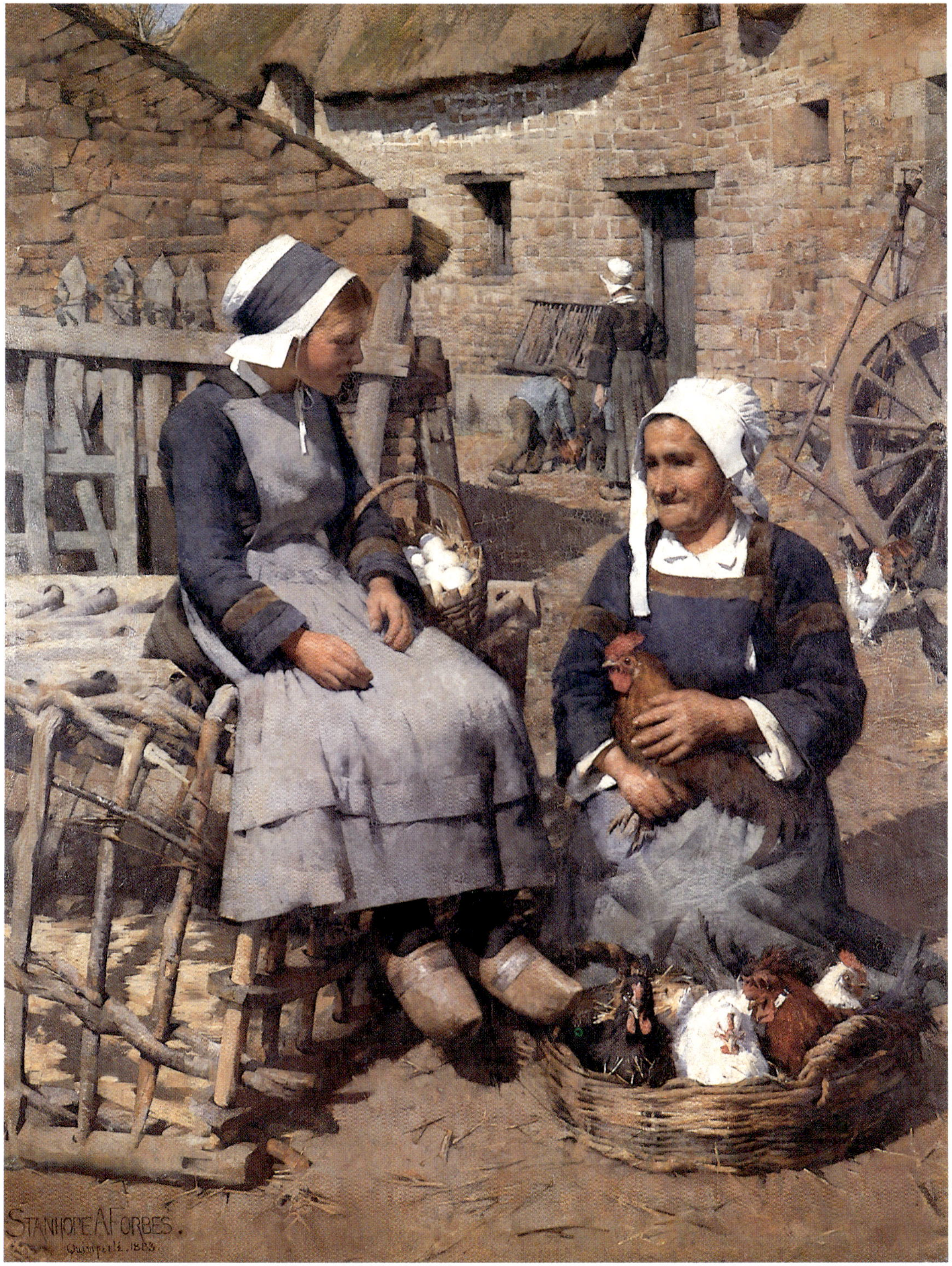

preferred it to Cancale because it was much more rural and thoroughly Breton:

> A beautiful rapid flowing river, a thickly wooded valley and in it a quaint old town with the whitest of houses and the queerest of roofs. Very steep streets crowded on market day, almost empty on other days. All the men dressed in regular Breton costume and of course the women in the most wonderful of coiffs and collars.

The only problem was the bad weather, which forced Forbes to devote his time to fishing and walking rather than painting. To Forbes' great consternation, La Thangue returned to England just two weeks after his arrival. Forbes himself felt at a loss to conceive of any place better for painting and praised the cheap living which cost him little over a pound a week! Later on, he was to reiterate its cheapness and artistic excellence, whilst adding: 'But O, how dull!'

In 1883 he exhibited two paintings at the Royal Academy, *The Church of St David, Quimperlé* (whereabouts unknown) and *The Convent* (1882). *The Church* was admired by a 'wealthy Liverpool swell' who found the price 'enormous', while *The Convent* was purchased by the collector J. Maddocks, after Forbes had asked his uncle, the original purchaser, to stand aside. *The Convent* shares the freshness of the *Street in Brittany* without the latter's awkwardness of perspective. As Betsy Cogger Rezelman has stated in her thesis on the Newlyn Artists (Indiana University, 1984), this was probably the time when Forbes came closest to the work of Manet and, in particular, Manet's *Argenteuil* (1874) and *A Bar at the Folies Bergère* (1881–2, Courtauld Institute Galleries, London) which he probably saw in the Salon of 1882.

The Convent has a lightness and simplicity in which nothing is forced and comes together as a whole, unlike many of Forbes' later works. The composition is built up of a series of horizontal bands, but any sense of monotony is relieved by the verticals of the trees and the curve of the river with its superb reflections – something to which Forbes was to return time and again when painting

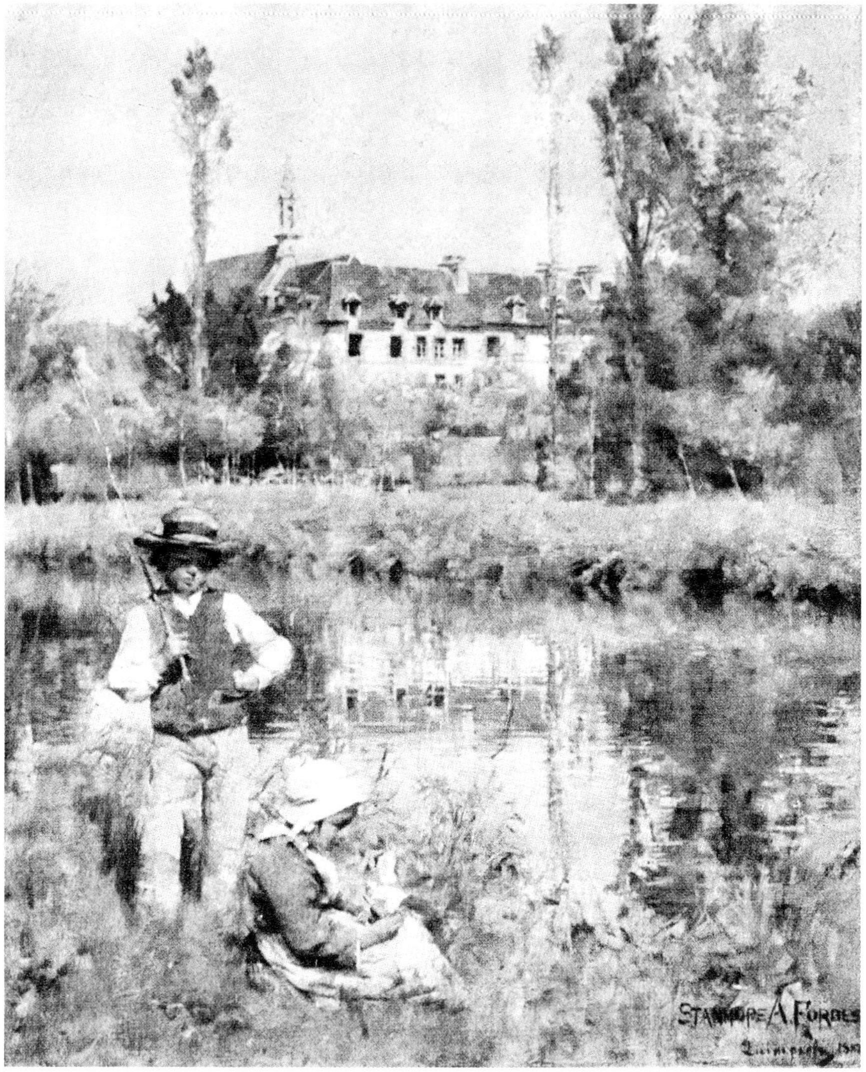

THE CONVENT (1882)
Stanhope Alexander Forbes

Oil on canvas, size and location unknown.
Reproduced in *Life of Stanhope and Elizabeth Forbes* by Mrs Lionel Birch, 1906

the harbour at Newlyn or Mousehole. The two children in the foreground appear to be included more as a device to complete the composition rather than from any desire to depict real children. The atmosphere of the painting is one of calmness and serenity, despite the fact that Forbes told his mother that he was frequently harassed by crowds of small children and had to resort to the gendarmes for protection! Betsy Cogger Rezelman quotes a telling remark penned in the catalogue of an exhibition held at Dowdeswell's London Gallery in December 1890, now in the Victoria and Albert Museum: A viewer has written in the catalogue beneath *The Convent*: 'This was when Forbes knew how to paint light.'

Forbes returned to Quimperlé for the last time between July and November 1883. His two Royal Academy submissions for that year were *Preparations for the Market, Quimperlé* (1883) and *Fair Measures – a Shop in Quimperlé* (1883, Milmo-Penny Fine Art). Both paintings, however, lack the clarity and freshness of *A Street in Brittany* and *The Convent. Fair Measures* portrays a very simple vegetable shop. In the foreground on the cobbled street, an elderly peasant woman weighs out potatoes beside a small cart of vegetables, while in the background, through the open shutters of her room, a younger woman dispenses soup to a child. All are dressed in the characteristic blue and white Breton costume. There is, however, something a little unsatisfactory in the rather squat scale of this work, with its hunched up figures. The painting was originally in the collection of R.A. Foster, London, who may well have purchased it at the Royal Academy of 1884. *Preparations for the Market* is a more contrived painting in which the background with its wheel, stonework, fencing, pen, and so on, appears as an opportunity to explore pattern and texture. It has been suggested that he was influenced in this by Henry La Thangue's *Study in a Boat-Building Yard* (1882, Maritime Museum, Greenwich).

Unlike *The Street* and *The Convent*, the figures are unidealised and the observation of the features of the old woman and the young girl are much closer to the work of Bastien Lepage and the other French realists. It is, however, the attention to detail which prevents the viewer from reading the painting as a whole, the eye constantly being drawn back and forth. Further, the shadows are confusing in that those beneath the thatched roof in the distance denote one time of day, while those of the old woman, another. It is probable that Forbes was aware of these problems when he told his mother that the 'big picture' was not altogether successful. He informed her, however, that *The Vegetable Shop* was his best. At a private view held in his parents' house in November, he wrote, 'So the picture is pronounced unique and the general verdict is satisfactory.' Presumably, he was again referring to *The Vegetable Shop*.

CHAPTER THREE

NEWLYN AND ITS ARTISTS

In the latter part of the nineteenth century Newlyn was a thriving fishing village, situated about a mile to the west of Penzance. From early times Newlyn had provided a safe anchorage for boats, and by 1873 it was the main fishing centre for Mounts Bay, with a fleet of 400 boats engaged in the pilchard and mackerel industries.

The influx of visitors into West Cornwall began after the completion of the railway between Penzance and Truro in 1852 and the building of Brunel's great bridge at Saltash in 1859. These two projects opened up Cornwall to the rest of Britain. Penzance was at the height of its prosperity in the 1880s, with a large harbour, a market, and good public buildings. These provided a marked contrast to the more basic conditions in Newlyn, described by Frank Richards in an article of 1895:

> The street scenes in Newlyn lack nothing of subject for the painter; paved with cobblestone, some of the narrow streets are occasionally strewn over with fishheads and entrails, so that one's progress in going 'up' or 'down'-a-long is sometimes considerably facilitated by an alarmingly quick slide to an unexpected destination.

The only remaining relic of Newlyn's origins is the Old Quay, repaired in 1435. The rest of the village dates from after 1595 when it was sacked by the Spaniards. It comprises many picturesque little houses and streets situated on the side of a hill overlooking Mounts Bay, or clustered around the mouth of the River Coombe. Indeed these were seen as two very distinct areas, Newlyn Town and Street-an-Nowan, separated from each other by a narrow causeway only passable at low tide. At high tide, Newlyn Town could only be reached by climbing the steep route known as Paul Hill. In 1908, the harbour road was completed, thus linking these two separate areas.

The artists who moved to Newlyn were captivated not only by the attractive setting of the village and its streets but also by its inhabitants, as Forbes wrote in 1913:

> In my keen hunt for motives, I soon stumbled upon Newlyn, a village which seemed the very object of my search. Here every corner was a picture and more important from the point of view of the figure painter, the people seemed to fall naturally into their places and to harmonise with the surroundings.

Village life revolved around the fishing industry and its allied trades. Mackerel fishing was carried on in winter and spring up to 100 miles out in the Atlantic where the fish were caught using drift nets. During the summer, fishermen would be away for as long as three months, following shoals of herring in the North Sea. Pilchards were caught nearer home. A 'huer' would be on the watch in the village for shoals of pilchards and, once sighted, he would shout 'Heva, Heva'. The fishermen would then catch the pilchards using a seine net held between two boats, and pull it to shore.

The whole pattern of life was greatly affected by fluctuations in fishing. Forbes recorded a glut of fish in 1884 not long after his arrival. At other times, fish were less plentiful and there was hardship in the village. Disasters at sea also affected the whole community and Walter Langley's paintings, in particular, dwell on the more tragic aspects of fishing life. Those not involved in the fishing industry became miners or quarrymen, working at the tin mines of St Just or the stone quarries at Penlee, Sheffield, New Mill, Lamorna, and Castallack.

The West Cornwall peninsula had attracted artist visitors since the early nineteenth century, notably, J. M. W. Turner, Lionel Constable, Samuel Prout, and James Inchbold. It was only in the latter part of the century, when artists were seeking to live in colonies, that they began to stay there for any length of time. The first to visit was Caroline Yates (later Caroline Gotch) who may have come on the recommendation of a fellow Slade student, the Falmouth-born, Henry Scott Tuke. She was visited at Newlyn both by Gotch and Tuke, and married the former at St Peter's Church, Newlyn in 1881. However, the couple did not settle in Newlyn until 1886. Another early visitor was the Birmingham artist, Walter Langley, who must have been there prior to 1880 when he sold five views of Newlyn at auction. Langley was the first to settle in Newlyn, in 1882 when he was given a commission for a year's work there by a Birmingham photographer. He was closely followed by another Birmingham artist, Edwin Harris and, in 1883, Wainwright, the Birmingham watercolourist, visited Newlyn. In September of that year, Tuke found there were already about ten artists in the Newlyn colony, including Langley, Wainwright, Gotch, Millard, Norman Taylor and Frank Bramley. Bramley had studied with Wainwright and Harris in Antwerp, while Wainwright and Millard had met Tuke and the Gotches in Paris.

Forbes, however, discovered Newlyn by chance. He was on a tour of Cornwall in search of a suitable place to settle and paint, and wrote to his mother in January 1884 from the Union Hotel, Penzance:

> so that unless I prefer a place called Newlyn within a mile of this town and which I have just run over to see, I shall probably put up at Porthleven. I sleep here tonight, go over first thing tomorrow morning to Newlyn, judge it, return then to Falmouth and back again to whichever place I decide upon finally.

His next letter is a eulogy on Newlyn, where he has already settled: 'Newlyn is a sort of English Concarneau and is the haunt of a great many painters.' He knows some personally, others such as Langley, Gotch and Warterlow, by reputation:

> The man I returned from Brittany with last year, (Leghe) Suthers has been here all last summer and (Ralph) Todd, the young fellow that fell in love and got engaged . . . at Quimperlé last year is here and offered to share a sitting room with me. I declined this, however, for I know but little of him. I have however found very nice rooms and a studio . . . (built by a painter here out of an old sail loft) for 15/- a week including attendance, cooking, lights and in fact everything but coal and food.

Initially, he found his new companions a little uninteresting but was encouraged by the arrival of Alexander Chevallier Tayler and the return of Tuke later that year. Both Tuke and Tayler had studied under Laurens in Paris in 1881 and remained friends ever since. The same year, Forbes referred to Frank Bodilly who may well have come to Newlyn to visit Caroline Gotch, his sister-in-law. Another incomer, Blandford-Fletcher, whom Forbes had met in Paris, joined him in his lodgings with Mrs Maddern at Bellevue. Forbes wrote in September saying that 'they are flocking in here each day' while the *Cornishman* of that month noted that there were no less than twenty-seven artists residing in Newlyn. The year 1885 saw the arrival of Percy Craft and his wife, the Batemans, Henry Detmold, Frank Bramley, W. B. Fortescue, Fred Hall, and the Norths. It is possible that Bramley had visited earlier and then returned, this time to settle. Another important arrival of that year was Elizabeth Armstrong chaperoned by her mother. She had probably heard of Newlyn through Harris, whom she had met in France. The Garstins arrived in 1886. Garstin may well have met Bramley and Hall at Verlat's and Detmold and Tayler in Paris; he was also a great admirer of Forbes' painting *A Fish Sale on a Cornish Beach* (1885). It was appropriate, too, that Frank Wright Bourdillon, who had expressed admiration for the work of 'the younger men who have studied in France and Italy', should find his way to Newlyn in 1887. Henry Meynell Rheam, a first cousin of Tuke's, was, as has been noted, imported to Newlyn to bolster the artists' cricket team against the St Ives artists, and subsequently remained there. Other artists who stayed in Newlyn included John da Costa, F. McNamara Evans and Frank Richards, as well as a host of amateurs and short-term visitors. Both Napier Hemy and Ayerst Ingram who, like Tuke, later settled in the Falmouth area, visited Newlyn for brief periods.

Initially most of the artists lived and kept studios in Newlyn. The married ones such as Langley and Harris rented houses, and Forbes recorded that Harris paid '£20 a year for a charming house with a garden and studio attached'. The unmarried artists took rooms and had to rely on the cooking of their landladies. Forbes lodged with a Mrs Maddern at Bellevue on Newlyn hill and found this much to his liking: 'The rooms are good, especially the sitting-room which is large and looks towards the sea . . . but the great attraction of this place is the situation which is worth anything in this relaxing and fishy place.' Mrs Maddern's house seems to have been one of the more popular lodgings and Tayler, Fletcher, Bourdillon, the Crafts, Detmold, Fortescue and Ingram all stayed with her at some time. Forbes formed close friendships with some of his fellow lodgers, and in particular with Tayler, whose company he especially enjoyed. He referred to him as 'a ray of sunshine in the house' and lamented his frequent departures from Newlyn.

Most of the artists left Newlyn for Christmas and summer holidays as well as visiting London for the Royal Academy and other important exhibitions. Forbes' family connections with the railway meant that he could travel with ease, and Tayler too, went off for long periods of time, often in order to fulfil commissions. Fred Hall increasingly spent time at Porlock on the Somerset coast where he had a studio, while Elizabeth Armstrong and her mother took rooms in St Ives between summer 1887 and February 1888. As a Canadian and a woman, she preferred the mixed cosmopolitan society in St Ives. Indeed, these were unsettled times for many of the artists – Langley and Harris left Newlyn for a year, and several others contemplated leaving. It seems that sales were not good and their work was not receiving the reviews for which they had hoped. However, the tide may have begun to turn with the purchase for the nation by the Chantrey Bequest of Bramley's *A Hopeless Dawn* (1888).

Studios were usually converted fish-lofts. Elizabeth Armstrong's first studio was rented from a fisherman who still used it on occasion for its original purpose: 'At times it was invaded by a red-bearded Cap'n and a troop of fisher lads . . . who proceeded to beat or mend their nets chanting all the time Moody and Sankey hymns or popular ditties.' Bramley's first studio consisted of a room over a basement. This served as a school and also a potato and turnip shop, run by a remarkable woman with no arms. She had an elephantine voice and Stanhope Forbes used to marvel that Bramley was able to work there at all. Bourdillon described his first studio in Newlyn as 'pregnant with the odour of the promiscuous pilchard'.

Social life was very important for the artists, both as a relaxation and because of a very real need to be with their fellow artists. Initially they met together in the homes of the married artists such as the Langleys or the Harrises and later in the homes of the Garstins, the Gotches and the Forbes. Forbes described one such occasion in July 1885 at the Harrises:

> Wonderful dinner, beginning with ducks and ending with a joint. After dinner, music. Little Bateman plays the flute beautifully. When they had departed about 11 o'clock, Langley sat down and played dance music and we had a little dance – quadrilles, waltzes, polka, etc. Mrs Harris pronouncing me quite a good dancer.

On another occasion Forbes and Tayler gave a dinner party for the Crafts and the local curate and his wife, for which his landlady provided an extremely sumptuous feast consisting of 'lamb and mint sauce – capon sauce Madderne – maccaroni cheese – tartes aux frais – fruit and dessert. Saumur for the ladies'.

Several of the group played instruments. Langley played the banjo and Fortescue the cello, the instrument that Forbes himself was to take up after his painting of *The Village Philharmonic* in 1888. Bateman played the flute, Elizabeth Armstrong and Mrs Bateman the piano, while the Gotches and Percy Craft sang.

A dinner for twenty was held at the Gotches to celebrate the purchase of Bramley's painting *A Hopeless Dawn* by the Chantrey Trustees. An earlier occasion held by Forbes in 1886 at Belle Vue gave rise to a myth amongst the local inhabitants that spirits had been heard singing solemn music at 2 o'clock on a Tuesday morning. The reality was a solemn procession of artists, led by Langley playing his banjo and singing, 'As we went home by the light of the moon.'

Another binding force within the group was the amateur theatricals in which nearly everyone took part, either acting or painting the scenery. The first reference to a performance of two short plays with songs and recitations was in 1885. The Newlyn Amateur Dramatic Society was formed the following year and performances were usually held in St John's Hall, Penzance. Percy Craft was the manager of the group, with Mrs Garstin as secretary and Forbes as treasurer. Despite his pre-stage nerves Forbes loved acting, and Garstin's performance that year was described in the local paper as good enough to make a 'budding barrister blush'. By 1890, the performances were so successful that the play of that year, *A Scrap of Paper*, was performed in Falmouth. Tuke told his sister:

> The drill hall was filled with the nobility and gentry of the neighbourhood and the whole thing was a vast success. Mrs Gotch came in for the lion's share of the evening's honours, everyone being charmed with her. We finished with supper, Gotch, Garstin, Tayler, Craft, Millard were all here and spent the next day in visiting the studios.

Another activity involving nearly everyone, was cricket. In the words of the one-time Newlyner, Frank Richards:

> Newlyn versus St Ives is the match of the year, generally terminating in the victory for the home team over their friendly opponents.
>
> Bramley is our captain and with Forbes, Langley, Tayler, Harris Rheam, Blackburne Da Costa, myself, etc., with Gotch and Mackenzie as umpire and scorer and Fred Hall, caricaturist, we make up not so bad a team, playing the first match at home, the return at St Ives, succeeding always in gaining a good day's rest from our work and a good day's fun.

These activities helped to foster a sense of comradeship and belonging within the group as a whole. The artists were very supportive of one another both in their work and in their personal lives. Forbes' letters home were full of concern for the success of all the artists at the Royal Academy, and Bourdillon's letters best exemplify the agony experienced by all when waiting to hear whether their paintings had been included and, if so, whether they had been well hung: 'I believe this insatiable need and failure to produce saleable work is good for one's development, though sometimes it goes near to engendering despair.'

For the very vulnerable, the group situation also introduced an element of competition and Bourdillon felt unable to continue painting his very sensitive landscapes and interiors, turning instead to historical and costume scenes: 'You see I am rather driven to this costume work for down here there are lots of clever fellows who do the village business so much better than I.'

On a personal level the artists were particularly supportive of each other. Richards wrote:

> A more good-hearted lot of men you wouldn't meet in a day's or rather a life's march. I have good reason to say this having experienced a long illness at Newlyn, whereby their mettle well proven, they are as big and as noble as their work.

Mrs Harris' illness in 1887 attracted similar support. Edwin Harris' wife died in 1887, presumably of cancer. Several of the artists' wives nursed her, including Mrs Garstin who was pregnant at the time, while the men, notably Tayler, Bramley, Garstin and Forbes kept Harris company at night. This was in spite of the fact that these were vital weeks for finishing work for the Royal Academy.

Forbes gradually became, in Garstin's words, 'the centre and rallying point of the Newlyn colony'. Although not the first to settle, the success of his paintings and, in particular, of *A Fish Sale on a Cornish Beach* led to recognition of the group as a whole, and outsiders generally looked to Forbes as the leader. Garstin went on to point out in his perceptive article of 1901:

> No one has done so much to hold the little community of Newlyn together as Mr Stanhope Forbes. His nature is an unusual compound of enthusiasm and scepticism, of strong opinions and generous deference to the ideas of others, the whole blended and kept sane by an unfailing sense of humour.

Garstin also recognised the importance of Forbes' family background in the moulding of his character and it was apparent that a degree of natural and unassuming authority came easily to Forbes in the small community at Newlyn.

Forbes was the only one of the group to marry a fellow Newlyn artist. He met Elizabeth Armstrong at the Harrises soon after her arrival in 1885 and reported to his mother:

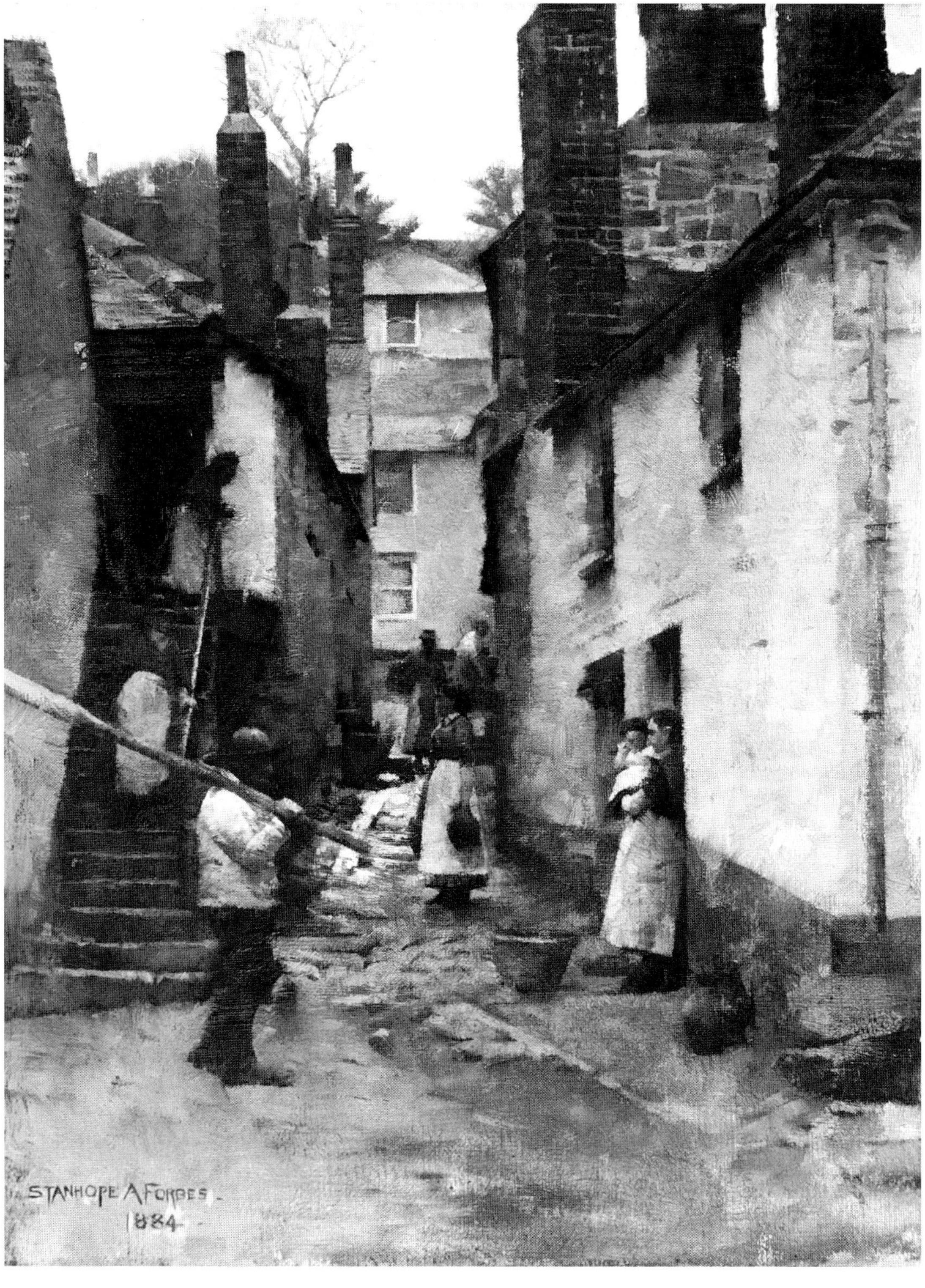

> She cannot be said to be pretty but is a nice and intelligent and ladylike girl. I had a long and interesting talk with the Canadian girl about Pont Aven and all my old friends there, for she, Miss Armstrong, was staying at Julia's whilst I was at Metayers.

Within six months they were engaged although not without some opposition from Forbes' mother, who disapproved of his marrying a fellow artist. Forbes fell deeply in love: 'I fear love-making and painting don't go together. Stannie has not done much of the latter,' complained his Aunt Alice when she visited Newlyn in 1886. 'And oh! to say he is silly over Miss Armstrong is to say nothing and does not care who sees him.' Aunt Alice was also shocked to find Miss Armstrong even 'less religious than her intended husband'. The pair did not marry until August of 1889 after the sale of *The Health of the Bride* (1889) to Henry Tate.

But how did the local people view the artists? It seems that on the whole they were proud of their artist colony: 'Again Newlyn is favoured by the presence of many artists', wrote a reviewer in *The Cornishman* of 1886. Over the following years *The Cornishman* followed the artists, their progress at the Royal Academy and also their acting prowess with enormous interest, often writing at some length.

Forbes was amazed and appalled at the narrow-mindedness of the local Primitive Methodists when he first came to Newlyn. The artists were attacked for sketching on Sundays and one unfortunate Sabbath-breaker actually had his painting slashed. Models would not sit for 'wicked young men who broke the Sabbath' and landladies were equally intractable: 'I am told Mrs Maddern would run me out bag and baggage if I were to paint or otherwise break the day.' Nevertheless, a genuine

OLD NEWLYN (1884)
Stanhope Alexander Forbes
Oil on canvas, 14½ x 11¾in (37 x 28.5cm)
Private Collection

relationship existed between Mrs Maddern and her artist guests and Forbes himself gradually began to warm to the local people despite their strictness: 'I know some charming families, little ménages that do you good to see', he told his mother on one occasion.

Generally, it seems that the villagers had good reason to be grateful to the artists. A writer from *The Cornishman* reported:

> So strong is their attachment to the old village that they are building themselves studios all over it. We have much to thank them for. They are circulating money and as a whole are ever ready to assist in anything which pertains to the wellfare of the town.

One of the ways in which they circulated money was their constant use of models who, Forbes complained, were more expensive than in Brittany. Adults could earn 6d an hour and children 4d. Some local people became almost professional and their faces occur again and again in the paintings. William Glasson and John Henry Tonkin were favourite models of Forbes', appearing in both *The Lighthouse* (1893) and *The Village Philharmonic* (1888), while Langley favoured the care-worn features of 'Old Grace', who appears in *Motherless* (1895), *'Never morning wore to evening but some heart did break'*, (1894), and *Anxious News* (1883).

Models were not always kindly treated. Forbes wrote of one who had to stand in a particularly awkward pose: 'The perspiration drops off him and falls to the ground like rain dripping off the trees. I think I ought to be whipped but the picture must be done.' Despite this apparent harshness, Forbes became a familiar and much loved figure in the village. Writing in 1939, he recalled how one model, known as 'Squeaking Jan', had paid him a great compliment. There had been riots in Newlyn over the difficult problem of fishing on a Sunday and Forbes had been away at the time. Jan was reported to have said: 'Ah, if Mr Faarbes had been there, it would never 'ave 'appened.' On another occasion Forbes was painting his model out-of-doors and the weather changed. His model, William Glasson, said, 'If I had may way, I'd 'ave the sun shine on 'ee all the time!' Forbes sometimes had to contend with local ignorance, however. On one occasion he left a small boy in charge of his painting for a few minutes and returned to find the latter happily seated on top of it! Fortunately no damage was done.

Several of the artists were genuinely concerned about social conditions in Newlyn, and Gotch and Garstin wrote to the papers about the amount of illness amongst the poor to try and alert the so-called 'sanitary commissioners of Newlyn'. The artists participated in local affairs, exhibiting at the opening of the new Penzance art museum in 1887. Forbes was called on to speak at a luncheon at the School of Art, where, he told Elizabeth, he was 'placed among the swells', and Langley spoke at a local prize-giving. They all joined in the village celebrations on the opening of the piers in 1886 and 1894 and at the Queen's Jubilee in 1887.

The most obvious example of the co-operation between the artists and the local inhabitants was the Newlyn Industrial Class. This was begun in 1890, with the financial support of Mr T. B. Bolitho and the help of the artists Gotch, Bramley and Craft. It was run by J. D. Mackenzie and was intended as a means of training and occupying the younger fishermen in their spare time. Although Mackenzie had come to Newlyn in 1888 as a painter he is now remembered almost exclusively for his work with the class. In particular he is noted for his outstanding beaten copper work, known as *repoussé* work (see page 88) and for the designs carried out by his students. His pupils produced small domestic pieces such as candlesticks, water jugs, tea caddies, and pots, pin trays and sconces. He was also concerned for the religious welfare of the people and taught in Sunday Schools in both Newlyn and Penzance.

Another event involving the whole village was the annual private view held in Newlyn before sending the paintings to the Royal Academy: 'Each year in March, we would collect our works together in these studios and hold what Simon the Tanner used to call "that there private interview".' The practice was begun in 1889, and in 1890 Bourdillon described the 'private view' in some detail.

> From 1.30 to 2.30 we had invitees from the village, i.e. our landladies, models, etc. from 2.30 to 5.30 all the top knots and bigwigs and from 5.30 to dusk the doors were opened to everybody who wanted to come in. There was a rush and dust and heat! How the ladies bore it I can't think, for I know I was tired enough. We must have had a thousand people there altogether.

Forbes looked back nostalgically on these private views and felt that the public preferred them to the Passmore Edwards Gallery exhibition. 'The Meadows', where they were held, 'would be crowded with people from far and near, who would make quite a picnic of it, looking through the studios, chatting on the grass, drinking tea and eating cake provided for them in the open air.'

The opening of the Passmore Edwards Gallery in 1895 was to change all this. It was a generous recognition of the number and achievement of the Newlyn artists, which may well have been prompted by the original private view in 'The Meadows'.

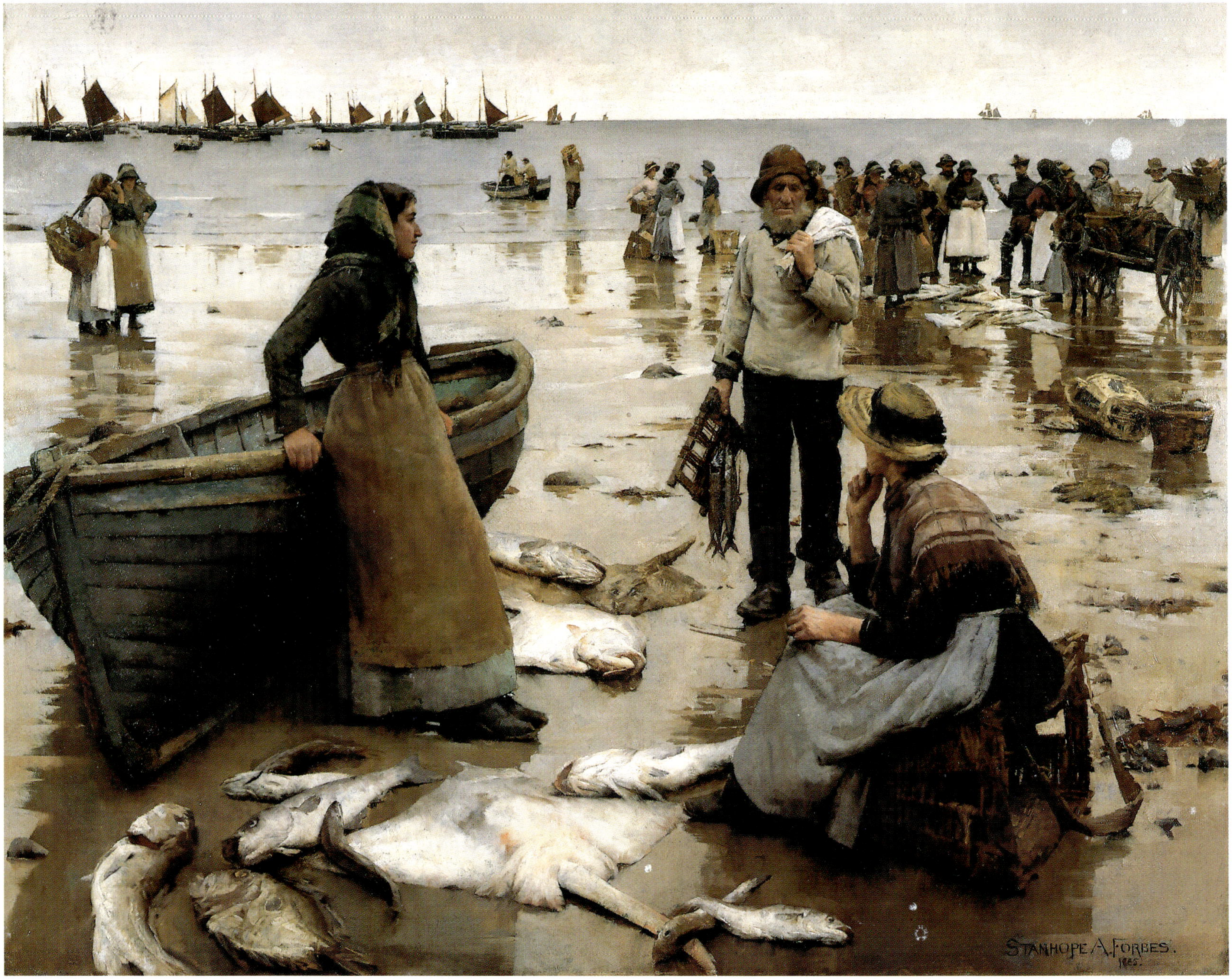

A Fish Sale on a Cornish Beach (1885)
Stanhope Alexander Forbes

Oil on canvas, 47¾ x 61in (121 x 155cm)
City of Plymouth Museums and Art Gallery

CHAPTER FOUR

FORBES IN NEWLYN 1880–1890

During the 1880s Stanhope Forbes produced a series of paintings of Newlyn life that were probably the most successful of his entire career. As we have seen, it was the sale of *A Street in Brittany* (1881) to the Walker Art Gallery in Liverpool in 1882 which made him decide to give up portraiture and concentrate on *plein air* work: 'I must do plein air or nothing. It is the only way to achieve success. To stick at one branch of art and make it your own.' It was only by painting thus that Forbes believed it was possible to capture the true effects of light and atmosphere and 'that quality of freshness, most difficult of attainment by any other means and which one is apt to lose when the work is brought into the studio for completion'. He even suggested that the success of a painting was in inverse ratio to the degree of comfort in which it was painted. Norman Garstin added that 'your work could not be any good unless you caught a cold doing it'.

Forbes was, however, only too aware of the enormous problems involved:

> To plant one's easel down in the full view of all and work away in the midst of a large congregation needs a good deal of courage; but it takes even more to boldly ask some perfect stranger to pose for one under such very trying conditions. But our principles demanded it and, convinced of their virtue, I strove always to be consistent to them.

Indeed of all the Newlyn artists, Forbes adhered to these principles with the greatest consistency. But they did not prevent him from accepting Arthur Bateman's offer of a studio glasshouse in the centre of Newlyn during the later 1880s. Studios were built for Forbes, Bramley, Todd, Millard, Garstin, and Bourdillon, providing a degree of warmth and shelter together with plenty of light.

Forbes, however, never sacrificed composition and taste for realism and all his paintings are extremely well organised, excluding anything which could be considered coarse or vulgar:

> whether it be purely decorative or frankly realistic a picture should never cease to be a piece of decoration; but as the laws which govern design and composition all spring from nature, the most uncompromising of realists will in his work unconsciously demonstrate some use of them.

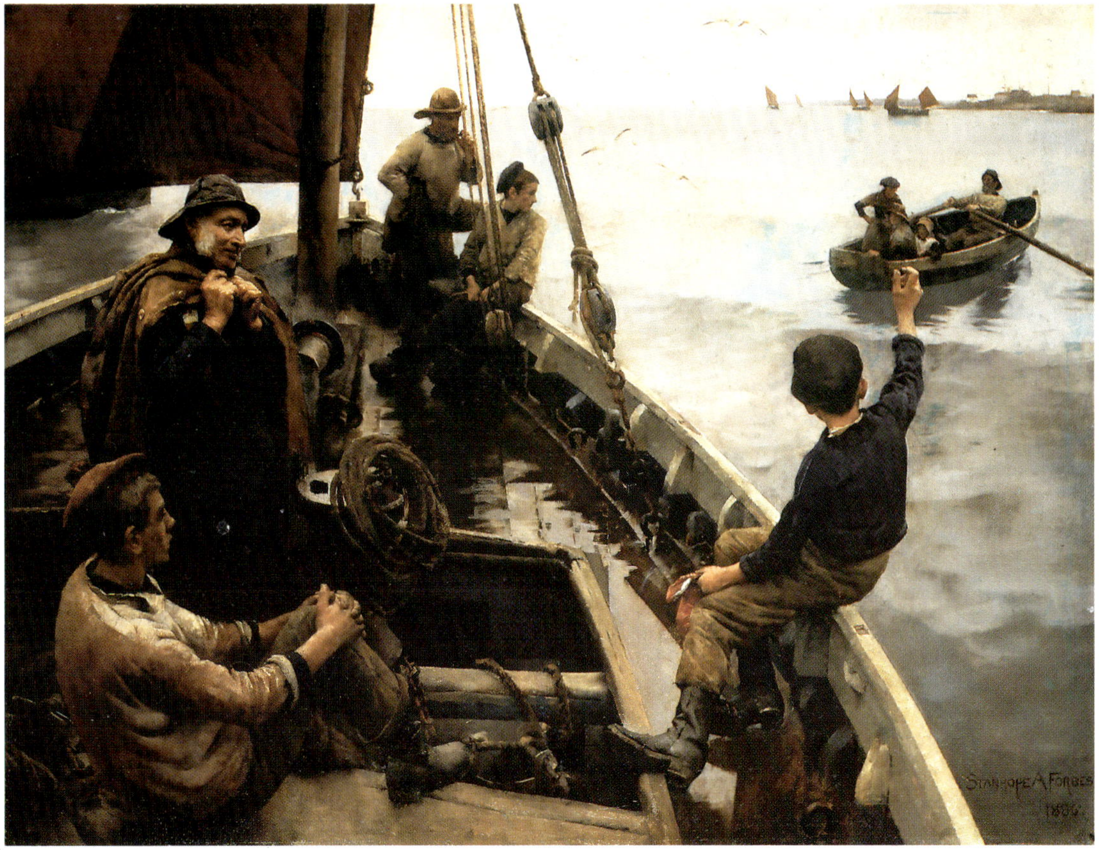

OFF TO THE FISHING GROUNDS (1886)
Stanhope Alexander Forbes
Oil on canvas, 44½ x 60in (113.5 x 152.5cm)
Trustees of the National Museums and Galleries on Merseyside (Walker Art Gallery)

He also felt that 'by possessing artistic qualities' his paintings went beyond being 'mere records of the age we live in'.

Along with most of the Newlyn artists, Forbes employed square-ended brushes. These were originally used in France and enabled artists to cover large areas of canvas quickly when painting out-of-doors. They gave the work a textured appearance and blurred the outlines. These effects are particularly noticeable in the Newlyn work of the earlier 1880s. Norman Garstin described the effect as being similar to an atmospheric envelope:

> We seek to represent not only the man but, as it were, his very atmosphere, and not only his surroundings but his surroundings under certain specific conditions, and it is in making this atmosphere as much a part of the picture as the mere actualities, that our chief claim to an original view of nature lies.

Forbes found that his Breton subjects were not selling as well as he had hoped and decided that subjects from nearer home might have a greater appeal. Thus it was that he went to Cornwall in search of a similar painting ground and discovered Newlyn in January 1884. On his arrival Forbes, as we have seen, found lodgings and a studio, and soon settled down to work. He began a number of oil sketches including one of the '"shoot", a sort of little waterfall where the people all come to wash, fetch water, etc'. He told his mother that he had never seen so many nice-looking girls, though he added; 'unfortunately, the fringe flourishes on this soil and ruins many a pretty face'. He was soon complaining:

> One of the great drawbacks of this place is that the girls will not pose in the streets. You know I like to paint always on the spot. There is only one I found who does not mind, a great big rather handsome woman. But all the pretty little ones are too shy.

In preparation for his painting of the 'shoot', Forbes began to do a series of heads of the best-looking girls. He was also painting a little street scene, 'houses, steps, etc., and a whole host of sketches of boats, boys, sea and other fishy things. I am more pleased with the place artistically each day and have no idea of going elsewhere this year'. In April he was painting a picture of two boys on the sand, including a dead seagull and some more children in the distance. In April and May he visited his parents in London, and took with him the work he had done over the last few months. This included a street scene, a little panel of a boy with a boat, a little head of a girl and a sketch of a boy's head. Most of this work did not satisfy him: 'a very bad three months' work, it is true', he told his mother. But when she began to pressurise him about the money he was spending (he could hardly have chosen anywhere cheaper to live than Newlyn), and the need to produce saleable work, he told her firmly:

> I can honestly say I have never worked harder than I have here and it is not my fault if I am not doing good work . . . I shall bring home good things yet. The little head ought to fetch enough to pay off what I have spent so far.

In February 1884 we find the first of many references to the painting which was to absorb his attention for the rest of the year and which was to become one of the most crucial works that he ever completed: 'The wet sands and the fish and the people buying is what has determined me to stop but I don't know whether it is to be painted. I shall try, however, and you may soon hear I have started a huge canvas.' In another letter he wrote, 'Anything more beautiful than this beach at low water I never saw and if I can only paint figures against such a background as this shining mirror-like shore makes, the result should be effective.' He was, of course, planning *A Fish Sale on a Cornish Beach* (1885).

In February he had considered a canvas of 9 x 5½ft, but on his return from London he decided to cut this down to the more manageable size of 5 x 4ft. He went on to describe his idea for the painting: 'There will be a group of girls in the foreground with the fish, and in the distance the sea and boats. This is already designed and thought out, but to carry it out will be a long, difficult job.' There were also difficulties with models and the weather: 'I sallied forth to have another go at the large picture. I got blown about and rained upon, my model fainted . . .' He was also hindered by the fact that he could only paint when the sky was grey and the tide was out. But in August he was lucky enough 'to get a capital model' in Mrs Madderns' (his landlady) brother:

> who though rather more well to do than most of the men here doesn't object to sit for me and with a sou'wester and a white coat he looks a fine old salt and greatly increases the interest of my large subject.

By October of that year, he feared he would not finish the painting in time for the forthcoming Royal Academy and wondered whether to go on with it, or to take up another painting he had begun of a ropewalk, and send that to the Institute instead of the Academy. It was, however, the support of his fellows, in particular of Henry Scott Tuke and Chevallier Tayler that encouraged him to stick at the *Fish Sale*: 'Art is precious long, I find daily the struggle against almost insuperable difficulties becomes each year more trying. I have begun too much this year and cannot hope to finish everything.' In the end he finished both paintings in time.

Later that month he was more cheerful, declaring that he had had a couple of fair grey days and that the big picture was progressing: 'Mrs Moore, who you and Aunt [his parents had recently visited Newlyn] saw me painting, is now nearly finished. I have put in a new head with yellow straw bonnet and it has greatly improved the composition.' Another improvement to the original design was 'the addition of a donkey cart in the distance'.

By early December, the picture still required another dozen little figures in the distance 'or my story does not tell itself'. Forbes was gratified to find that Walter Langley, usually known as a stern critic, was extremely complimentary: 'Like everyone here he pronounces it a long way the best picture I have painted.'

This painting presents a degree of balance and clarity never before attained by Forbes. The cross-composition leads the eye from the three powerful foreground figures to the middle ground of the painting, showing on one side the auctioneer with his bell, surrounded by a group of fishwives; and on the other, two men unloading a small boat. The fish in the foreground are easily identifiable and form a still life in their own right. Forbes told his mother: 'One day I did a study of some fish for my figure canvas. Fancy three huge skate for 9d.' On another occasion he was not so fortunate. He was offered a turbot by a fishwife for 12/- who then suggested that if he only wanted it for an hour, he could pay 4/-!

The harmonious integration of the figures and the background is achieved by tonal means and further enhanced by the blurred edges resulting from the use of square-ended brushes: 'Beauty lies as much in the light, the atmosphere which surrounds all things as their actual form and fashion. There is nothing which cannot be transformed by the effect under which it is seen.' Forbes' ability to portray the wet sands with their superb reflections is a major feature of the work, particularly since it was these wet sands which had drawn him to paint the work in the first place.

As early as June 1884, Forbes received an understanding from Dowdeswells of Bond Street that they would purchase the finished painting. Although it was subsequently considered for purchase by the Chantrey Bequest (later to form the basis of the Tate Gallery collection) it was rejected because it was seen as 'too positively the outcome of a foreign school'. Forbes was then pleased to accept Dowdeswell's offer of 250 guineas.

The *Fish Sale* received great acclaim at the Royal Academy, bringing not only Forbes himself but the Newlyn artists as a group to the public eye for the first time. It was greatly admired for its 'fresh vitality', its 'gradations of greys' and its 'air of pearls'. The same critic (Wilfred Meynell) wrote of it in 1892, 'It was a picture, which besides being delightful in itself, awakened expectations and those expectations have since been realised. If it did not make an era in British painting, it began to make one.'

Forbes' Royal Academy submission of the following year, *Off to the Fishing Grounds* (1886), did not attain the same high degree of praise. The subject matter is more complex and it lacks the clarity and directness of the *Fish Sale*. Once more Forbes had to face the trials of *plein air* painting, 'I was blown about by the cold wind, my palette smashed in my hand, actually by the force of it. I came to the conclusion that painting was all a mistake.' He found it extremely stressful trying to live up to the promise of the *Fish Sale*, which, he admitted, he was beginning to hate, and rather galling to receive criticism from such artists as Walter Langley and Frank Bodilly.

However, encouragement and sound advice came from surprising quarters. General Peel Yates, a Newlyn worthy and amateur artist, visited Forbes in November and inspired him on: 'That's right my boy, keep on, it's going on well. Keep the water transparent! Don't lose the brilliancy of the sky. A little more tone in the foreground!' And in December, Forbes was visited by the Falmouth marine artist, Napier Hemy, who came to invite him to spend Christmas with him and his wife and to see Forbes' picture.

> I was very nervous of showing it to such a judge of marine subjects, but am glad to say that he liked it and pronounced it a better picture than the *Fish Sale* from which opinion, I must, however, continue to dissent.

Hemy advised Forbes to paint a rough sea and Forbes agreed to do so, adding 'nice prospect of sea sickness'.

The month of February was a particularly trying one for Forbes. He needed grey days without sun, rain or excessive cold – but if the weather was too favourable, the fishing boats went out and he lost his models. By 13 February he admitted to being 'nearly crazy with worry'. At the end of February, when he only had one month left in which to finish the painting for the Royal Academy, one of the boys refused to continue sitting: '. . . surely you must know that a figure once begun must be finished from the same model or else unpainted. O dear I am so bothered I can't settle to anything', he lamented to his mother. The weather in March was more accommodating and his model may have relented, for *Off to the Fishing Grounds* was 'all but finished' on 21 March.

This painting is characterised by the strong contrast between the darker foreground with the figures in the prow of the boat and the much lighter sea in the background with its very subtle tones. There is just a suggestion of movement in the sea, which would certainly have benefited from Hemy's suggestion to make it rougher. Unlike the *Fish Sale*, where the positioning of the figures cannot be faulted, here the foreground figures do not lead the eye into the painting so well, and the general effect is less restful to the eye.

Forbes' own feelings about the painting varied. On one occasion he told his mother that it was 'really in no way inferior if not really superior to my last one', and on another, 'I think myself now you will like it quite well as the *Fish Sale* though perhaps in detail it is not so good.' As Forbes feared, the criticism was unfavourable: Claude Phillips wrote a particularly severe piece in *The Academy*.

> Mr Stanhope Forbes in *Off to the Fishing Ground*, if he does not altogether disappoint the admirers he won last year, does nothing to enhance his suddenly acquired reputation. We have again the cool, harmonious grey tones founded on French models, the atmospheric effect, the freedom from affectation and sentimentality; but we have also the same want of mastery in rendering perspective, both linear and aerial, and what is more serious the same lack of genuine individuality, in the absence of which we do not venture to hope great things of an already skilful painter.

P. H. Rathbone was more enthusiastic and praised his thorough workmanship: 'the texture and movement of the sea is especially successful and

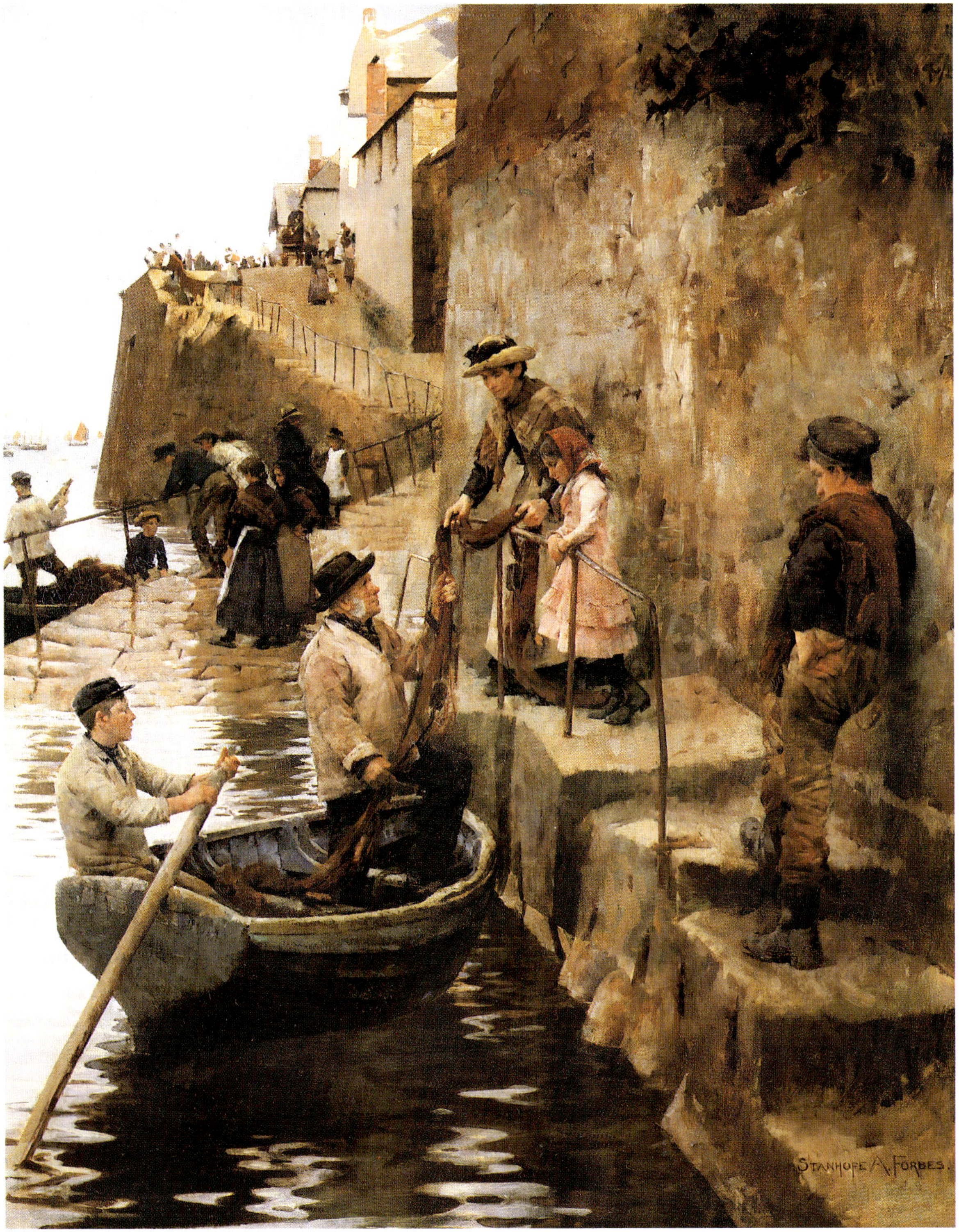

the boat full of life and stir'. However, even Wilfrid Meynell, the champion of the Newlyn School, felt that the painting 'was much outdone by better successors'.

Forbes, however, hoped to sell the painting for a much higher price than the *Fish Sale*. Dowdeswells offered him £325, with a promise to make it up to 350 guineas if he found another customer. Arthur Bateman, the amateur artist who funded the building of studios in Newlyn, offered £350 to induce Dowdeswell to buy, but the latter would not increase his offer nor would Forbes accept the £400 offered by another would-be purchaser called Gwiny. The painting was eventually purchased for £350 by the Walker Art Gallery in Liverpool.

Forbes' Royal Academy submission of 1887 was a complete contrast to *Off to the Fishing Ground*. It shows a procession of gypsies headed by a young woman carrying a child, and was entitled *Their Ever-Shifting Home* (1887). It is close in conception to a watercolour by Walter Langley entitled *Betrayed* (1887), which depicts a woman with a child in her arms being hounded from a village. It was obviously a common theme at the time and was echoed in Chevallier Tayler's paintings of pedlars, Percy Craft's *Homeless*, Blandford-Fletcher's *Evicted* (*c.*1895, Queensland Art Gallery, Australia) and Fred Walker's *The Lost Path* (1863). Forbes' painting was a composite one since the sketch for the background with the old sycamore trees was begun at St Ives in the summer of 1886, when he was on holiday there.

THE SLIP (1885)
Stanhope Alexander Forbes
Oil on canvas, 42 x 33½in (106.5 x 85.5cm)
By courtesy of the Richard Green Gallery, London

A delightful early work showing the area dividing Newlyn Town from Street-an-Nowan which was only negotiable on foot at low tide. The painting divides into three distinct areas: the boat with its lovely reflections and figures in the foreground, the middle distance showing the slip, figures and another boat and the far distance where the slip becomes a track and the figures and buildings are completely dwarfed. It was probably painted from a boat since Forbes could not have obtained such a close up view from the other side of the water.

Interestingly, Forbes' friend Robinson photographed the landscape setting for him and although he did revisit the site several times, he must have worked primarily from the original oil sketch and the photograph. He was, however, to complete the background at the top of Paul Hill in Newlyn:

> I have almost finished my roofs. Keyed up the sky and repainted the trees, but hardly touched the ground for I can't get better roads than the one I have here. It has no nice wheel ruts in it and that I must go for on Paul Hill, I expect.

He also found the gypsies at the top of Paul Hill in February of 1887:

> I am most fortunate for I have all but done the caravan and it quite makes the picture . . . it is very taking, this old van at the top of the hill. I have not yet got my gypsy people about but there will be a few tramping alongside *On the Tramp*.

He found the gypsies to be expensive models and had to work with an audience of nearly 300 while he painted! The gypsy woman in the foreground was probably painted as early as October 1886 when he told his mother that he was worried she would have a baby before he could complete the painting. He went on: 'The gypsy van will be a great difficulty but I hope to overcome it.' In November 1886, Forbes was criticised by 'Uncle Plummer' (a favourite model) for painting his model bare-headed in the garden: 'Ah Mr Forbes, you're a cruel man to keep a poor woman like that.' Forbes himself was photographed painting the large work in the garden of his house, wearing a thick coat with the collar turned up!

Despite compliments from friends such as Tayler, the painting failed to achieve much notice at the Royal Academy. He told Elizabeth Armstrong, 'My picture seemed to me to fall flat. I heard very few complimentary remarks and it seemed to me to astonish nobody. It looked very bad to me.'

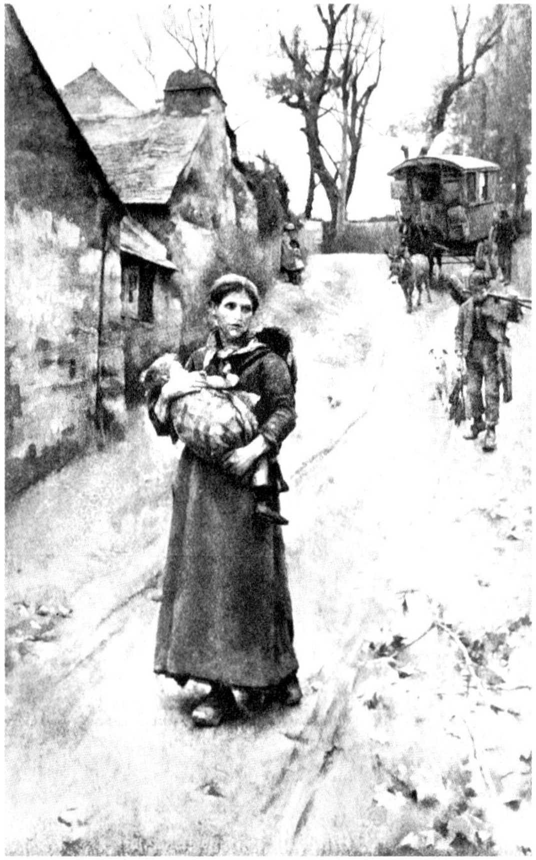

THEIR EVER-SHIFTING HOME (1887)
Stanhope Alexander Forbes
Oil on canvas, 70½ x 45¼in (179 x 115.6cm)
Art Gallery of New South Wales, Sydney

As well as painting and making sketches for these major works, Forbes also worked on other paintings such as *The Ropewalk* (1884) (sold to Aberdeen for £23), *The Slip* (1885) sold by Colnaghi's for £150, *The Bridge of Street-an-nowan* (1886) (whereabouts unknown), *Adam and Eve* (1886) (wherabouts unknown), *Lamplight* (1886) (whereabouts unknown), and *Palmistry* (1886) (whereabouts unknown). He had originally intended that both the Garstins should pose for the latter, but later decided 'that it would never have done' for Mrs Garstin to model. Nevertheless, Mrs Garstin and Elizabeth went to Penzance to choose materials for the dress for the model to wear: 'It will soon be made and I am sure will be very pretty. It will cost all told about 30/- . . . Poor Garstin finds the pose a trying one.' Forbes went to great lengths to produce the right effect:

> I have transformed one corner of my studio into a hall . . . the floor is stained and polished with beeswax and looks quite as good as parqueterre. The sofa is covered with old gold satin and the wall papered to look like a flattened wall.

His mother was required to obtain a lamp. Forbes referred to living in a 'perfect whirl of activity' at this time, for not only was he painting until 10.30pm, but afterwards was busy with rehearsals for the Newlyn artists' play of that year: *Freezing a Mother-in-Law* and *Cut off With a Shilling*. *Palmistry* was exhibited at the New English Art Club and eventually sold in Calcutta. He continued to paint a number of smaller works too. Having managed to sell his 'street scene' (possibly *Old Newlyn*, see page 20) of early 1884 to Dowdeswell, he painted a similar one in August of that year, and also several little scenes featuring boys with boats.

CHAPTER FIVE

FORBES' NEWLYN INTERIORS 1880–1890

The promise of *A Fish Sale* was totally vindicated in Forbes' work of the later 1880s when he painted three of his finest interior scenes – *The Village Philharmonic* (1888), *The Health of the Bride* (1889), and *By Order of the Court* (1890). Ill-health had forced him to turn to interior subjects, and this enabled him to study the subtle effects of differing light sources. The first two works were painted indoors, while the third was painted in his recently completed studio/glasshouse, and consequently displays a more even distribution of light.

Forbes painted *The Village Philharmonic* in the Fishermen's Institute near to the old bridge in Newlyn and, despite the fact that there was already an orchestral society meeting there, he chose and assembled the 'musicians' himself. A Mr White agreed to pose as the conductor, as long as his Stainer violin was included. In November 1887 Forbes told his mother that he had 'run a double bass to earth' and that his 'orchestra was being gradually completed'. The following month he informed her that he had himself started to learn the cello. Forbes apprised Elizabeth of this fact with some trepidation: 'I did something on Monday I ought not to have done, I had my first lesson on the cello. You won't be enlightened by the result I fear, I am put back to making all kinds of . . . sounds, shakes, tremors, arpeggios, etc.'

The subject of musical gatherings was a popular one at the time but more frequently, certainly among the work of the Newlyn artists, instrumentalists appeared alone, as in Elizabeth Armstrong's painting *The Accordion Player* (1888), or in F. M. Evans' *The First Steps* (1889, David Messum Fine Paintings).

The composition of *The Village Philharmonic* is characterised by its integration of natural and artificial light and its raised viewpoint, which may well be taken from Degas rather than from Lepage. The figures are placed so as to maximise the natural light from the little window. This illuminates the window area and falls with dramatic effect on to the end of the long, rectangular table and the floor nearby. The somewhat ragged looking choir, composed of men and children standing alongside the table, contrasts strongly with the more dignified players grouped around the music stand. The foreground violinist with his back to the viewer leads the eye directly to the window and choir on the left, while a diagonal also leads the eye to the cellist on his right.

Forbes has used artificial light sources to highlight, for example, the faces and hands of the cellist and conductor/violinist behind him, while the faces of the choir are subtly highlighted by the overhead lamp. A further lamp, out of the painting, gently accentuates the features of the two seated choir boys with their backs to us. As well as demonstrating a subtle blend of differing light sources, the painting also shows Forbes' strong powers of individual portraiture, particularly noteworthy in the features of the cellist but more subtly hinted at in the extraordinarily varied features of the choir, from the old man on the far left to the smallest child near the window.

The painting won a gold medal at the Paris Universal Exposition and was then purchased by the Birmingham Corporation. It is interesting that a watercolour study for the painting is in existence (Phillips, 15 November 1988 [9]), in which the details appear to be almost exactly the same although a great deal clearer. Forbes probably felt the need to plan the composition first before adding the dramatic effects of light and dark.

The contrasting light effects in *The Health of the Bride* (see frontispiece) are less dramatic. This may have been because it was painted in a better-lit room and also because Forbes particularly wished to concentrate on the individual details and features of the wedding party. The idea for the painting came to Forbes when:

> Standing in one of these inn parlours I had first thought of painting an anglers' meeting – you will notice one or two cases of fish on the wall [in *The Health of the Bride*] – but it occurred to me that a wedding party could be much more picturesquely grouped, even though one had to paint them in the smarter, more conventional Sunday clothes.

Although the subject of weddings was a popular one with Victorian audiences, artists tended to depict either the aftermath of the wedding service out of doors or the bride being prepared for the wedding. The depiction of the wedding breakfast was rarer.

Forbes' painting shows a very dignified and private occasion entirely lacking in the rough and tumble of Fildes' *Village Wedding* (1883, whereabouts unknown). He has so organised the composition that the faces and hands of all the participants are visible, and he has concentrated on a sensitive reproduction of their features. The table, with its vanishing point to the left of the toastmaster forms an essential framework around which to assemble the group and lead the eye into the painting. The old grandfather with his back to the viewer again helps to bring the viewer in, while the inclusion of the children adds a popular note. Indeed, it is the very sensitive depiction of all the different generations that make this such an appealing work, from the demure bride lowering her eyes to look at her posy to the old woman on her left with a small child's head peeping out beside her.

The highlights in the painting are created by the white cloth of the laden table and the pale costumes of the bride, the sailor proposing a toast, the woman on the left, and the small child with her back to us. The oranges in the foreground add a welcome tinge of warm colour. The light from the central window is counterbalanced by the reflection in the mirror on the right and the maid with her white apron and cap on the left. The reflections on the pile of cutlery and plates in the right foreground again introduce a lighter note.

Forbes stated that the painting was 'not carried through without infinite painstaking labour, or finished without much misgiving and doubt of its reception'. The work was very well received and the public delighted in deciphering it 'bit by bit, figure after figure, growing quite vociferous as to which were the parents of the bride and whether it was sherry or rum the old lady on the right was drinking'. The critics also praised Forbes' 'genuine observation of character and truth of detail, his handling of light and his avoidance of the usual smiling, pretty, plump bride'. While unknown to Forbes, the Chantrey Trustees were discussing whether to buy it or not, Forbes accepted an offer of £600 from Henry Tate at the private view. His action was rewarded five years later when Sir Henry Tate's collection was donated to form the basis of the present-day Tate Gallery in London. Another piece of good fortune which resulted directly from the sale of the painting was Forbes' own marriage to Elizabeth Armstrong in August 1889. Forbes told Mr Tate, 'it was inevitable after painting this picture'.

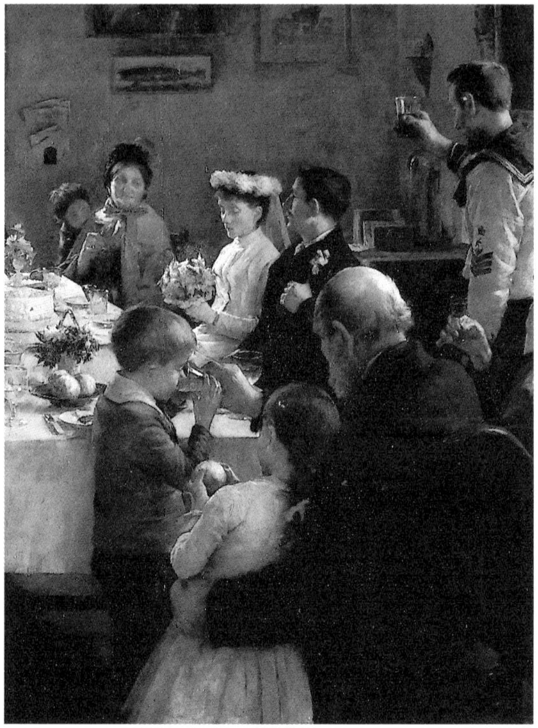

Detail from The Health of the Bride

By Order of the Court (1890) shares the latter's emphasis on characterisation to an even greater extent, where again all the participants were based on local models. Bourdillon's letters inform us that General Peel Yates modelled for one of the bidders (on the right of the painting) and that the other models were friends of the artist. The setting for the scene was based on a farmhouse, and the idea came from Forbes' own experiences – 'through attending so many of the auction sales at farms and country houses hereabouts in the hope of picking up odd things for my home and studio. All the details of the scene were stamped upon my memory, and I had no difficulty in painting them.'

As in the previous two paintings, Forbes has used the *contrejour* effect of figures seen in front of a window, although here the window is larger and the light more diffused. He also uses the same raised viewpoint as in the other two works.

It is probable that the story-telling element which has crept into this work and was not present in the previous two, was included to encourage a sale. It has also given Forbes an opportunity to explore a wide variety of facial expressions. Forbes deplored the incursion of modern 'luxury' into the traditional way of life in West Cornwall and the objects on the table may well have been intended to represent this alien manufactured element – with the possible suggestion that this precipitated the bankruptcy. A critic in the *Athenaeum* noted that the bidding for the clock was being contested 'between a woman of the better class and her poorer, more demonstrative neighbour'.

The painting was considered one of the best two paintings of the year and the critic in the *Saturday Review* felt that Forbes had 'narrowly escaped producing a great work'. Even Claude Phillips, who had been so critical of *Off to the Fishing Ground,* considered it 'the best piece of modern genre produced this year'. He went on to describe the scene, and concluded:

> The most delicate power of observation is revealed in the fashion in which each physiognomy is discreetly individualised; its business-like, eager character being just veiled with a shadow of genuine piety and regret. Mr Stanhope Forbes is thus making good use of his solid foreign technique, using it as a weapon in the expression of English scenes and English types. No fault can be found with the execution of the picture, save that its general tonality is unduly and unnecessarily sombre, and, wanting, too, in the kind of strength which it might have achieved without departing from its quakerlike reticence of colour. The glimpse of out-door sunlight obtained through the small window is however charming.

It was said that the success of this painting contributed towards the artist's election as an ARA in 1891. The painting was purchased by the collector Sharpley Bainbridge for £500.

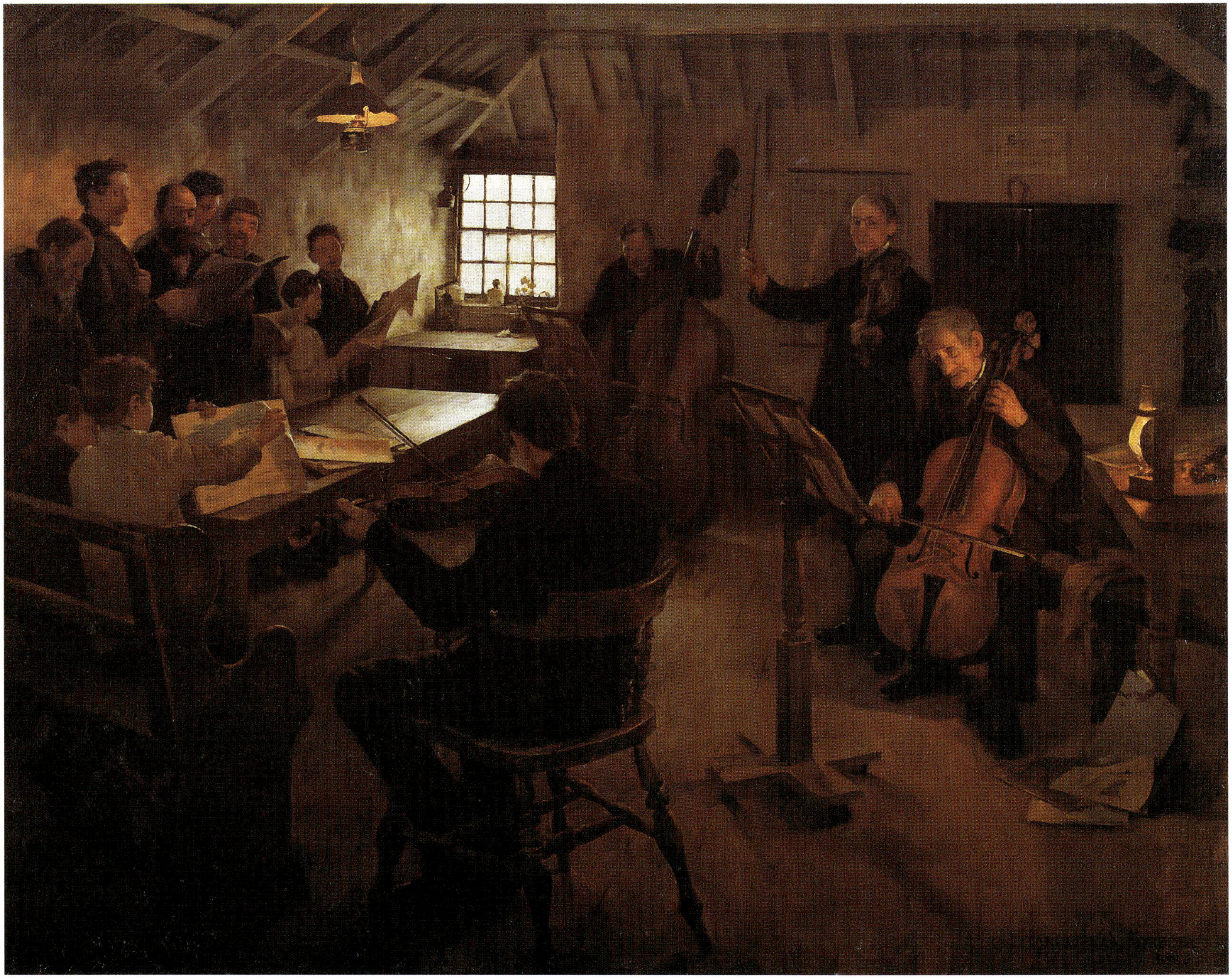

THE VILLAGE PHILHARMONIC (1888)
Stanhope Alexander Forbes
Oil on canvas, 51½ x 66½in (131 x 168.5cm)
City Museums and Art Gallery, Birmingham

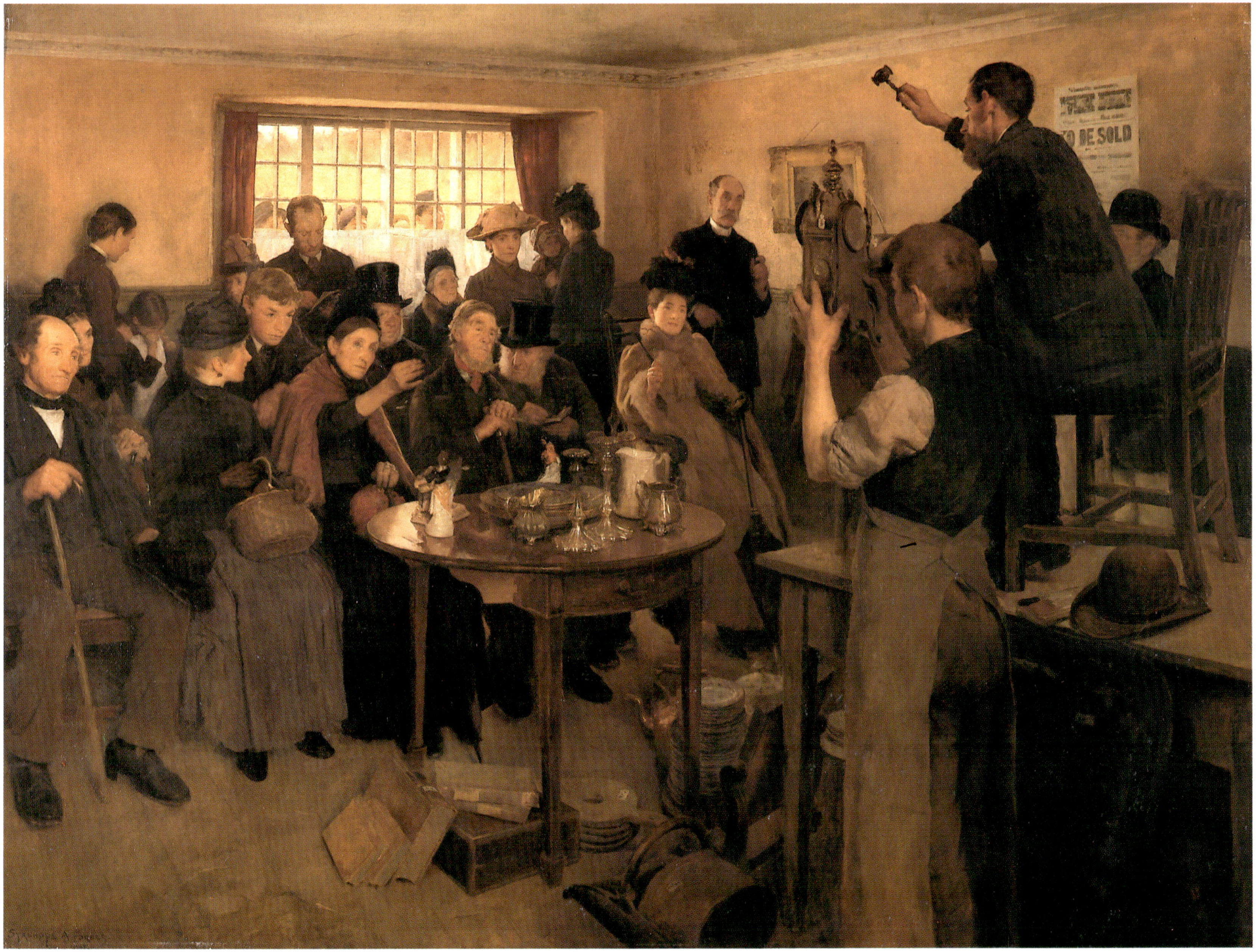

By Order of the Court (1890)
Stanhope Alexander Forbes

Oil on canvas, 60 x 80½in (152.5 x 204.5cm)
Trustees of the National Museums and Galleries on
Merseyside (Walker Art Gallery)

CHAPTER SIX

THE NEWLYN SCHOOL IN THE 1880s

The consistently high quality of Forbes' work during the 1880s provided example and encouragement for the majority of the Newlyn group and their successes and failures can be seen against the background of Forbes' steady output. His solid draughtsmanship, firm handling of paint and total commitment to village subjects served as an example for less successful members to follow, while the more able could develop their own individual styles within this framework.

It is undoubtedly true that being a member of a group gave the individual artists a great sense of support and encouragement, particularly when going through a difficult patch, and the group situation encouraged less consistent artists to give of their best. This may be the case with artists such as Ralph Todd, Leghe Suthers, Fred Millard and others whose work was not of such a consistent quality as that of Forbes and the major artists. On occasion they all produced very charming and well executed works. The same is true of Edwin Harris, whose work was of a more consistent quality but more limited in subject matter than some of the major artists. Bourdillon somewhat patronisingly described him as the 'master of the window seat scene', and indeed Harris carved himself quite a comfortable little niche while in Newlyn by painting interiors with pretty girls.

WALTER LANGLEY

Walter Langley (1852–1922) was an artist whose commitment to village life was quite as strong as Forbes' and his output was nearly as substantial. However, the fact that he used the medium of watercolour meant that he received far less critical attention. When Forbes came to Newlyn in 1884, Langley was already an established watercolourist who had been elected to the Royal Institute of Painters in Watercolour (1883). Forbes told his mother that 'Langley is the watercolour painter that Uncle [James Staats Forbes] goes in for', and added, somewhat patronisingly but not without a hint of envy, 'A rapid worker and sells all he does as fast as done.'

Unlike Forbes and the majority of the other artists, Langley came from a working class background. He was born in Birmingham where he attended school, and was apprenticed to a lithographer at the age of 15. At 21 he won a scholarship to South Kensington where he studied designing for two years. Most of his work at this time was in gold and silver, and some pieces produced between 1873 and 1876 are in a very ornate Renaissance style and drawn with great technical skill. On returning to Birmingham, Langley found that he did not enjoy business, and having spent much of his spare time painting, decided to take it up professionally. In 1881 he was elected an Associate of the Royal Birmingham Society of Artists and the same year was offered £500 for a year's work by a Birmingham photographer named Thrupp. It was this generosity which enabled Langley and his family to move to Newlyn, where he was actually one of the first to settle.

Langley's upbringing gave him a unique understanding and compassion for the sufferings of the people of Newlyn. As he wrote, 'It may be because I have worked my way up that I am interested in all who work.' Langley was a supporter of Charles Bradlaugh, one of the most radical socialist politicians of the day and his work was very much in keeping with his political beliefs. He was even more consistent than Forbes in his devotion to depicting the lives of the fisherfolk. Where Forbes continually sought stimulation from new subjects, Langley never tired of painting what were often remarkably similar subjects. These included a group of fisherfolk posed on the old quay, a young girl sorrowing for the death of her lover, an old woman seated indoors, quietly reflecting on her past life, and so on. Forbes usually tried to avoid disturbing subjects but Langley sought them out time and again. The author of an article on Langley in the *Moseley and Kings Heath Journal* of 1897 wrote:

> His interest, he remarked, has always been with the workers, and toilers; and although not what may be termed a pessimist, he is forever impressed with the signs of the struggle for existence which are so apparent throughout nature, and which entails here and there so much misery and pain.

Many of these scenes have now become his best-known works. One such painting is *For Men Must Work and Women Must Weep* (1883), based on Charles Kingsley's poem *The Three Fishers* of 1851. It has been suggested that this was Langley's favourite work and that one night, while reading Kingsley's poem,

> he heard a gun go off as a signal of distress. He went out into the black night – an awful storm was howling – and he saw the blue rockets being fired from Penzance as a signal to those who were at sea. The scene was to the last degree impressive – a fearful constraint to his cosy fireside – and the idea of the scene at once suggested itself.

The painting is an extremely powerful one and sorrow is expressed through the quiet monumentality of the figures. It is also a superb example of Langley's astonishing grasp of the medium of watercolour. His early training in lithography must have facilitated his ability to master detail and portray different surfaces and textures with such skill. This painting contrasts strongly with '*Disaster*', where the sea lashes up over the harbour wall and all is chaos and movement. *Disaster* was exhibited at the Whitechapel Art Gallery in the spring of 1902, where the following words were added in the catalogue:

> Whether in calm or storm the lives of the fisherfolk are never far removed from sorrow. The wives behind the feeble shelter of the pier are looking for their husbands' boat caught in the storm. All are full of fear, but the face of the woman in the front shows she has learnt the worst.

Langley was probably happiest painting less turbulent works such as *A Quiet Afternoon* (1882, private collection), showing an old woman in a reflective mood. Some of his paintings of children, such as *I think I'll Be a Sailor* (1884, private collection), showing a boy lounging in the grass and contemplating a toy boat, add a lighter note.

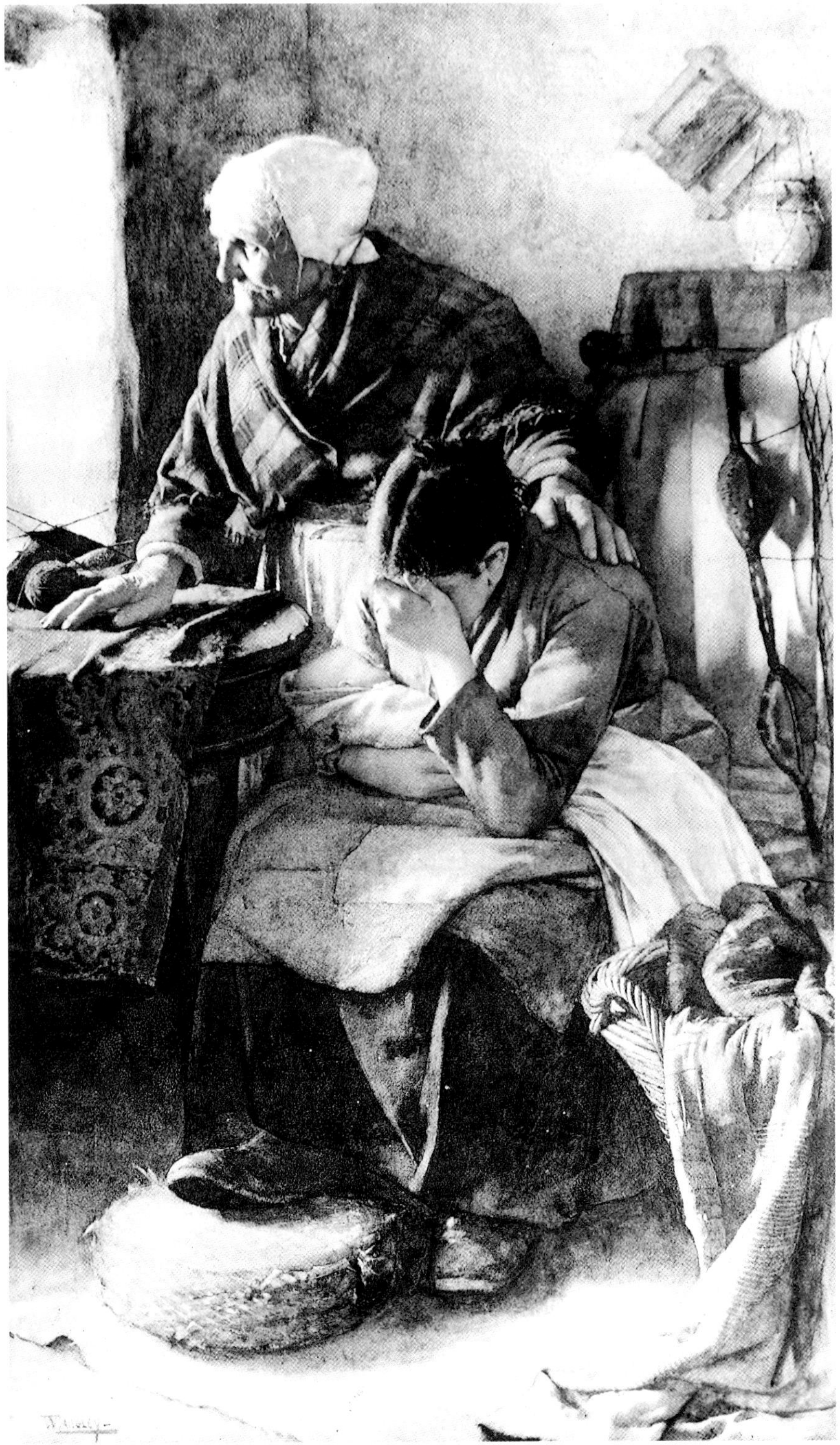

'FOR MEN MUST WORK AND WOMEN MUST WEEP' (1883)
Walter Langley
Watercolour, 36 x 20½in (91.5 x 52cm)
City Museums and Art Gallery, Birmingham

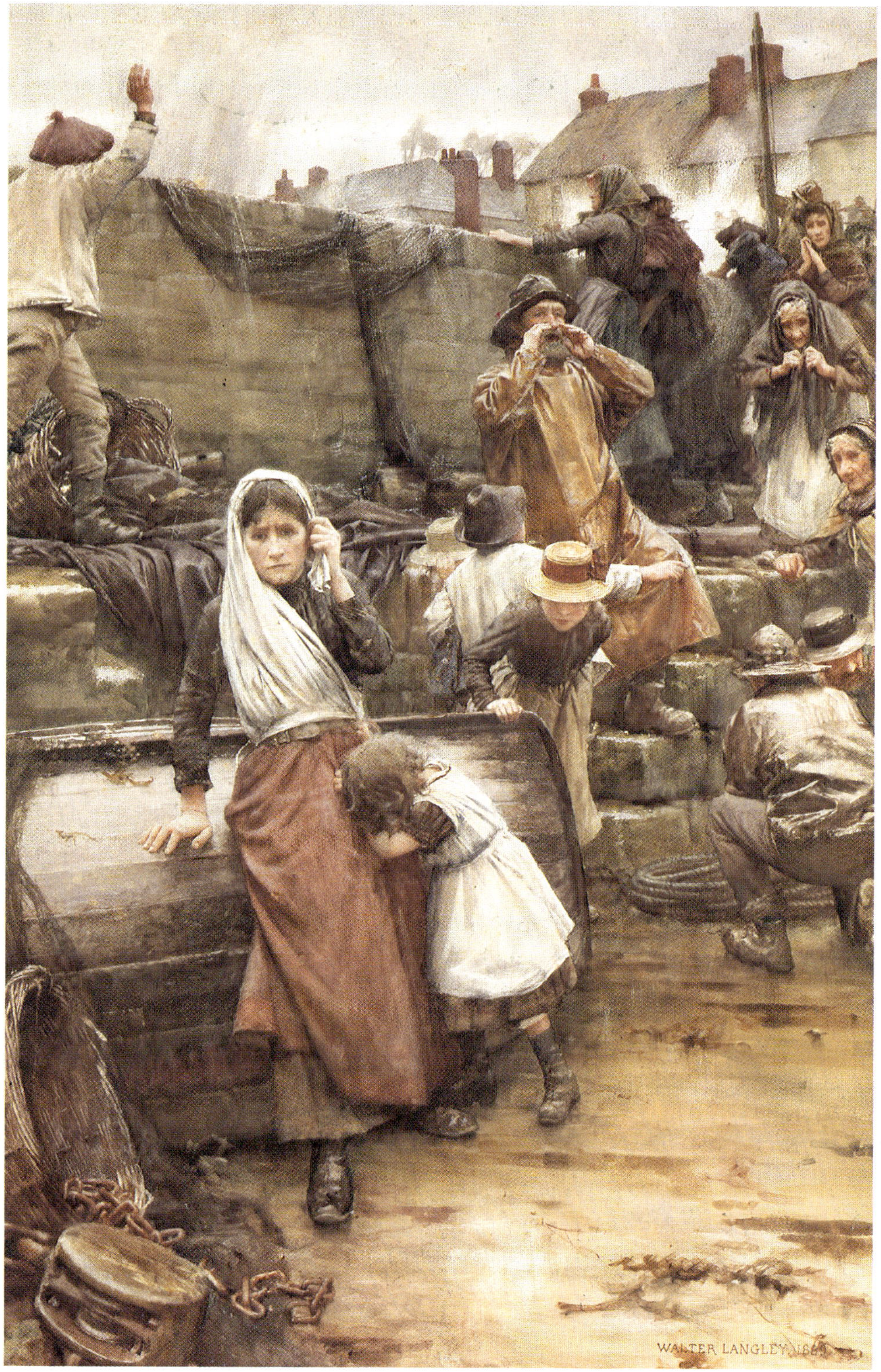

HENRY SCOTT TUKE

Although he lived in Falmouth and only spent very brief periods in Newlyn (September to November 1883 and May to December 1884), Henry Scott Tuke's (1858–1929) work of the 1880s was very similar in both subject matter and style to that of the other Newlyn artists. Tuke was particularly drawn to Newlyn at this time, and wrote to his sister: 'Newlyn is looking more bewitching than ever, I only wonder why I didn't come down sooner, it is now simply reeking with subjects.' Forbes soon recognised Tuke's calibre, both as companion and artist, and was very glad of his presence in Newlyn. *On the Cliff, Newlyn* (1884) shows two local models, Phil and Janie Harvey, posing against the railing beside some drying fish, with Newlyn harbour in the background. However, much as he liked Newlyn, Tuke stated in 1895 that his primary aim was 'to paint the nude in the open air', and conditions in Newlyn were hardly conducive to this. However, at Falmouth, which he knew well from childhood holidays, there were 'quiet beaches, some of them hardly accessible by boat, where one may paint from the life model undisturbed'. Falmouth was also an excellent centre for sailing, Tuke's favourite sport.

During his first years in Falmouth Tuke had some difficulty in obtaining models, but in 1886 he discovered Jack Rowling, 'a young quay scamp', who was to pose for *Our Jack* (1886, Royal Cornwall Polytechnic Society) and *The Promise* (1888). The latter was painted in an orchard and shows Jack with his sweetheart's

◁ *DISASTER* (1889)
Walter Langley

Watercolour on paper laid on stretcher,
47¼ x 29½in (120 x 75cm)
City Museums and Art Gallery, Birmingham

THE PROMISE (1888) ▷
Henry Scott Tuke

Oil on canvas, 22¼ x 26¼in (56.5 x 67cm)
Trustees of the National Museums and Galleries on Merseyside (Walker Art Gallery)

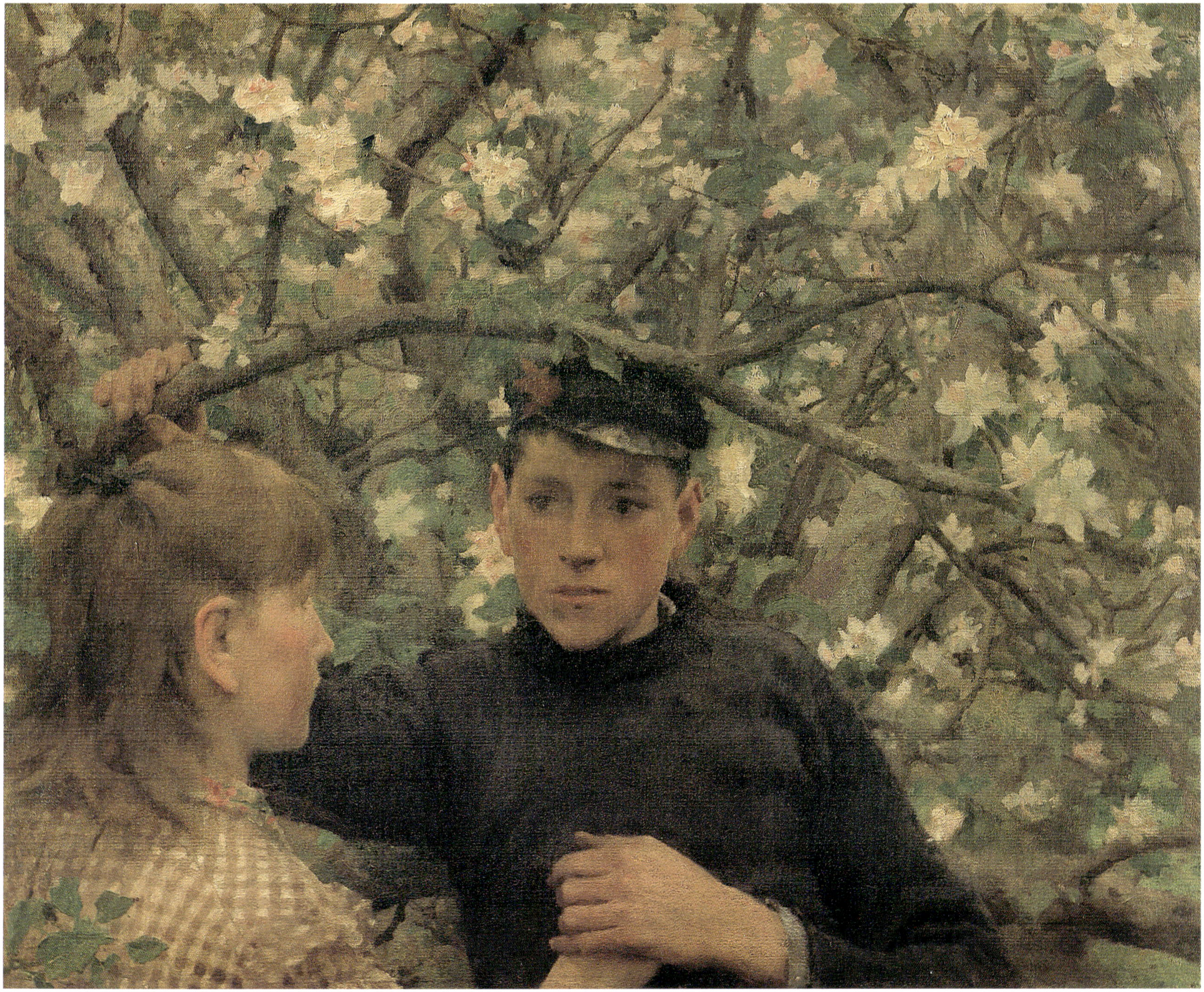

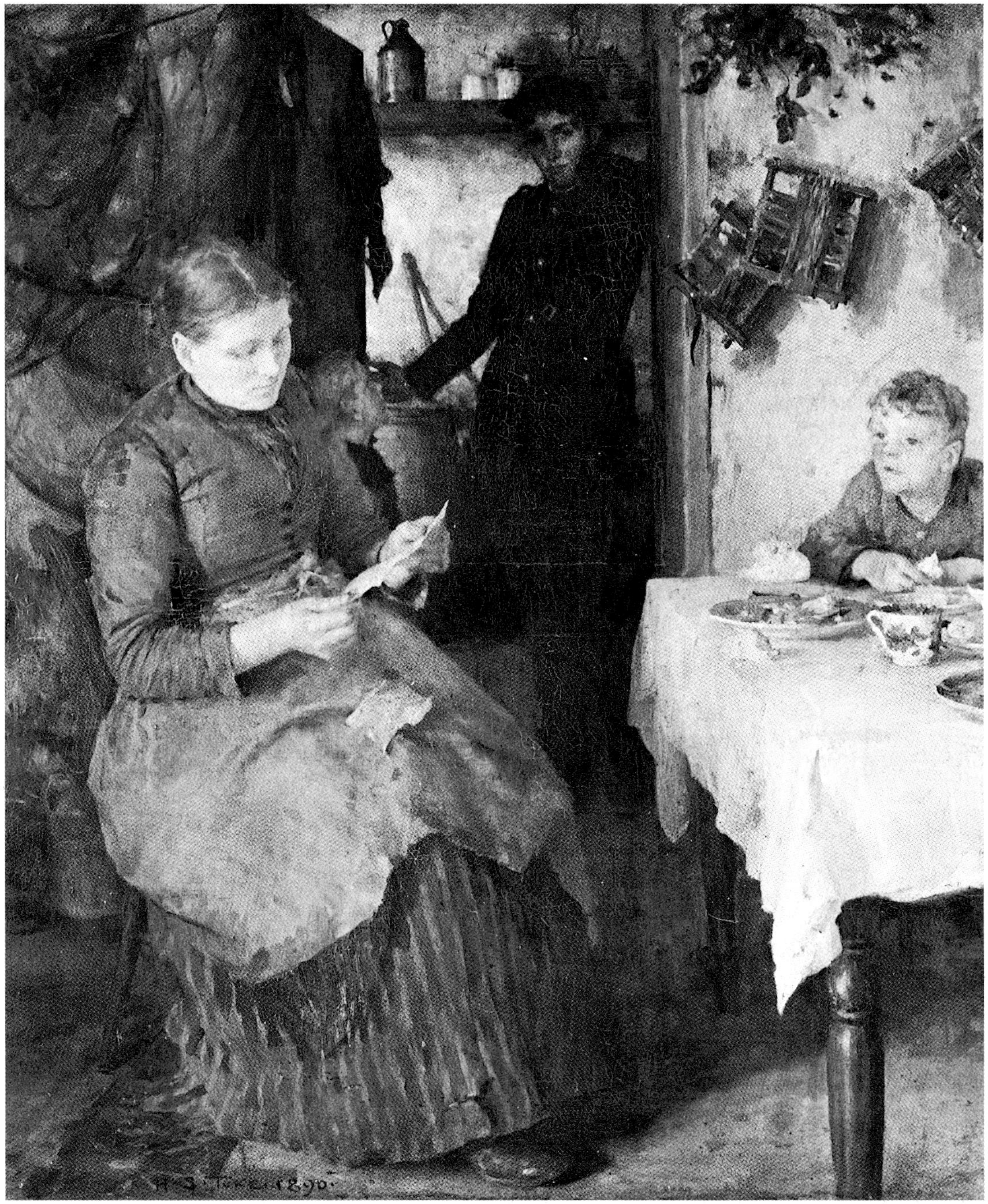

The Message (1890)
Henry Scott Tuke
Oil on canvas, 39½ x 35½in (100 x 90cm)
Falmouth Town Council

sister, Jessie Nicholls. Both paintings reflect the freshness and more subdued tones of the Newlyn and *plein air* artists. *The Message* (1890) is typical of a Newlyn interior and is a simple, homely scene showing Tuke's landlady and her sons. Tuke has made a particular feature of the small boy and the half-eaten meal on the table on the right.

Frank Bramley

Viewed beside the work of Forbes and Langley, the work of Frank Bramley (1857–1915) appears, with one exception, as less substantial and more decorative. The exception is, of course, *The Hopeless Dawn* (1888), the painting whose acclaim at the Royal Academy of 1888 and subsequent purchase for the Chantrey Bequest did more than anything to confirm the reputation of Bramley himself and of his fellow Newlyn artists.

Bramley's natural leaning was towards an exquisitely composed approach so well exemplified in *Domino* (1886) and *Weaving a Chain of Grief* (1887, private collection). Both are departures from the Newlyn realist ideals in that they are middle-class interiors, showing well-dressed women amusing themselves. Both gave Bramley ample opportunity to display his interest in composition and the juxtapositions of tone and form. In *Domino* he has delighted in painting the different planes of white and off-white material from the table-cloth and the woman's dress to the basket with white material elegantly displayed in the foreground. It is a painting in which everything included is 'essential', from the stairs with the light at the top, creating a feeling of space and depth, to the ruckles in the carpet in the foreground. Although greatly admired by his fellow artists, the subtleties of *Domino* were lost on the critics, one of whom described it as 'unfinished'.

The following year, 1887, Bramley decided to exhibit a more 'acceptable' work at the Royal Academy while reserving the more decorative *Weaving a Chain of Grief* for the New English Art Club, a less conservative exhibiting body. The latter work has an *art nouveau* emphasis on

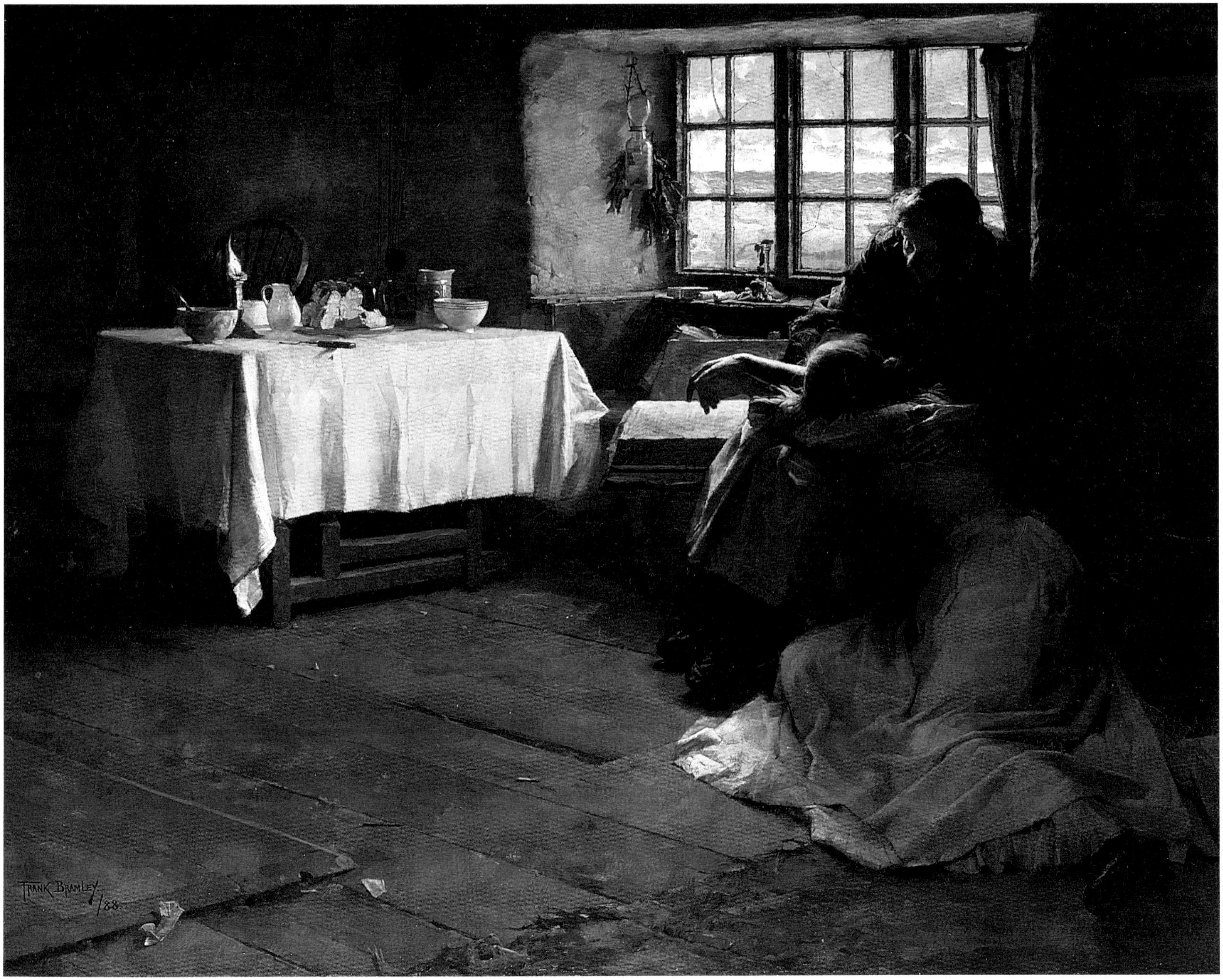

A Hopeless Dawn (1888)
Frank Bramley
Oil on canvas, 48½ x 66in (123 x 167.5cm)
Tate Gallery, London

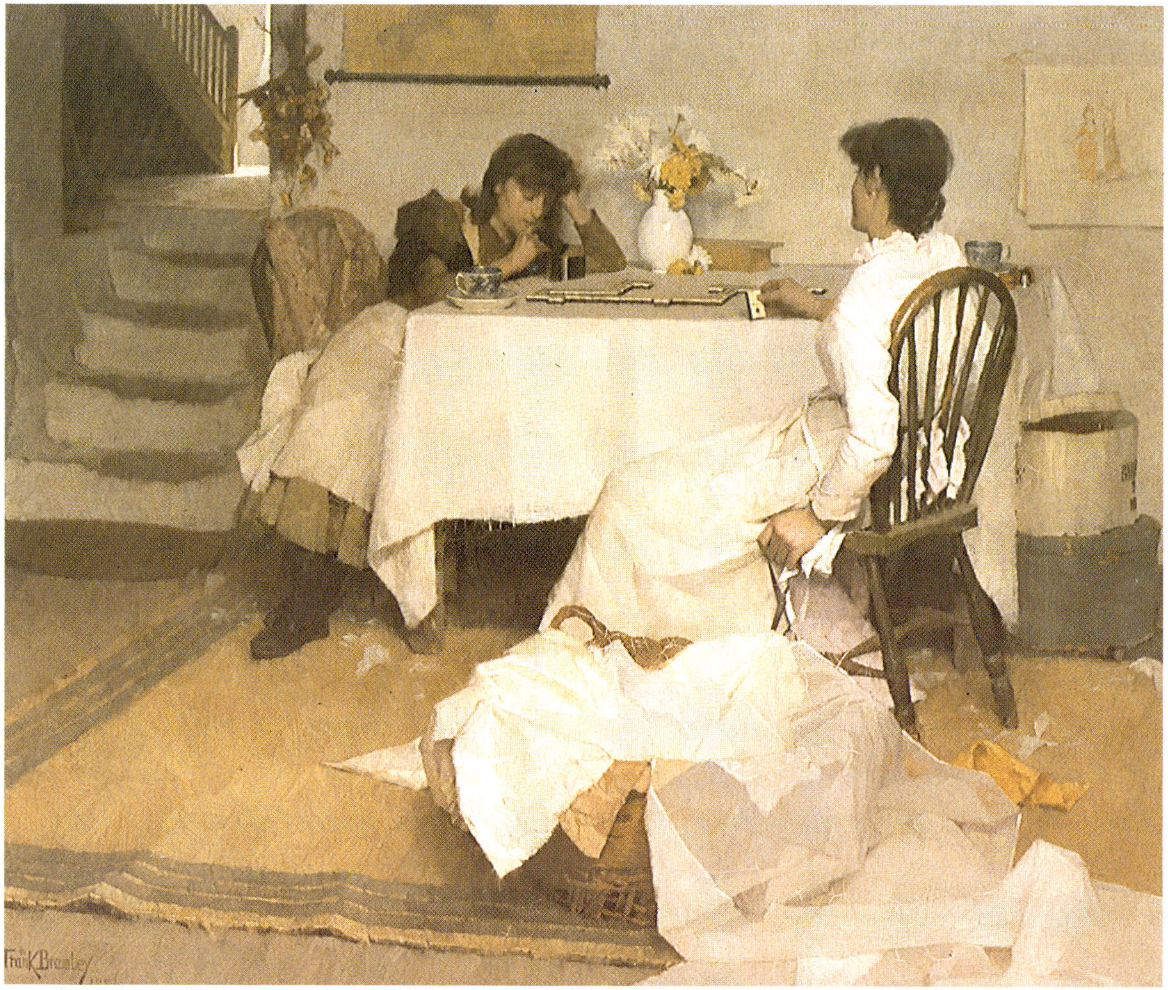

DOMINO (1886)
Frank Bramley
Oil on canvas, 35 x 44in (89 x 112cm)
Crawford Municipal Art Gallery, Cork

decoration expressed by the elegant trail of chrysanthemums in the foreground and the silhouetted shape of the girl in her black dress.

In *A Hopeless Dawn* Bramley has combined his artistic sensitivity with a much more realistic streak, producing a painting which is both simple, emotionally moving and superbly executed. The table set for a meal never to be eaten is especially poignant, while the two figures in the last stages of sorrow and exhaustion, the open Bible and the rough sea seen through the window, would move the most hardened of observers. The painting made a very strong impact on Bramley's fellow artists in Newlyn. Forbes told his mother in February 1888 that it was the finest picture he had ever seen: 'It will establish his reputation I feel shure (*sic*). The dramatic interest of it is so great that even the public will admire it and I need not say that it is freely drawn and finely painted.' A month later he wrote: 'Bramley's picture strikes me more than ever. I cannot describe how beautiful it is. If I were a rich man, I should lose no time in going for it.' Writing in the *Art Journal* in 1889 Alice Meynell described it as 'a perfect blend of simple but profound human drama and of beautifully executed and very carefully observed effects of light and of colour and tone'.

As we have seen, the purchase of *A Hopeless Dawn* for the Chantrey Bequest was a great cause for celebration in Newlyn and a reception was held at the Gotchs' house in Bramley's honour.

NORMAN GARSTIN

The arrival in Newlyn in 1886 of Norman Garstin (1847–1926) was considered by Forbes to be an important addition to the group. Garstin was not only a social asset, renowned for his dry wit, but he soon came to be regarded as the intellectual of the group. His writings are extremely fluent and perceptive, and his views on art were undoubtedly more advanced than those of the other Newlynites. Garstin was always more concerned with spatial and tonal relationships in painting and he found these issues easier to explore in small panels, many of which are quite Whistlerian in their approach. In *Saint's House and Field, Tangier* (1885) Garstin has created a great sense of space and depth using the simplest of means. It is not surprising, however, that to many Victorian patrons accustomed to highly finished academic paintings, Garstin's panels may have appeared as mere sketches and were therefore not saleable.

The Garstins were in fact in straitened circumstances and with a wife and family to support (there were two sons and a daughter – Crosbie, Denys and Alethea), Norman Garstin was under constant pressure to sell his work. Forbes told his mother in 1887:

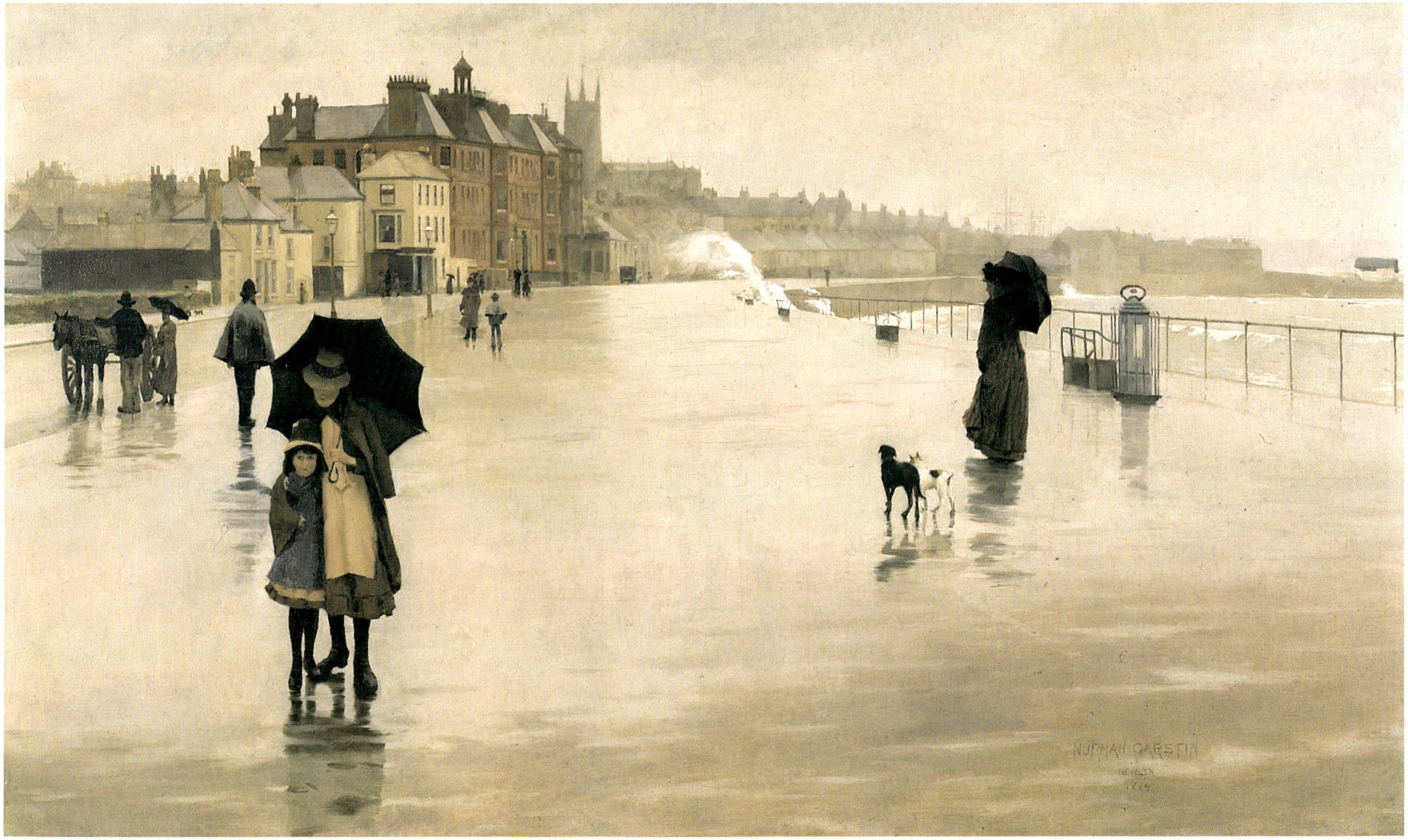

The Rain it Raineth Every Day (1889)
Norman Garstin
Oil on canvas, 37 x 64in (94 x 162.6cm)
Penzance Town Council, Penzance and District Museum and Art Gallery

> They have £80 a year each which between them they manage somehow. It must be a tight squeeze, but old Garstin ought to sell a few of his pictures soon. He has like me just received a cheque from Aberdeen, but his is for £3 for 3 pictures.

It was undoubtedly financial difficulties which forced Garstin into taking sketching parties abroad in the summer and later, into painting works which were not his true métier, in order to achieve sales. One such painting, *A Stranger* (1890, National Gallery of Modern Art, Dublin), combines an element of story-telling with a more painterly representation of landscape in the background. In the foreground, two Lepage-like children are debating whether they dare cross a stone stile occupied by a mysterious-looking tramp and his dog.

It was a tragedy that Garstin's masterpiece, *The Rain it Raineth Every Day* (1889) was never hung at the Royal Academy, being in Bourdillon's words, 'crowded out at the last minute'. The painting shows Garstin's great skill in rendering space and depth which he learned from his intense study of Japanese painting. It is further enhanced by the wet reflections on the promenade and the skilful positioning of the figures, which appear almost as if in silhouette, creating a photographic effect. The painting was not sold and was presented much later to the Penzance Corporation.

THOMAS COOPER GOTCH

Thomas Cooper Gotch (1854–1931) was one of the first artists to visit Newlyn with his then wife-to-be, Caroline Burland Yates, who was also an artist, but they did not actually settle there until 1887. During the intervening years they came and went between Newlyn, France, London and Winchelsea. In 1884 they visited Australia and were closely involved with the formation of the Anglo-Australian Society of Artists. This undoubtedly accounts for the number of Gotch's paintings which were exhibited and sold in Australia.

Gotch's nomadic living arrangements were reflected in the variety of styles and approaches with which he experimented during the 1880s. Like Bramley, he had a natural inclination toward decoration but of a more colourful, symbolic kind. His first painting, entitled *Monseigneur Love* (1880), which was described in his notebook as 'a man with bow, woman plucking arrow', demonstrates this interest. Similarly, *Destiny* (1886, Art Gallery of South Australia, Adelaide) is full of symbolic content. He also painted Newlyn subjects at this period, such as *Work and Play* (1882, whereabouts unknown) showing a woman in a fish cellar peeling potatoes and a boy and girl sailing a boat in an earthenware pan. *Mental Arithmetic* (1883) was painted in Newlyn and sold to a Gotch relation in Australia, who presented it to the National Gallery of Victoria. Although the figures are well painted and the work is in the *plein air* tradition, the composition appears a little contrived and lacks the feeling with which Forbes and Langley invested their work.

'Twixt Life and Death (1890, whereabouts unknown, reproduced in *Studio* XIII, No. 60, March 1898, p.78) shows a woman in despair standing with her two children at the door of a cottage in the foreground, while in the background crowds of people can be seen watching a vessel in distress at sea. The intensity of this subject is unusual for Gotch, being more reminiscent of Langley's painting *Disaster*. *'Twixt Life and Death* was sold in Melbourne in 1892 to the well-known collector George McCulloch for £300. Throughout his life Gotch painted landscapes in which he demonstrates a powerful feeling for mood and atmosphere. However, like Forbes, Gotch was also a highly competent portrait painter and this probably proved a more reliable source of income.

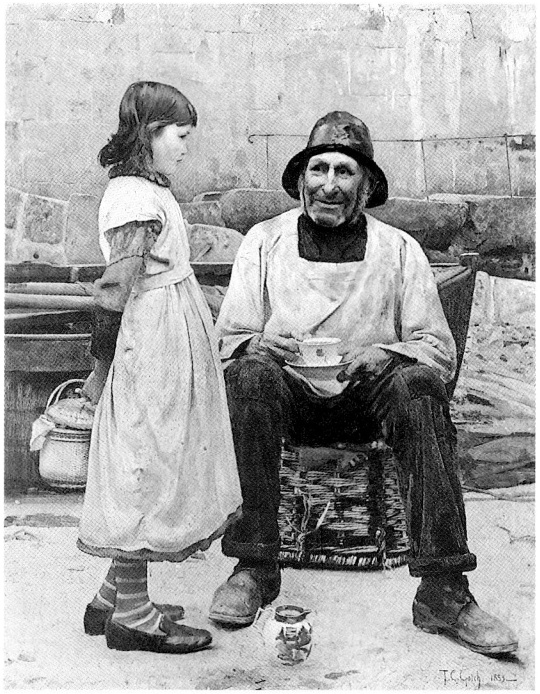

MENTAL ARITHMETIC (1883)
Thomas Cooper Gotch
Oil on canvas, 58½ x 46½in (148 x 118.5cm)
National Gallery of Victoria, Melbourne

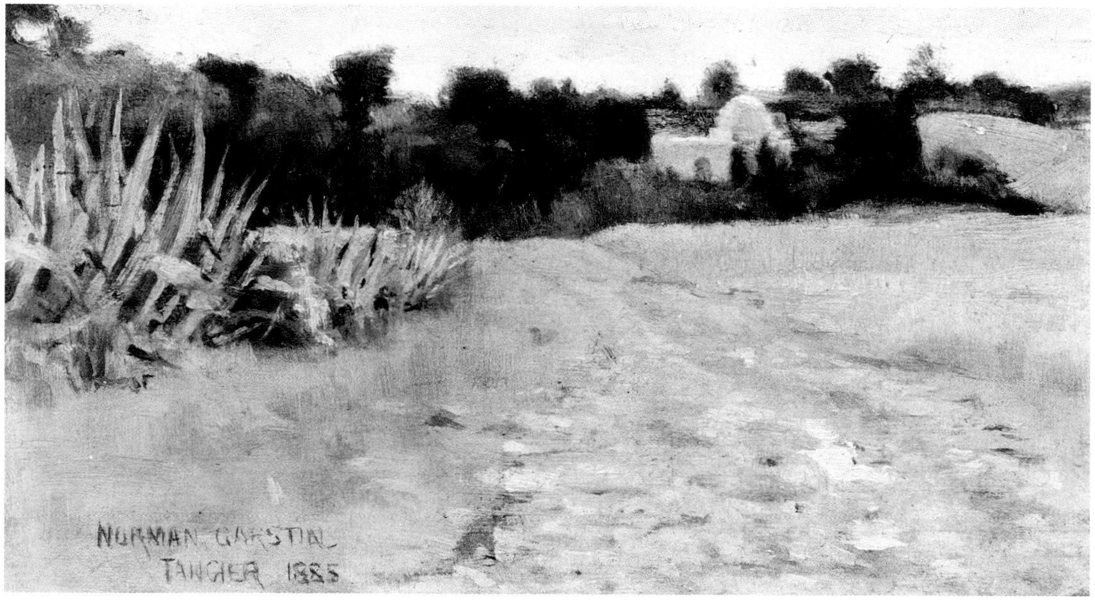

SAINT'S HOUSE AND FIELD, TANGIER (1885)
Norman Garstin
Oil on panel, 5½ x 9½in (15 x 24cm)
Plymouth City Art Gallery

FRANK WRIGHT BOURDILLON

Frank Wright Bourdillon (1851–1924) was a close friend of Garstin's. Like his friend, he started painting later in life and was one of the last of his generation to arrive in Newlyn. His work shows a delicate sensitivity in the handling of paint and a harmony of composition. *The Jubilee Hat* (1887) is an example of Bourdillon's sensitive interpretation of a typical Newlyn subject. Unfortunately,

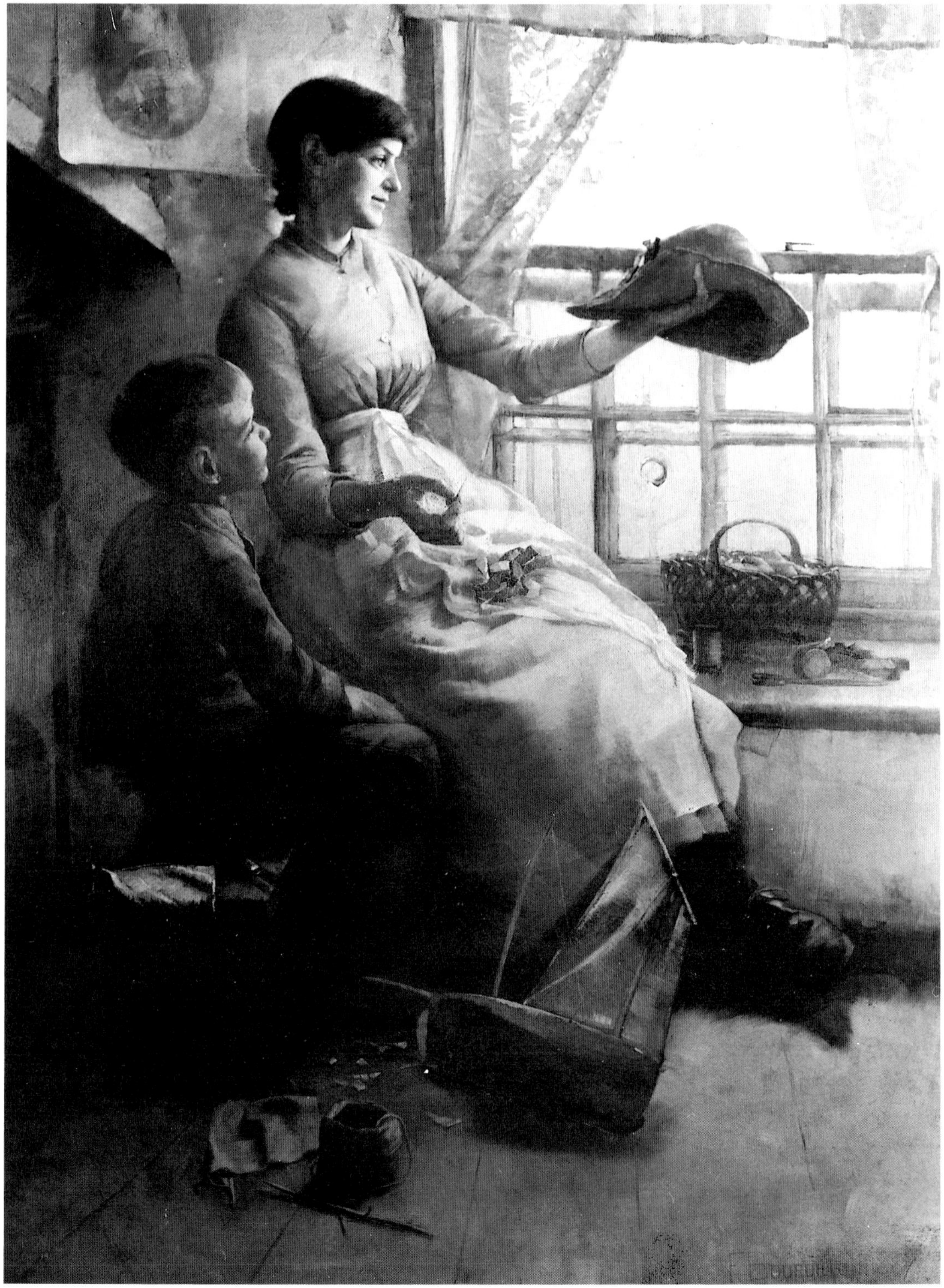

the British public seemed to appreciate Bourdillon's paintings about as much as Garstin's and his highly-strung and not over-confident temperament was affected by lack of success: 'I believe this insatiable need and failure to produce saleable work is good for one's development though sometimes it goes near to engendering despair.'

ALEXANDER CHEVALLIER TAYLER

Alexander Chevallier Tayler (1857–1926) was another artist who had difficulty in selling his paintings but, unlike Bourdillon, he had a more easy-going temperament, and was probably one of the most sociable of the group. Indeed Bourdillon, in his conscientious way, feared that Tayler's over-active social life was hindering his progress in painting. Tayler was the artist whose company Forbes most enjoyed and the latter discusses in a letter with his mother why it was that the artists he found most congenial seemed to have the greatest difficulty in selling their work. He went on to suggest that they probably lacked the 'grit' or ruthlessness to push themselves and their work forward, which might have made them less congenial as companions.

It is certainly true of Tayler that he appeared less consistent than some other Newlynites. On occasion, he could produce some very freshly painted work such as *A Girl Shelling Peas* (1886, Penzance Charter Trustees), and paintings such as *Bless O God These Gifts to Our Use . . .* (whereabouts unknown: *Art Journal* 1889, p.99), which Forbes considered his best painting and was confident that it would sell. It depicts a simple Newlyn interior with grace being said around a table and a typical cottage window in the background. In the foreground a young mother rocks a cradle.

Forbes reported some initial difficulty over the sale of *Not Lost but Gone Before* (1886, Williamson

THE JUBILEE HAT (1887)
Frank Wright Bourdillon

Oil on canvas, 36 x 27in (91.5 x 69cm)
Private Collection

Art Gallery and Museum, Birkenhead), a typical Victorian genre scene in a similar vein to Arthur Hughes' *Home from the Sea* (1883, Ashmolean Museum, Oxford). Although painted *en plein air* in an actual Cornish churchyard, the painting seems to look backwards rather than forwards. Tayler was further distracted by the necessity of fulfilling commissions elsewhere, which meant he was frequently coming and going from Newlyn and, much to Forbes' disappointment, spent the year of 1887 in Venice doing some paintings for Tooths, presumably for a fixed salary. It seems that sociabilities apart, Tayler never really found a niche in Newlyn.

FRED HALL

Another artist who found his niche away from Newlyn was Fred Hall (1860–1948). He has been described as 'something of a mystery' and despite frequent references to him in Forbes' letters, it is not possible to gain a very full picture of his personality. Like Tayler and Gotch he worked in a variety of styles during the 1880s. In the first place, he was a superb caricaturist and his individual portrayals of his fellow artists are most successful (now in the Tate Gallery). However, despite his special talent in this area, he never pursued it as a career, possibly put off by the return of Phil May, the well-known cartoonist, from America.

Hall produced charming paintings in the Lepage tradition, such as *In the Kitchen Garden* (1887, private collection), showing a girl with a goat among a field of cabbages, with some buildings in the background. *Home from the Fields* (1886) has a more contrived composition, although it is beautifully executed. It does appear from Forbes' letters that towards the late 1880s Hall was considered an animal painter, and his two Royal Academy submissions of 1888 are both anecdotal scenes based on the legend of the killing of the goose that laid the golden egg. They soon sold, and it may have been to their sale that Forbes was referring when he told his mother, 'Fred Hall is back, his purse full of money. He has been very fortunate lately.'

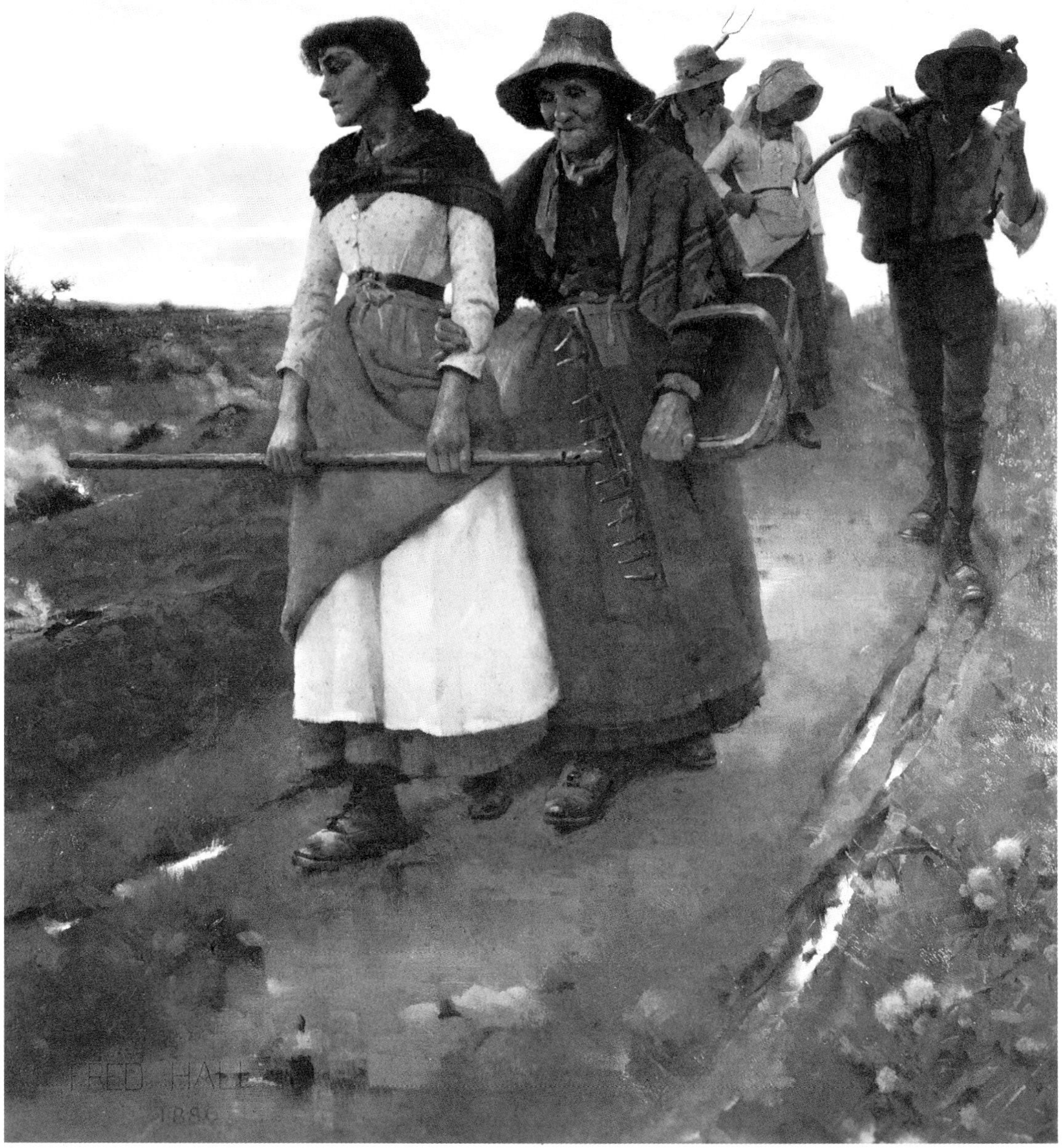

HOME FROM THE FIELDS (1886)
Fred Hall
Oil on canvas, 46 x 36in (117 x 91.5cm)
By courtesy of David Messum, London

CHAPTER SEVEN

ELIZABETH FORBES

Elizabeth Armstrong (1859–1912) was one of the most talented and interesting of the Newlyn artists, and her very feminine sensitivity and lightness of touch contrasts with her husband's more solid approach. She worked with equal authority in a wide variety of media, including pastel, drypoint, oil, gouache, watercolour and a mixture of gouache and charcoal which was unique to her. Her output, though not as large as her husband's, was high and did not lessen after her marriage to Forbes and the birth of their son, Alec, despite her many additional duties. She exhibited widely, wrote, and illustrated articles as well as helping her husband run their School of Painting.

Born near Ottawa in Canada in 1859, Elizabeth was the daughter of William Armstrong, a Canadian government official who died when she was young. Much the youngest in a family which otherwise contained boys, she was left to her own devices a great deal and, being very shy in company, derived pleasure from more private activities such as reading, drawing and observing nature. Like the Forbes, her family was used to frequent moves which prevented the accumulation of many books and objects, and from an early age she used to cherish random scraps of poetry which interested her. Again like many lonely children, she was much given to day-dreaming.

Elizabeth recorded that she was close to her father, who adored and understood his youngest child. He encouraged her in her artistic interests and engaged an old Abbé with some Beaux-Arts training to give her her first drawing lessons. Soon after he sent Elizabeth, with her mother as chaperone, to a school in England. Tragically, two months later he died of a stroke.

Elizabeth and her mother went to live with an uncle in Chelsea. The house was situated next door to Rossetti, whom Elizabeth greatly admired but never met. She was sent to the South Kensington Art Schools at an early age – later regretting this, feeling that she was too young to follow the school routine and that her fellow students were too old to provide real companionship and

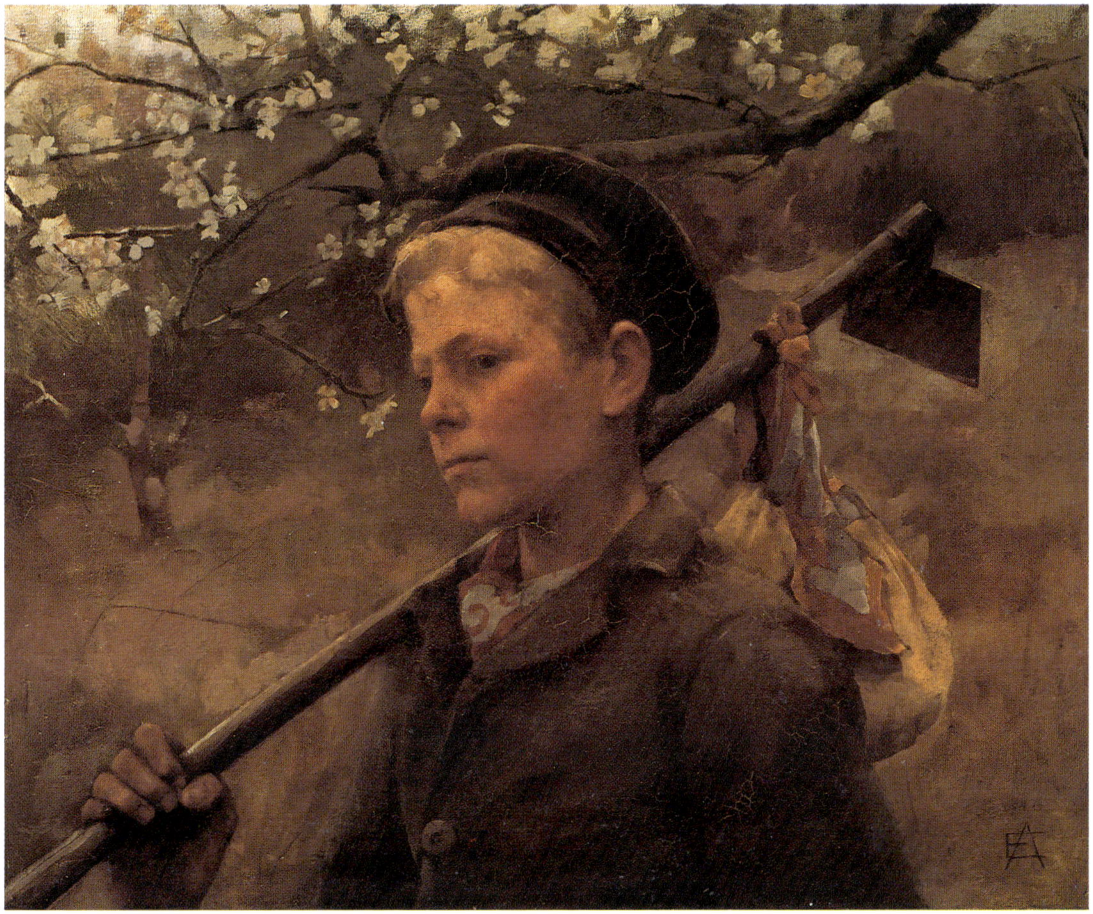

BOY WITH A HOE (c. 1882)
Elizabeth Forbes
Oil on canvas, 19 x 23in (48 x 55.8cm)
Private Collection

understanding. However, she loved visiting the museums and was particularly attracted by a Madonna attributed to Michelangelo. She began to discover novels at this time, and avidly read *Romola* by George Eliot, which she found in some dusty forgotten copies of *The Cornhill Magazine* in her uncle's attic. She also read Ruskin and Carlyle in her uncle's library.

Elizabeth went back to Canada with her mother about 1878, and for the first time in her life was able to enjoy an active social life. They went on to visit some friends in New York where Elizabeth soon became involved with the Art Students League and went on to spend the next three years studying with them. The teachers were mostly young artists who had studied in Europe and were full of 'revolutionary' ideals such as painting *en plein air*. Under their influence, her early enthusiasm for Ruskin's *Modern Painters* was soon eclipsed by a fascination for the paintings of Millet and Lepage. On the advice of a favourite teacher, William Chase, she went to study at Munich rather than Paris, but found that the fact she was both Canadian and a woman weighed heavily against her and she spent five unhappy months there. Nevertheless, she was influenced by the work of an American artist there named Frank Currier, whose energetic drawings of windblown trees with interlacing boughs and whose imaginative use of charcoal may have sparked off some of her own lively studies.

In 1882, she persuaded her mother to accompany her to Pont Aven in Brittany of which she had heard good reports from friends in the Art Students League. She joined a lively and cosmopolitan group of individuals whose Bohemian lifestyle made her feel very much at home. The group gave her support and encouragement and she started exhibiting her work there. Later, she sent small watercolours to the Royal Institute in London, which met with immediate success. It was while staying at the Hotel des Voyageurs in Pont Aven that she heard news of a young Englishman, Stanhope Forbes, working nearby at Quimperlé, whose work was described as 'very strong'. She did not meet him, however, until she went to Newlyn in 1885.

Elizabeth's uncle, Dr Thomas Hawksley, had always taken a great interest in her career and hoped to establish her in London. Elizabeth, on the other hand, hated the restrictions of town life and longed to escape to the country. In the summer of 1884, she joined the Art Students League in Zandvoort, Holland, and produced some very fine etchings and paintings. Despite her enormous skill as an etcher she had to relinquish it when she left London and moved to Cornwall because facilities were not readily available. During her two-and-a-half years in London she became a regular exhibitor at the Grosvenor Gallery, the Royal Institute, and Suffolk Street.

In the autumn of 1885 Elizabeth and her mother moved to Newlyn. Stanhope Forbes first met her at the home of Edwin Harris (whom she may have met in Pont Aven) and, as has been said, confided to his mother that she was 'a nice, intelligent and ladylike girl'. It has been suggested that they were engaged within six months but, until their marriage in 1889, Elizabeth spent much time either in London working on her etchings or at St Ives, where she felt at home in the more cosmopolitan atmosphere. From the correspondence between the two at this time it appears that Elizabeth was both a hard and a quick worker. On one occasion Forbes told her not to stoop too long over her copper plate while on another he suggested that when they were married, he would see she didn't work too hard. Once, when going through a difficult period with his own work he wrote, 'You could have knocked off a dozen charming little pictures in the time I have wasted lately.'

Her hardworking nature did not prevent her, once in Newlyn, from joining in with the other artists and taking part in the dramatic society and other group activities. She was popular with the other artists and may well have enjoyed her position as one of very few women in the community. The other artists also admired her work. Bourdillon thought her 'a nice girl before [her marriage] but she is nicer still now', and went on to add that such was the popularity of the couple that they had to keep their wedding day a secret in order to avoid a crush in the church.

Stanhope and Elizabeth were married in St Peter's Church, Newlyn, and spent their honeymoon on Dartmoor with rod and line. Afterwards they went to live at Cliff Castle in Newlyn, where Elizabeth had previously been staying with her mother. In 1893 they moved to Trewarveneth Farm at the top of Paul Hill before finally settling at Higher Faugan, a house which they designed and had built for themselves in 1904.

Unlike Caroline Gotch, wife of Thomas Cooper Gotch, who gradually painted less in order to concentrate on looking after her husband and her home, Elizabeth was as prolific as ever after her marriage, and exhibited her work extremely widely. As well as exhibiting her work at the Royal Academy from 1883, she showed work in Glasgow, the Grosvenor Gallery, the Society of British Artists, Birmingham and the New Gallery, and also exhibited at the New English Art Club in 1889. In 1893, the year that Alec, her son, was born, she won a gold medal in the oil painting section of the Chicago Exposition. She also found time to write poetry and articles as well as editing a magazine produced by the Newlyn artists in 1907, called *The Paperchase*. The Forbes had a great reputation for hospitality and were frequent hosts to their students, providing many musical and social evenings in their home at the Faugan.

One source of contention between Elizabeth and her future husband was her admiration of and friendship with Whistler and the Sickerts. The friendship was based on her admiration for their work and possibly on a need for technical help with her own etchings, but Forbes deplored both artists and wrote on one occasion that he hoped 'she had seen the last of Whistler for some time, however amusing he may be'. Forbes probably felt ill at ease with artists of whose work he did not approve, although it is interesting to note that later in his life a Whistler etching was to become a treasured possession!

Elizabeth's etchings clearly demonstrate a strong Whistlerian influence and were praised by the marine artist Napier Hemy, who said that 'they were as good as any that are done nowadays'. She did a series of drypoint etchings based on the almshouses in Zandvoort in 1884, while others show children, old women and a self portrait (see page 4). All are characterised by superb draughtsmanship and great delicacy of line. A critic writing in *The Studio* in 1894 praised her etching of *A Dutch Girl* (1884):

> No detail to complete the effect is lacking, yet nothing obtrudes itself. The figure has no air of being a posed model, but is instinct with movement; the line of wool that connects the stocking with the ball on the floor, seems still for a second only ere it moves again. The drawing of this particular line seems to me to be in itself a proof of rare power. To find one to measure it against you must turn to one of Whistler's Venice etchings, where a telegraph wire, apparently as unimportant as this thread plays a very vital part in the scheme of the design. The pleasure derived from refined work with repressed emotion is always keen, and when, as in this etching, one's first enjoyment is amply reinforced by more minute study, you feel tempted to praise it unreservedly, for the cumulative effect is not so often met with that it can be disregarded.

Several of these etchings were exhibited at the Royal Academy, and gave her admission to the Royal Society of Painter Etchers.

It was probably while painting in Brittany that she discovered her special aptitude for and delight in representing children. Although children would have been considered an appropriate subject for a woman to paint at this time, Elizabeth seems to have more than warmed to her subject. Her *Boy with a Hoe* (1883) is a particularly delightful example, showing the head and shoulders of a young boy carrying a hoe over his right shoulder, and a tree in blossom in the background. *A Zandvoort Fisher Girl* (1884) is another delicate and subtle example of her style during this period.

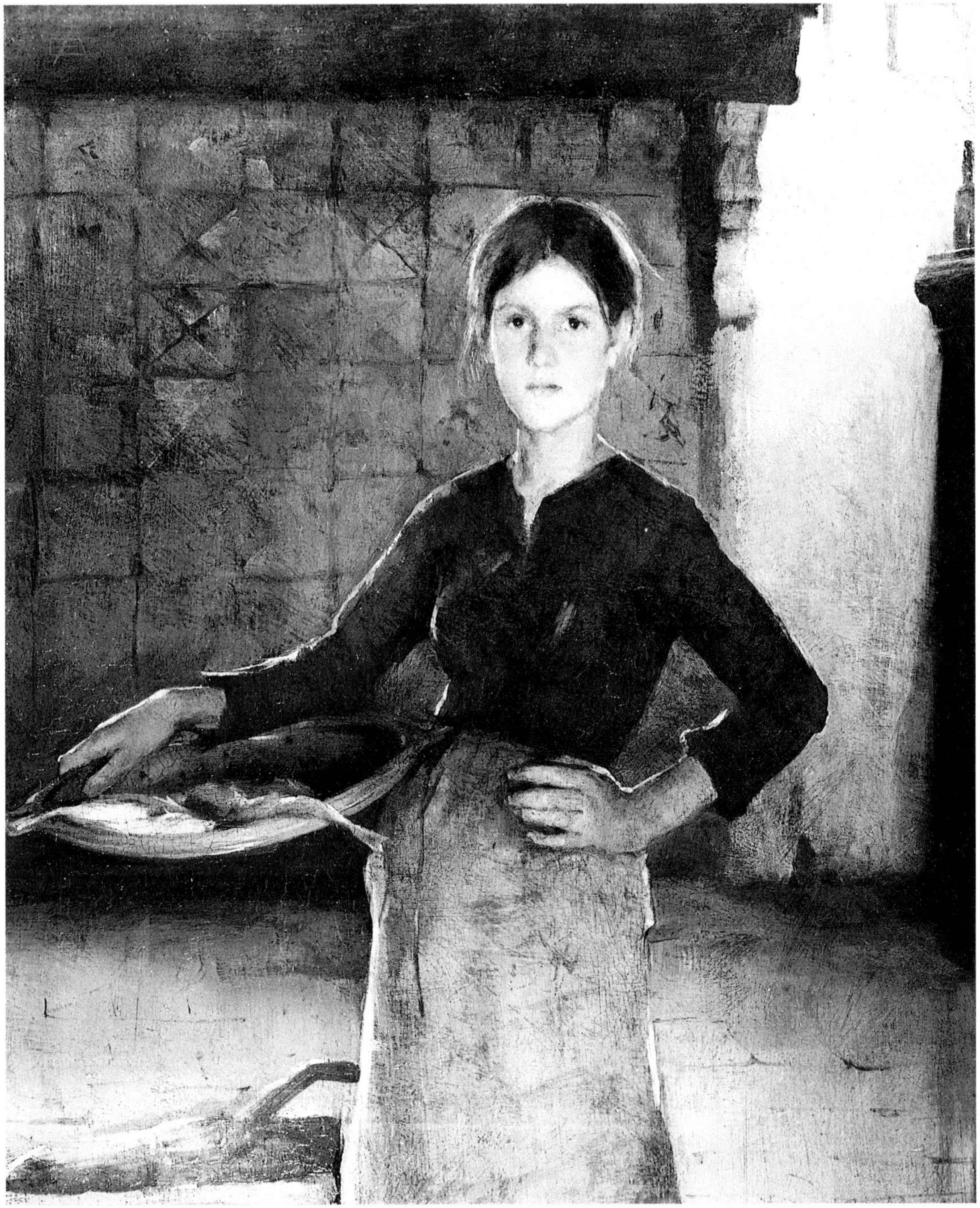

A Zandvoort Fisher Girl (1884)
Elizabeth Forbes
Oil on canvas, 26½ x 21in (67.5 x 53.5cm)
Newlyn Art Gallery

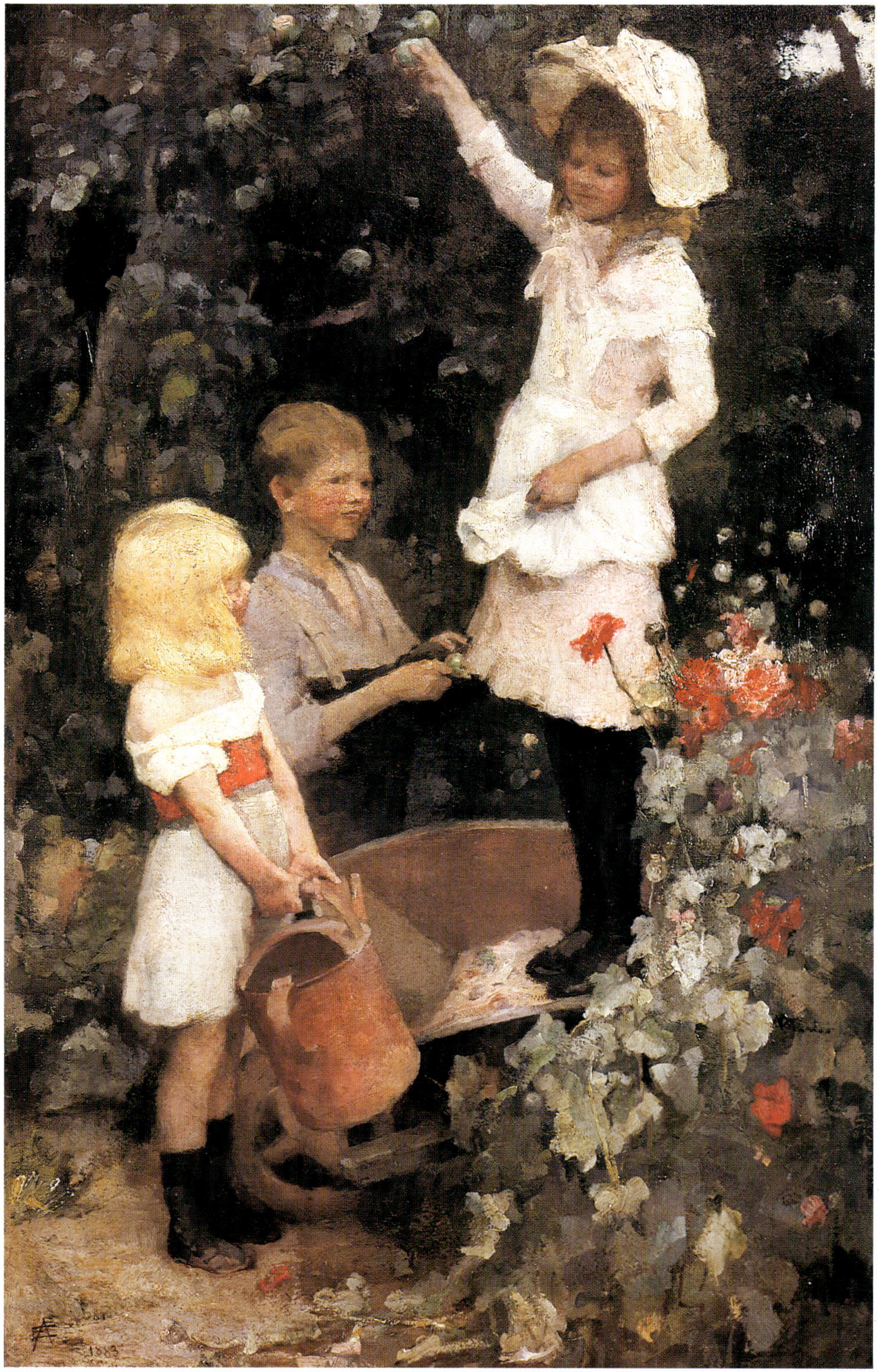

One of her first and most popular works painted in Newlyn is *School is Out* (1889) (p48) showing the schoolroom at the nearby village of Paul and described by Bourdillon as 'a jolly picture of children being let out of school'. She portrays the children with a real sympathy and understanding of their movements and poses, and their faces, though generalised, are full of charm. The painting relies for its light source on the window to the left, with its striking reflections on the floor. The open door to the right leads the eye out to the world beyond the schoolroom. The composition is so organised as to focus on the small boy who is being kept behind and a diagonal runs from him to the head teacher at her table and the little girl beyond, in front of the window. The rest of the children are placed to the right of this table – one group throwing amused glances at the recalcitrant and another silhouetted *contre jour* in front of the open door. Elizabeth has obviously enjoyed painting the details of their clothing from the tam o'shanters worn by the elder children, to the large white bonnet worn by one of the younger girls positioned in front of the teacher's desk.

Two small panels probably dating from her early years in Newlyn (*c.*1885-6) *The Critics* (private collection) and *The Forge* (David Messum Fine Paintings) are again characteristic of Elizabeth's style in their delightful portrayal of children. Indeed, it seems that where other Newlyn artists such as Hall, Tayler, and Bourdillon struggled to find their own characteristic subject matter and style within the Newlyn context, Elizabeth never wavered in her depiction of children, whether indoors or outdoors.

THE APPLE PICKERS (1883)
Elizabeth Forbes

Oil on canvas, 34 x 26in (86.5 x 60cm)
Private Collection

A particularly delightful work and typical of all Elizabeth's paintings of children with its interest in movement, gesture and attractive costume. The little girl standing on the wheelbarrow is seen in bright light, in strong contrast to the dark apple tree behind her. The geraniums in the right foreground balance the composition – their strong reds bringing out the red of the little girl's bodice on the left. Probably painted in Brittany.

A series of three interiors of the early 1890s, *Mignon* (1890, Sydney Art Gallery, Australia), *A Game of 'Old Maid'* (1891) and *A Minuet* (1892), have a more sophisticated flavour. The success of *School is Out* and her marriage to Forbes probably gave Elizabeth greater confidence, enabling her to explore these more refined interiors. Mignon (taken from Goethe's *Wilhelm Meister*) is portrayed with tasteful delicacy, playing the lute in a room full of theatrical properties. In the other two interiors, the compositions are both based on a diagonal, and light falls on the floor through the gaps in the diaphanous curtains. In *A Game of 'Old Maid'* the children are beautifully observed, the young girl sitting slouched across her chair in the manner of young children, while the two older girls are doing their best to look grown up. The boy, who is scoring, stands with one leg wrapped around the other. In *A Minuet*, she has observed the exaggerated movements of the child learning to dance, and a direct diagonal runs from her to the rather bored little boy in the window seat who cannot resist turning round to watch. The costumes are particularly well painted.

The more mysterious qualities of two paintings, *The Witch* (1891, whereabouts unknown) and *Moorland Princesses* (1893, whereabouts unknown), give a foretaste of her later, more imaginative works, while stylistically, *At the Edge of the Wood* (1894, Wolverhampton Art Gallery), depicting a pair of rather awkward lovers in a wood, is still very close to the soft *plein air* work of Lepage. The delightful *Jean, Jeannet and Jeannette* (1891, City Art Gallery, Manchester) was painted in a similar style after a visit to Brittany with her husband.

In *A Fairy Story* (1896) the square-brush technique is gradually replaced by a more flickering one showing some awareness of the Impressionism of Manet, in common with her

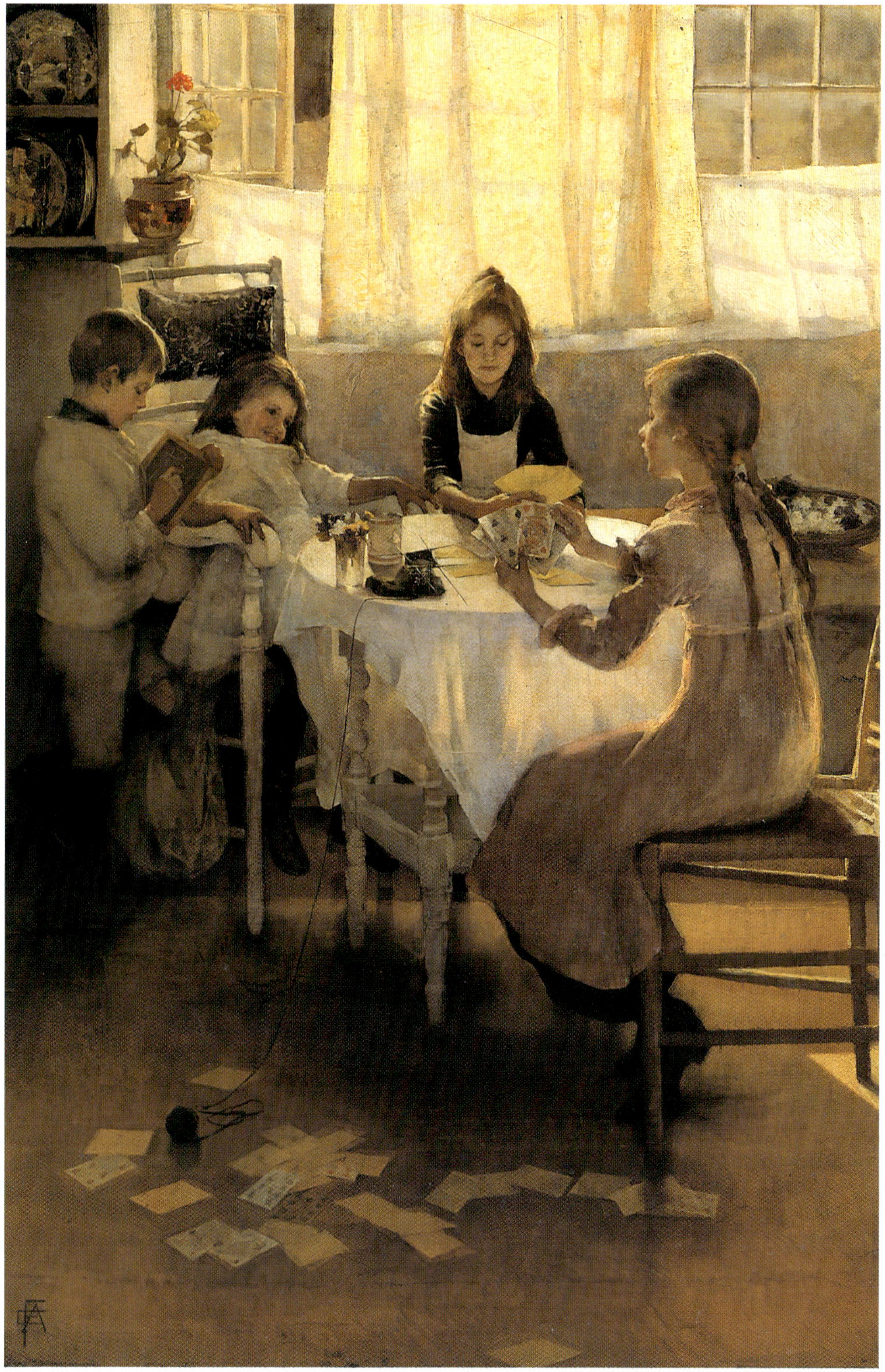

A GAME OF 'OLD MAID' (1891)
Elizabeth Forbes
Oil on canvas, 40 x 25in (101.5 x 63.5cm)
Private collection

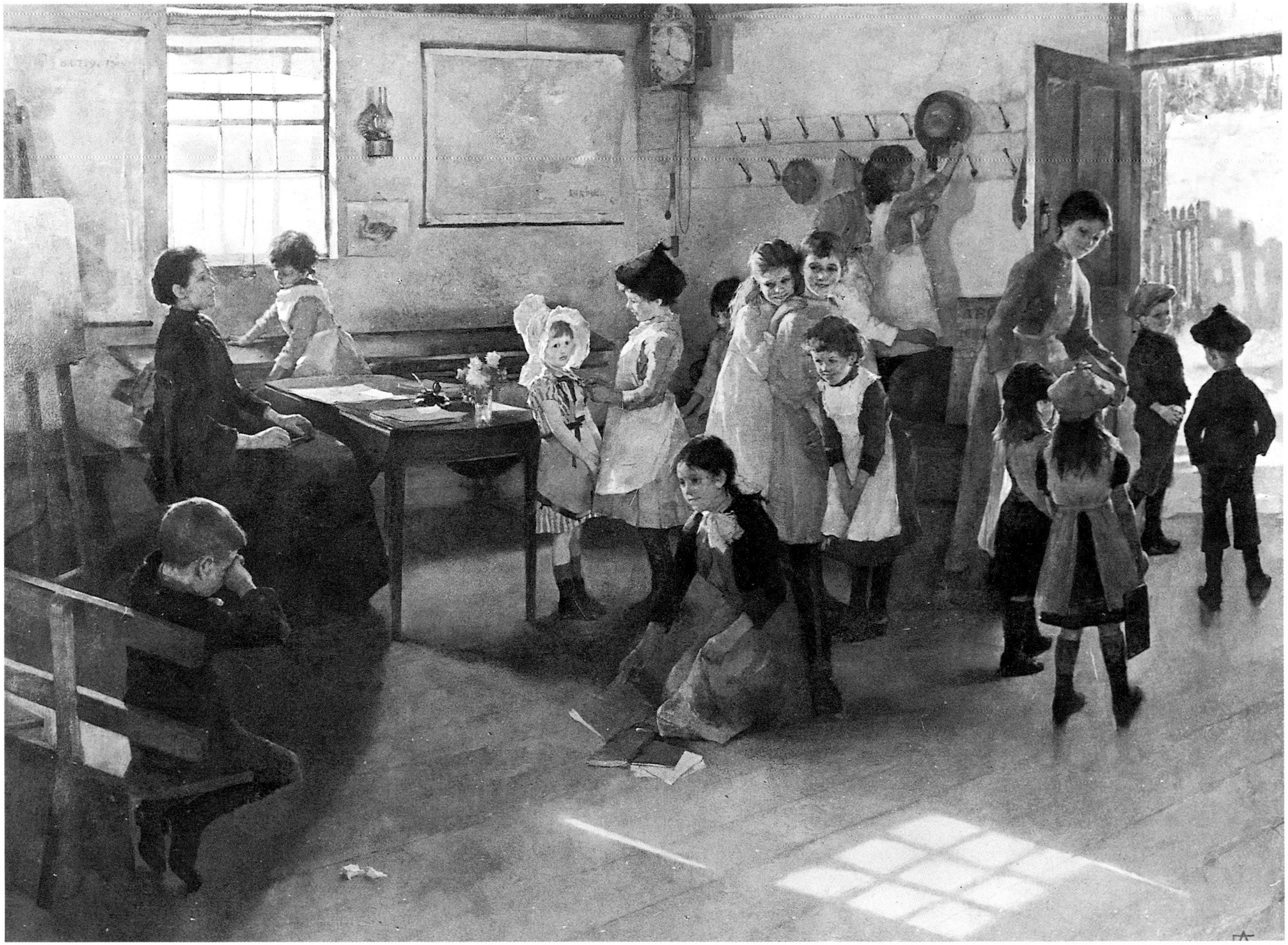

SCHOOL IS OUT (1889)
Elizabeth Forbes
Oil on canvas, 41½ x 46¾in (105.5 x 119cm)
Penzance Town Council, Penzance and District
Museum and Art Gallery

husband's work of the period. This and a delightful portrait of her son Alec aged four standing on a chair and framed by an enormous Newlyn copper plate (1897), are further examples of her more conventional work at the time.

Her increasing interest in literary and fairy story paintings was probably encouraged by the changes in style of several of the Newlyn group away from realism towards more aesthetic or poetic styles. The countryside of West Cornwall, with its mysterious woodlands and rugged moorland, seems to lend itself to a more imaginative approach. Examples include *A Dream Princess* (1897, whereabouts unknown) showing a country boy asleep on a grassy bank beside a waterwheel (probably the miller's son), dreaming of a princess wearing a beautiful medieval costume, *Imogen* (1898, Plymouth City Museum and Art Gallery) and *Hop O' My Thumb* (1898, whereabouts unknown), showing a procession of children in a wood.

Her son Alec was the model for *Hop O' My Thumb* and also for Myles, the hero of King Arthur's Wood, a story which she began about this time but did not publish until 1904. The book was dedicated to 'my little friend and comrade, Alec . . . with his mother's love'. It is a simple story which blends contemporary country life with chivalric legends. The story is based on the little copse near the Forbes' home at Higher Faugan. Myles, as a knight, overcomes various other knights and rescues the Lady of the Castle Perilous. She described Myles entering the enchanted wood:

> The little boy jumped over, and oh! on the other side of the stile was a whole new world. Instead of open spaces and wide sky, here a green delicious light quivered under thick leaves . . . Great beeches, like bronze giants with lifted arms glowing red in the low sun, stood foot deep in the cool flood of bells and their faint hyacinth odour filled the place as the scent of incense fills a cool dim church.

Some illustrations were carried out in her own imaginative blend of charcoal and watercolour. Others, such as *The Black Knight* (illustrated in *Life of Stanhope and Elizabeth Forbes* by Mrs Lionel Birch), demonstrate a strong sense of pattern and design akin to the art nouveau book illustration of the period, whilst still retaining a sense of individuality. The decorative qualities of *A Knight in Armour* (*Art Journal* 1904 p.384) give some idea of this illustrative work.

Upon submitting a portfolio of drawings for the book to the Royal Watercolour Society in 1899, Elizabeth was immediately elected an Associate. The book was published by E. Everard, Bristol, in 1904 and was enthusiastically received. It was praised by a critic writing in *The Studio*:

> To few, indeed, is it given to retain after their first youth the consciousness of the deep mystery that lies hidden beneath the simplest and most familiar forms of natural beauty; while even rarer are those who combine with that consciousness the power of giving expression to it in a form that appeals alike to the child-like and simple-hearted, the experienced and the travel-worn . . . That Mrs Stanhope Forbes is the possessor of these rare gifts is already well-known to all who are familiar with her exhibited paintings; but in the ideal fairy story, with its exquisite illustration, each one of which is a poem in itself, that she has recently published, she will come into touch with a far wider public . . . Mrs Forbes has been especially fortunate in the interpretation of her exquisite watercolour and charcoal drawings. In the former her fine sense of colour is brought out with wonderful force; and in the latter, for which the subtle gradations of tone with the warmth so characteristic of the original medium, are rendered with exceptional fidelity . . .

None of the other Newlyn artists shared Elizabeth's remarkable ability to evoke this magic world of childhood and Forbes himself, with his rigid adherence to realism, appreciated his wife's special talents, describing these works as 'charming and beautiful paintings which combine such lovely imaginative qualities with almost unrivalled technical skill and artistic feeling'.

On a Fine Day (1903, location unknown; illustrated Mrs Birch) shows a group of five ladies in exotic medieval costumes dancing in the Cornish countryside. There is a strong contrast between the brilliant sunlight which illuminates the landscape on the far side of the water and the rest of the painting which is in shadow. A sketch for this work shows that she altered the position of the dancing girls quite drastically, but also shows a greater sense of movement. The painting is based on some lines by the Italian poet Franco Sacchetti. A more melancholy work, *The Leaf* (date and location unknown, illustrated Mrs Birch) is based on a poem by Leopardi, translated by Rossetti, while *Will 'o the Wisp* (date and location unknown, illustrated Mrs Birch) which shows a girl gazing into a pool in the heart of a woodland, is charged with mystery and the mood of the *fin de siècle*.

Many of her later outdoor paintings were carried out from a movable studio, rather than worked up indoors from sketches made on the spot. A photograph in a *Studio* article of 1895 shows her painting in the open doorway of a wooden shed placed in a wood. The object of her study is a goat, tethered to a nearby tree.

In 1900 Elizabeth held an exhibition entitled 'Children and Child Lore' at the Fine Art Society in London. She also included works executed on the Forbes' recent visit to Spain, such as *A Shepherd of the Pyrenees* (reproduced in *Studio* vol 18, 1899, pp25–34). The simplicity, accuracy and imaginative qualities of her drawing put these works in a very different category from those of her more prosaic husband. In the preface to the catalogue of an exhibition held in 1904 at the Leicester Galleries and entitled *Model Children and Other People*, she described the problems of using children as models:

> Humorous, quaint and pathetic are the little irresponsible folk, the volunteer models of the village and countryside. When the painter, filled with energy and anticipation, emerges at the day's beginning, they are already watching afar off . . . If permitted to carry the painting kit it becomes a triumphal procession. Desperate their ambition to be 'put in the picture' . . . But their

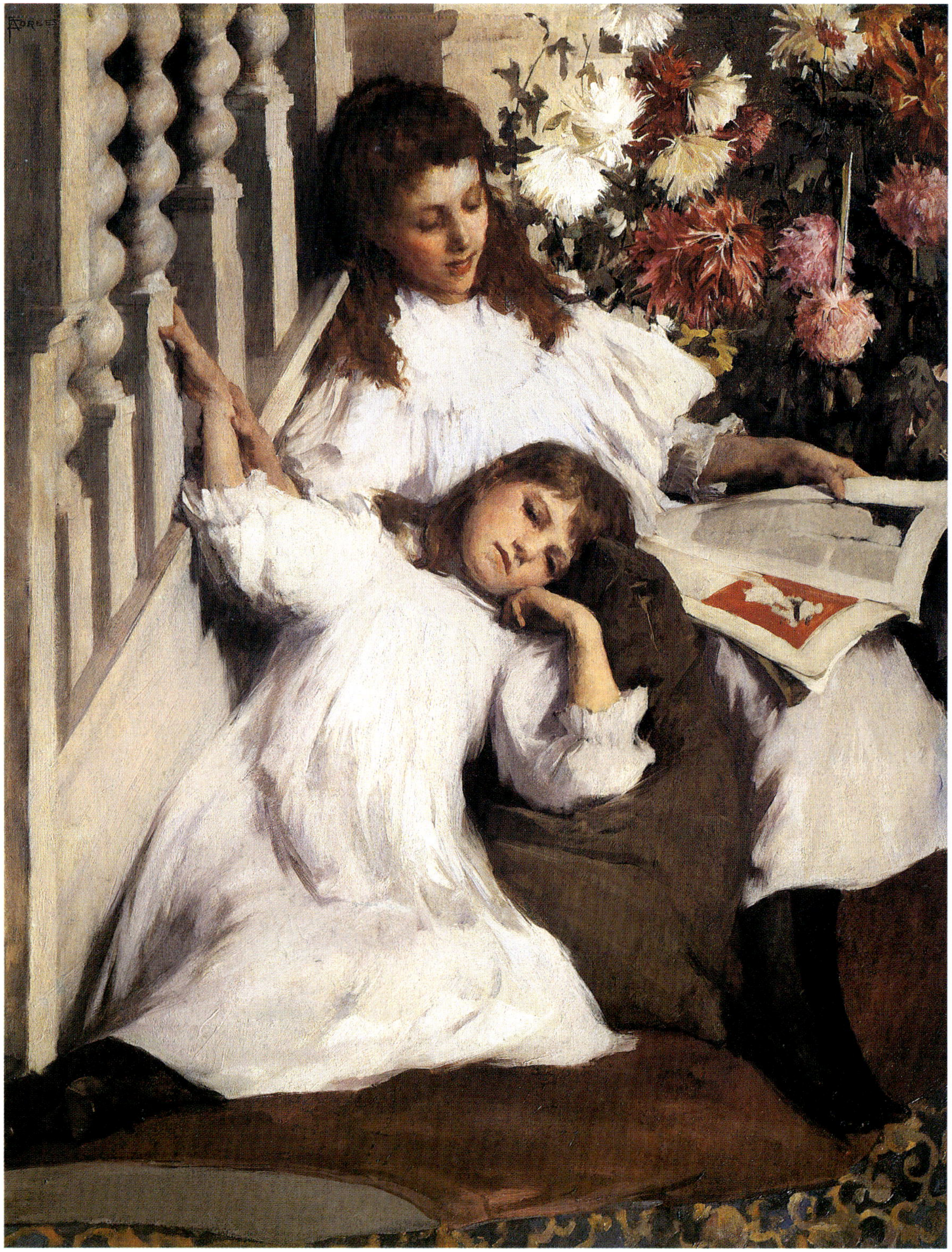

playmates, the wind and the sun, call too loud to be resisted . . . The smiling mouths begin to droop at the corners and the little restless feet refuse to be still. Then it becomes a duel *à l'outrance* between artist and model, till at last, with the conviction that inextinguishable hatred has been kindled in those childish breasts, the painter, now weary and browbeaten, returns on his road. But the children keep no grudges; the same row of eager, smiling eyes watch for his coming next day, and the duel begins anew . . .

One of the main features of this exhibition was the group of original drawings for the book *King Arthur's Wood*. The woods continued to fascinate Elizabeth after 1900 when she used them as a setting for further paintings, such as *The Poet and Some Country Girls* (1904, whereabouts unknown) and *The Woodcutter's Little Daughter* (1905, whereabouts unknown) which shows a little girl kneeling before a tree laden with glowing candles in the middle of a wood. *The Ford* (1908, Phillips 5-6 March 1987 (59)) is less symbolically charged, showing a woman with a child fording a stream at the edge of a wood. *The Half-Holiday* (1909, private collection) shows the youthful Alec reading under the shade of a tree. Elizabeth continued exhibiting until her death in 1912; her Royal Academy submission for that year was *Blackberry Gatherers* (1912). The painting shows no evidence of diminished powers but is, on the contrary, a lively and exuberant work, using the much brighter palette of the second generation of Newlyn artists. Her early death was a tragic loss to her husband and her son, and to the very wide circle of admirers of her work.

◁ *A Fairy Story* (1896)
Elizabeth Forbes

Oil on canvas, 47½ x 38in (120 x 96.5cm)
By courtesy of the Richard Green Gallery, London

Blackberry Gatherers (1912) ▷
Elizabeth Forbes

Oil on canvas, 33 x 39½in (84 x 100cm)
Trustees of the National Museums and Galleries on Merseyside (Walker Art Gallery)

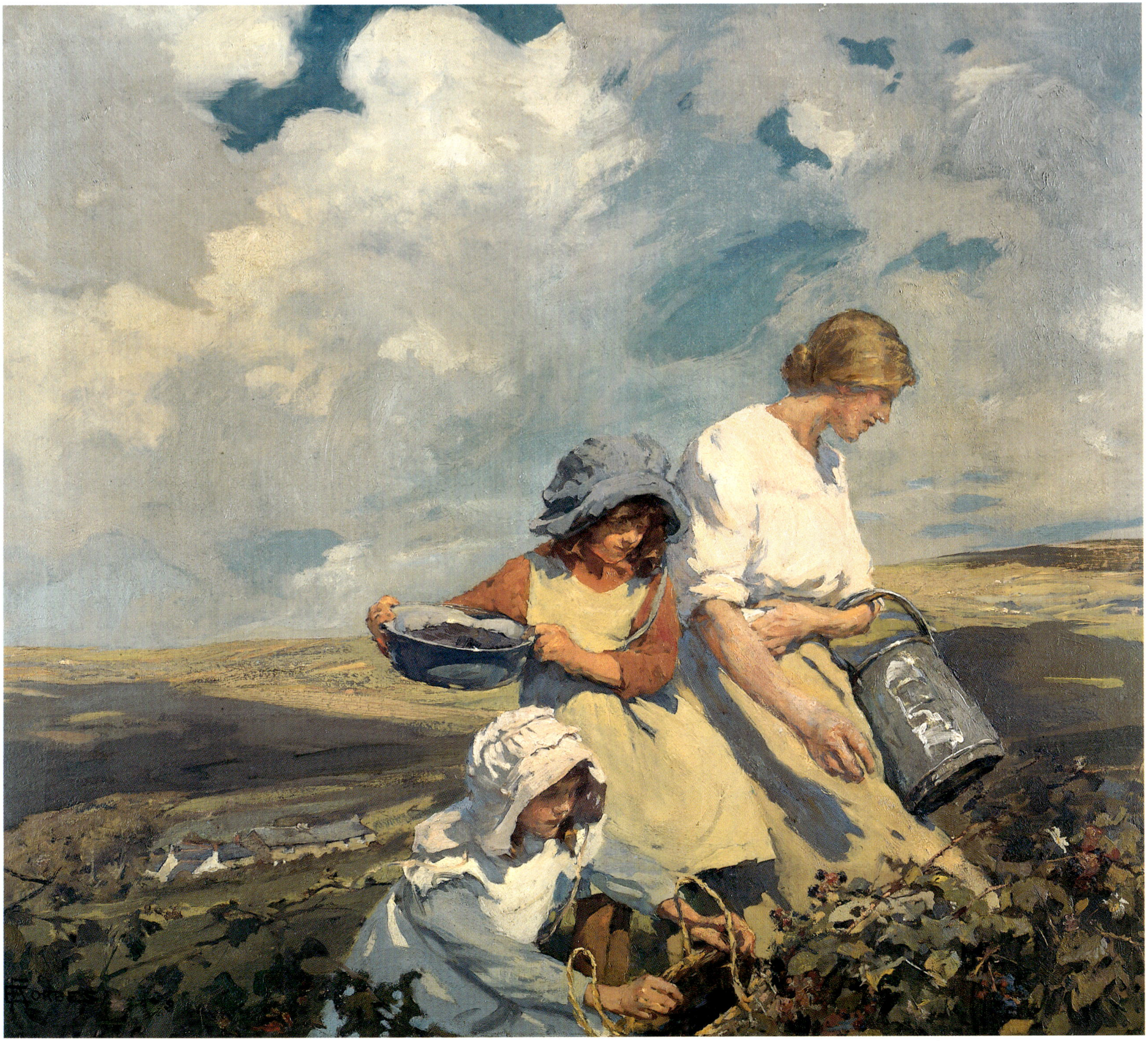

CHAPTER EIGHT

FORBES IN NEWLYN 1890–1900

During the 1890s, when several members of the group were going through major upheavals and stylistic changes, Stanhope Forbes continued to produce a succession of large works concentrating on the life of Newlyn. The encouragement of official honours in the form of an Associateship at the Royal Academy, the example and companionship of a hard-working wife, and the birth of his son were all factors which spurred him on to work at this time.

Unlike so many of the other Newlyn artists, apart from Walter Langley, Forbes realised that the depiction of scenes of village life was his métier and he stuck to it unwaveringly throughout his life, never tiring in his pursuit of new subjects and scenes within the Newlyn context. Indeed, he appeared to have a monopoly of these subjects making less confident artists such as Bourdillon feel that he should turn to costume pieces because, as he wrote, 'other fellows do the village business so much better than I'. Forbes had found his niche. His paintings were obviously popular and sold well. He was a well-liked and much respected figure in Newlyn, on good terms with his models and his fellow artists alike, and he felt that he was daily adding to the store of knowledge of local ways of life: 'It was borne in upon us that here was a life in which we were in thorough sympathy and which it was more or less our duty to transcribe and to leave the record for posterity.' His satisfaction came from a repetition of excellent draughtsmanship, well-studied light effects and tonal relationships together with the stimulus of new and very different subjects: 'Not only the fishing village itself and the life of the fisher folk, but the country round Newlyn, the moorlands, the little valleys or coombes, the Cornish farms and the agricultural life of the country would occupy many painters.'

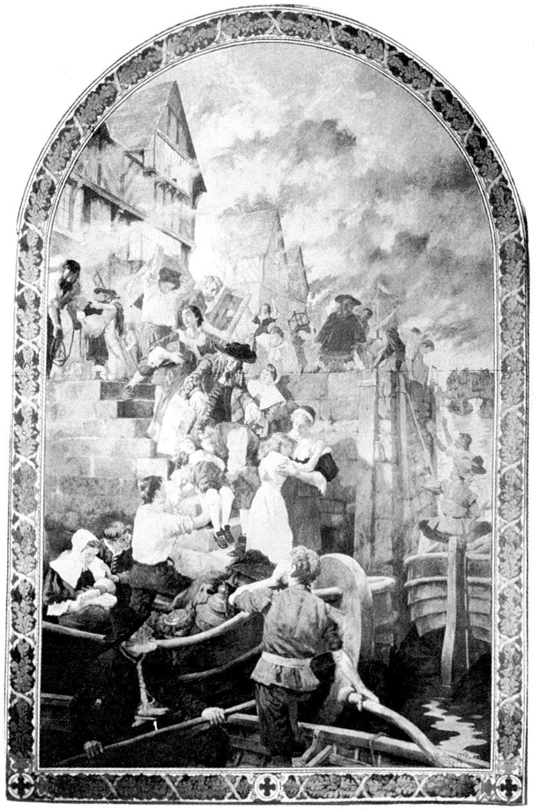

THE GREAT FIRE OF LONDON (1897)
Stanhope Alexander Forbes
11ft 1in x 17ft 6in (340 x 530cm)
By courtesy of the Joint Grand Gresham Committee

Unlike so many of his contemporaries, Forbes saw no need to go beyond the representation of everyday reality, nor did he appear to wish to change or develop stylistically, although inevitably changes did occur in his work. In the first place, the square brushwork and softened outlines of the 1880s gradually gave way to a harsher, more flickering effect. On the whole, Forbes did not seek out compositions with large numbers of figures such as *The Health of the Bride* (1889) and *By Order of the Court* (1890), but instead painted subjects with fewer models, frequently using the same models over and over again. This tendency may have been connected with the difficulties of obtaining a wide range of models, but it meant that he was not able to indulge his special powers of characterisation to the same extent, and possibly made for less interest in the works. Toward the end of the 1890s we find that his figures have become much smaller in relation to the landscape, thus again leading to a falling off of interest. Forbes, however, still employed the same restrained colour range, with the emphasis on tonal harmonies as in the previous decade.

We learn from Forbes' early letters to his mother that the people of Newlyn had very strong religious beliefs and that many of them were Primitive Methodists, undoubtedly the legacy of John Wesley's many visits to Cornwall in the eighteenth century. Forbes initially found the people 'narrow-minded' and 'bigoted', and the penalties imposed on would-be Sabbath breakers have already been noted. He soon came to realise that the Chapel was a central feature in the life of the village. As the Newlyn historian, Ben Batten wrote, 'It is no exaggeration to say that for most of them Chapel in all its aspects was the equivalent, in modern terms, of a religious sanctuary, a social club, a youth club, and a choral society all gathered at various times under one roof.' Yet despite this Forbes tended to eschew religious subjects. He was himself a sceptic and his Aunt Alice, writing to her daughter after a visit to Newlyn in 1886, was shocked to find that Elizabeth Armstrong was even 'less religious than her intended husband'. Forbes' main criticism of Tayler, his favourite companion, was that he would go to church every Sunday, and on another occasion we find him complaining that 'poor Garstin' was dragged to church every Sunday by his wife.

Nonetheless, it seems that Forbes was fascinated by the Salvation Army and attended a meeting early in 1884, when he told his mother that 'what they do call a "free and easy" was going on. "I love Jesus" was being sung to a music hall tune'. Perhaps it was the relative newness of the subject, for the Salvation Army had been founded only 13 years before by General Booth. Penzance became one of their main spheres of activity and Booth visited the town twice in the early 1880s. During the early years, Salvationists were scorned and members were attacked; and when a group met together in public, large crowds would immediately gather to watch.

Forbes perhaps shared this almost voyeuristic fascination and wished to express this in his painting *Soldiers and Sailors; The Salvation Army* (1891, private collection). The action takes place on the north pier, built in 1888, and we know that all the models were actual Salvationists. The faces of the women Salvationists are thin and full of frenzied other-worldly fervour. They are singing and playing various instruments, in contrast to the male Salvationists who, apart from the two drummers, are standing solemnly, even a little sheepishly, grouped around their flag. In the background is the harbour and boats. Forbes has chosen the more natural gestures of the bystanders and children in the foreground as a foil to the intensity of the Salvationists. In particular, the little girl eating an orange and half-turning to look at a dog in the foreground, and the children's faces peeping out from underneath the upraised arm of the drummer, restore a human element to the painting. The children are very well observed, the younger ones being strongly reminiscent of Elizabeth's paintings of children. The contrast is further enhanced by the black of the Salvationists' clothing and the white pinafores and coloured dresses of the children. The painting was probably bought by the collector George McCulloch, as it was listed in his collection in 1892.

Interestingly, in 1891 both Bramley and La Thangue painted religious subjects, Bramley *For of Such is the Kingdom of Heaven* (1891, Auckland City Art Gallery, New Zealand), and La Thangue, *A Mission to Seamen* (1891, Nottingham, City Art Gallery and Museums). La Thangue's painting is closest to Forbes' in that it shows a peripatetic preacher addressing the fishermen and their families on the quay at Bosham. The composition of this work was criticised in *The Graphic* for being 'ill-balanced', and Forbes' and Bramley's paintings received similar treatment from other critics. It is a strange coincidence that all three should have been painted at an angle, rather than looking directly at the subject with the sea behind as in Tayler's *The Departure of the Fishing Fleet, Boulogne* (1891), shown at the Royal Academy the same year. It does, however, seem unlikely that they should have collaborated and must remain a strange coincidence.

In Bramley's painting *For of Such Is the Kingdom of Heaven*, showing a child's funeral procession in the village, the emphasis is not on the sadness of the scene but rather on a delight in the act of painting the women and girls in their attractive white dresses and hats, the flowers and the village bystanders. For Bramley, unlike Forbes, the subject matter was totally secondary to an aesthetic pleasure in the act of painting and the design of the composition.

The idea for Forbes' Royal Academy submission of 1892, *Forging the Anchor*, may well have been originally suggested by a painting by Lepage of a similar subject, although it is unlikely that he ever saw Lepage's painting. In terms of organisation and strategy this was an enormous undertaking for Forbes, who initially attempted to paint it in an actual forge 'amid the gloom, smoke and noise' but this proved impossible. He then had to use all his ingenuity to coax the unwilling blacksmiths into his studio where he had created a smithy of his own.

It was unfortunate that the painting should have coincided with the year that Forbes was made an Associate of the Royal Academy. This drew extra attention to him and left him at the mercy of critics such as George Moore, for whom the painting was the epitome of everything he most despised. The composition is well organised, centering on the anchor and the four men who are working on it, investing them to some degree with the 'heroism' of labour. Further interest is added by the light from the furnace, which illuminates the face of the boy stoker. But the characterisation and human interest to be found in *By Order of the Court* is lacking, this painting having become more of a record of an event, evident in Forbes' attempt to include every possible detail of the tools and equipment that would have been found in a smithy. It is this attention to detail which so infuriated Moore, and he compares Forbes unfavourably with George Clausen, whom he praises for shaking off the influence of Lepage:

> Stanhope Forbes, however, still continues at the point where Bastien Lepage began to curtail, deform and degrade the original inspiration. Mr. Clausen, I said, overcame the difficulty of the trousers by generalisation. Mr Stanhope Forbes copies the trousers seam by seam, patch by patch; and the uglyness of the garment bores you in the picture exactly as it would in nature

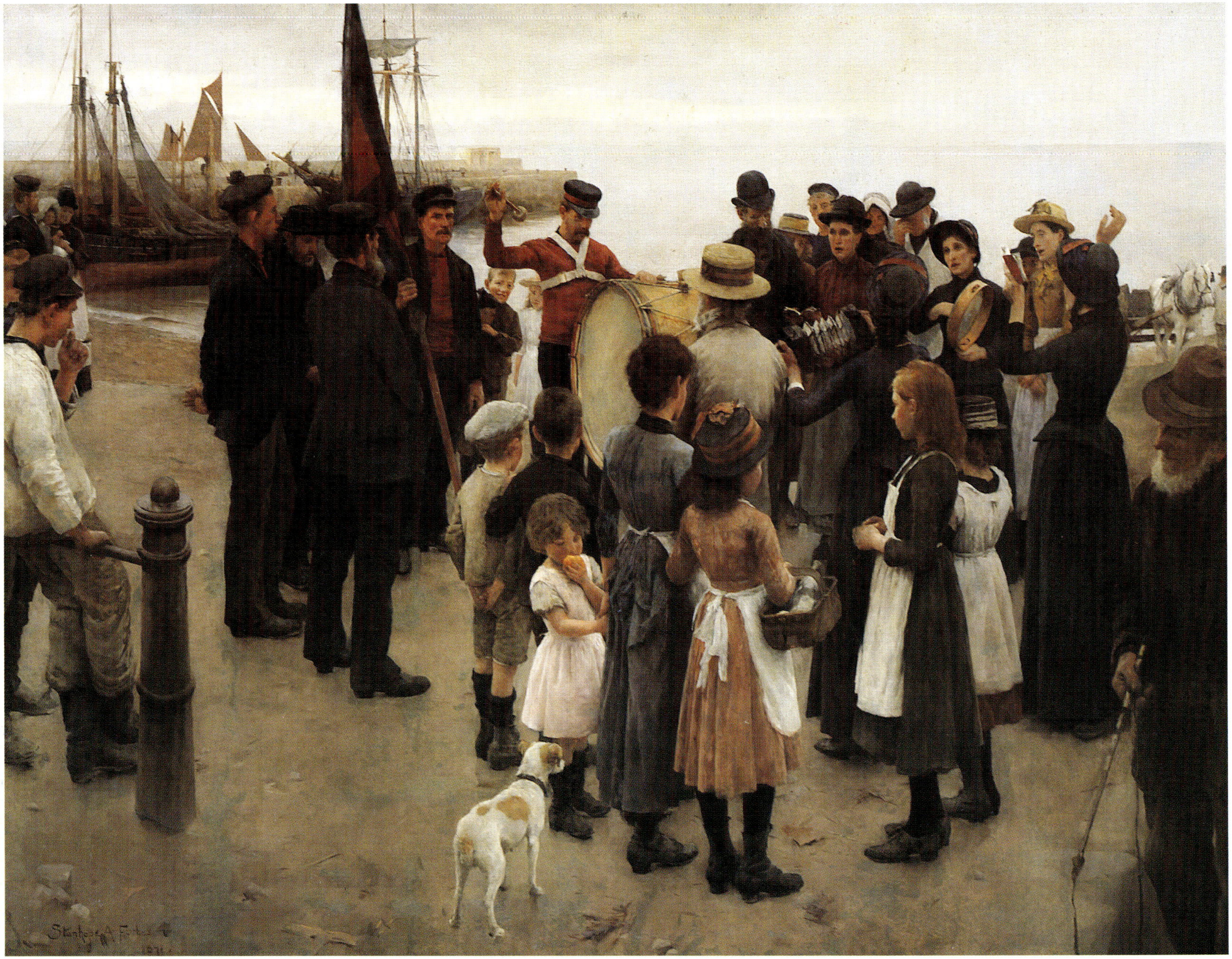

SOLDIERS AND SAILORS;
THE SALVATION ARMY (1891)
Stanhope Alexander Forbes
Oil on canvas, 59 x 78in (150 x 198cm)
Private collection

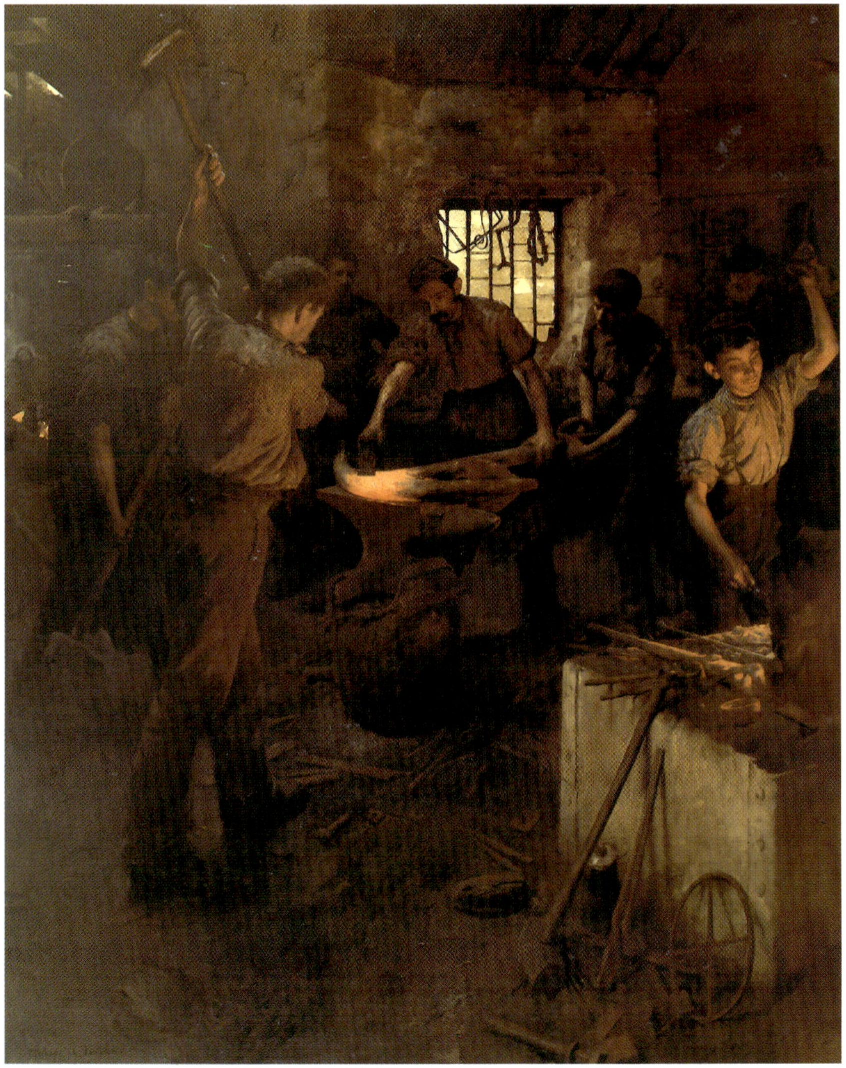

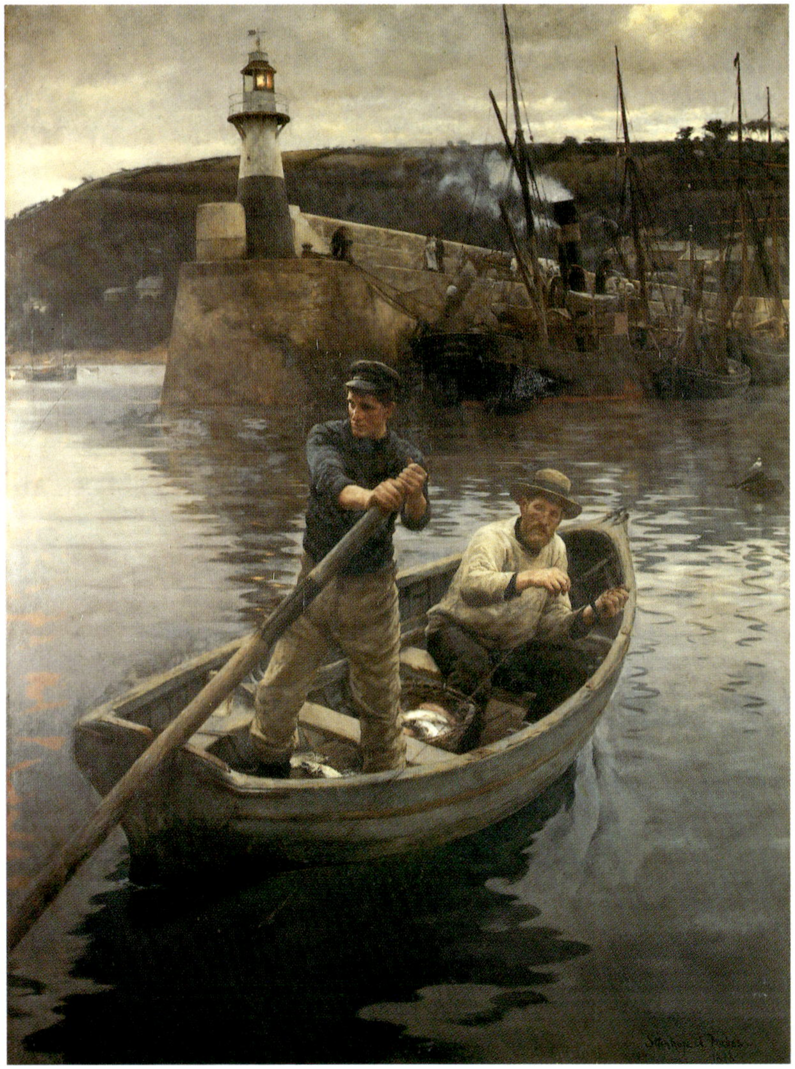

> . . . I should not be surprised to learn that Mr Stanhope Forbes had had a forge built up in his studio, and had copied it all as it stood.

He added that Forbes' painting lacked 'an element of mystery'. A hundred years of dirt have now added this 'element of mystery' to the painting, creating dramatic light effects by concentrating the darks and the lights. Other critics were more generous. *The Thunderer* termed it one of the most remarkable works exhibited at the Royal Academy that year, and *The Athenaeum* praised 'the breadth and vigour of the whole [which] justifies us in saying that this is by far the best work of Mr Forbes, who, retaining all that is good in the dogmas of the so-called Newlyn School, has accepted the larger principles of a greater school.'

Forbes' Royal Academy submission of 1893, *The Lighthouse*, was on a similar scale to *Forging the Anchor* and the conditions of its execution were probably nearly as unpleasant. Forbes recalled the small lighthouse at the end of the pier, 'which I can never contemplate without certain uneasy sensations. For off that pier head, day after day for

(Left) *FORGING THE ANCHOR* (1892)
Stanhope Alexander Forbes
Oil on canvas, 84½ x 68in (214.5 x 173cm)
Ipswich Museums and Art Galleries

(Above) *THE LIGHTHOUSE* (1893)
Stanhope Alexander Forbes
Oil on canvas, 90 x 68in (228.5 x 173cm)
Manchester City Art Gallery

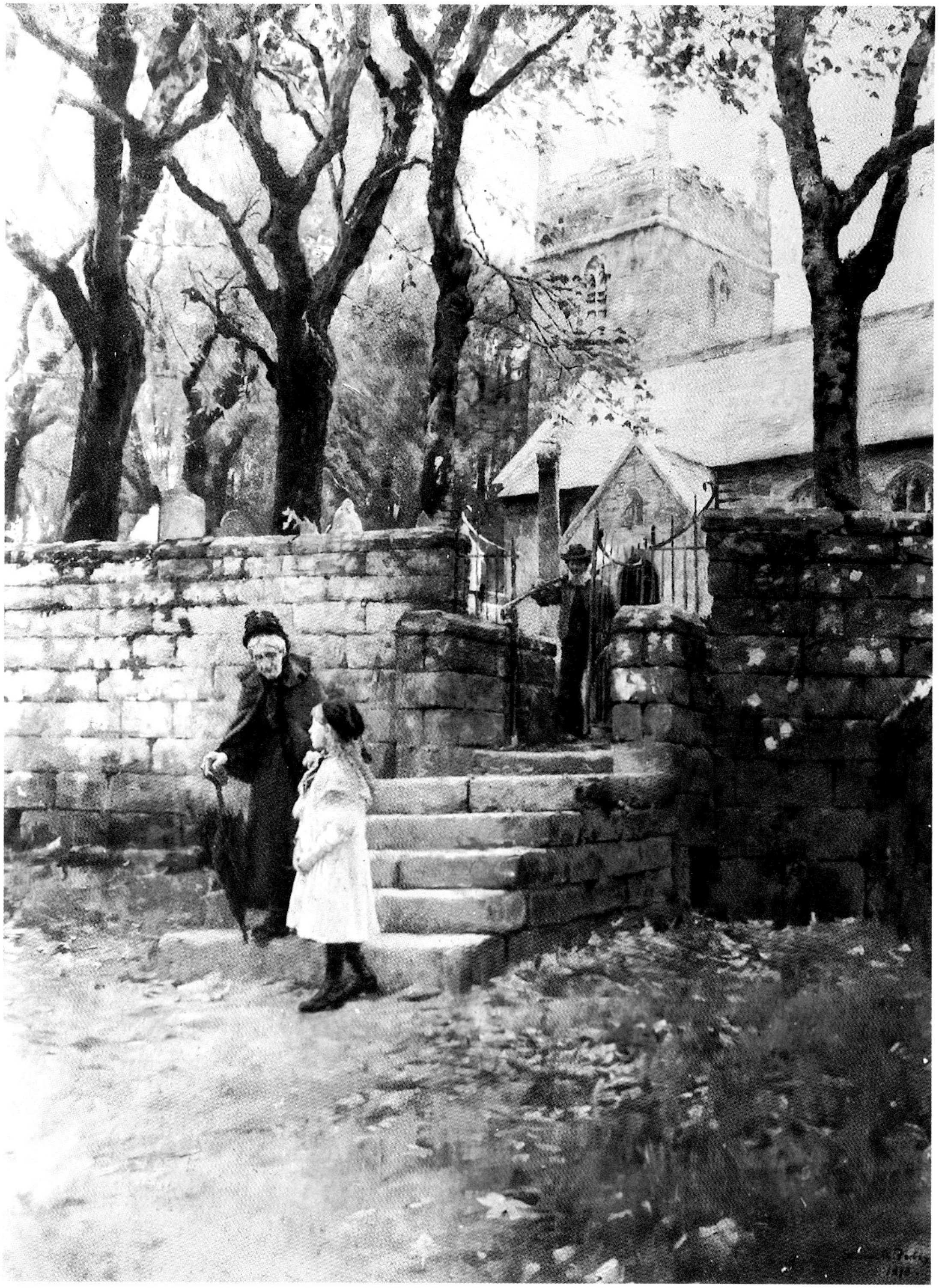

months, I painted in a crazy old fishing boat which lay at anchor there and with unsteady hand endeavoured to dodge the motion of the waves.'

The Lighthouse centres on a small fishing boat at the entrance to the harbour, and captures the bold features of the younger fisherman who wields the long oar while the older man deftly dangles his fishing line into the water. For Forbes it was one of many opportunities to paint the ripples and reflections on the water in Newlyn harbour, the eye being carefully led into the work by the diagonal positioning of the boat. A writer in the *Cornish Telegraph* for April 1893 recorded that '*The Lighthouse* is said to have attracted attention among the artists who have seen it and freely predict that it will prove to be one of the great successes of this year's Royal Academy'. The painting was then exhibited at Manchester and bought by the City Art Gallery there.

In 1893 the Forbes moved to Trewarveneth Farm at the top of Paul Hill. This move encouraged Forbes to look further afield for his subjects, and over the following few years we find him turning inland. He could hardly have been unaware that mining and quarrying were major aspects of the Cornish economy, and would undoubtedly have watched the teams of horses as they hauled massive lumps of granite into Newlyn, to be shipped from the harbour. *The Quarry Team* (1894, private collection) expresses the bleakness of this dreary job with the team of solid cart-horses pulling an enormous slab of granite – the size of which makes one wonder how it was ever moved – on a makeshift cart driven by a man inured to the hardness of his lot, while three of his fellows trudge wearily along the road behind the cart. The bleakness of the landscape and the lowering grey sky add to the oppressive effect of the scene and one feels that here Forbes has come nearest to the social realism of his French contemporaries (this

OCTOBER (1898)
Stanhope Alexander Forbes
Oil on canvas, 67 x 55in (170 x 139.5cm)
Private collection

painting contains echoes of Courbet's *Stonebreakers*). *The Quarry Team* is a far cry from the glorification of labour in *Forging the Anchor*. Ironically, an extremely popular print was made from this painting, which adorned the walls of many middle- and upper-class homes.

Forbes also turned to farming scenes over the next few years, painting *The Smithy* (1895, whereabouts unknown), *The New Calf* (1896, whereabouts unknown), and *Across the Stream* (1897). *The Smithy*, showing a horse being shod, is a similar painting to *Forging the Anchor* yet, by placing two bystanders watching the horse being shod and in the background three lads of varying ages gathering around the furnace, the atmosphere created is more informal and relaxed. *The Smithy* was painted entirely on the spot, and was awarded a second class gold medal in the Paris International Exhibition of 1899, as well as a first class gold medal at Munich, where the German government hoped to purchase it for the National Collection. However, it had already been bought by Richard Burke, a well-known Irish master of foxhounds.

The same attention to detail and the concentration of dark and light is also a feature of *The New Calf*, where the faces of the farmer's family, who have turned out to see the new arrival, are lit by a glow from a light source out of the painting. In *Across the Stream* the figures, which have shrunk to very small proportions, are dwarfed by the stream as it gushes over the rocks and the landscape beyond. It was painted near Buryas Bridge, a subject Forbes had earlier executed in 1890, where again the figures were small in comparison with the bridge and surrounding countryside (*Buryas Bridge*, private collection). Buryas Bridge was also the setting for his painting *Nomads* (1904, Laing Art Gallery, Newcastle).

In 1897 Forbes was commissioned to paint a panel illustrating the Great Fire of London by the

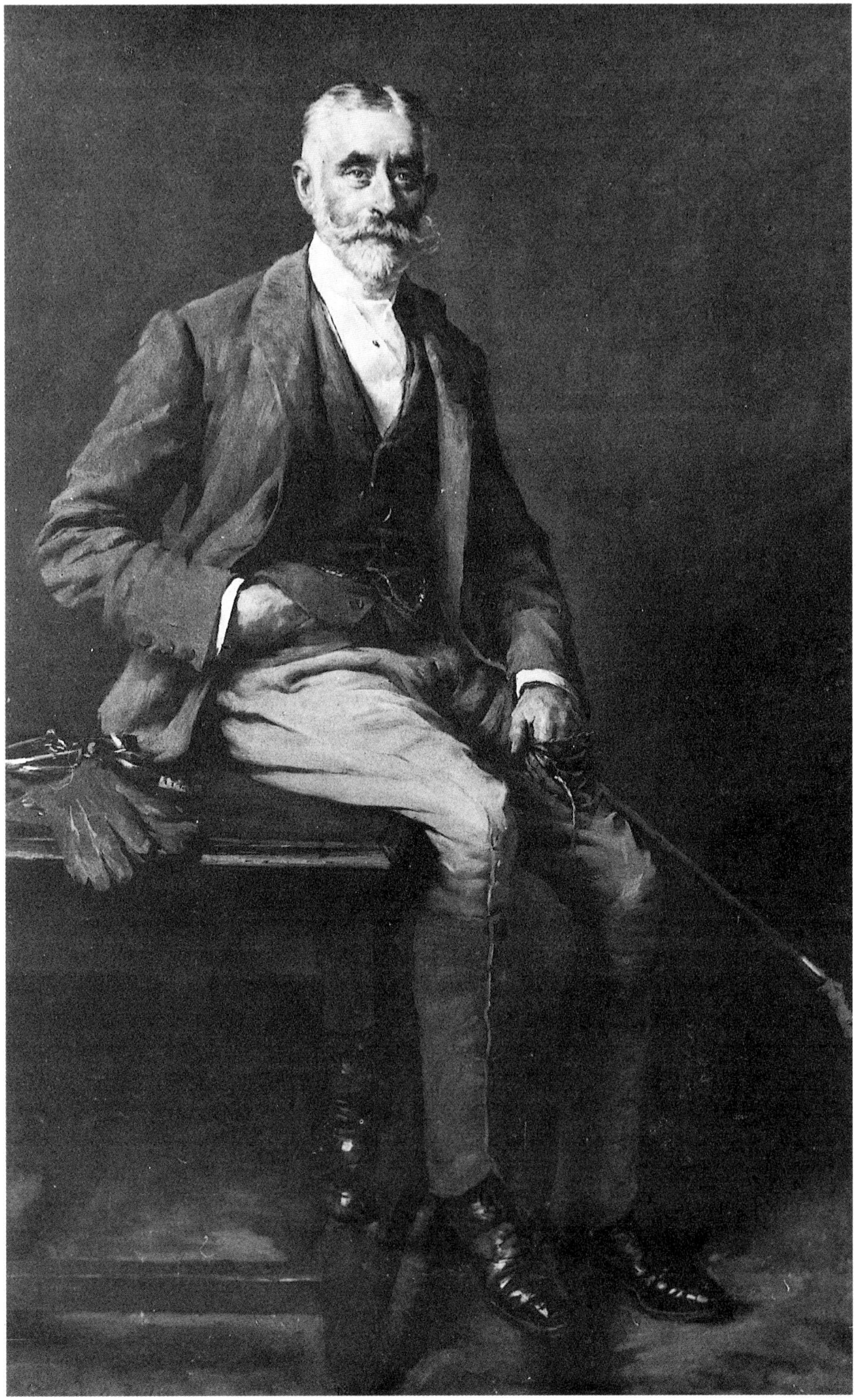

RICHARD BOLITHO (1896)
Stanhope Alexander Forbes
Oil on canvas
Private collection

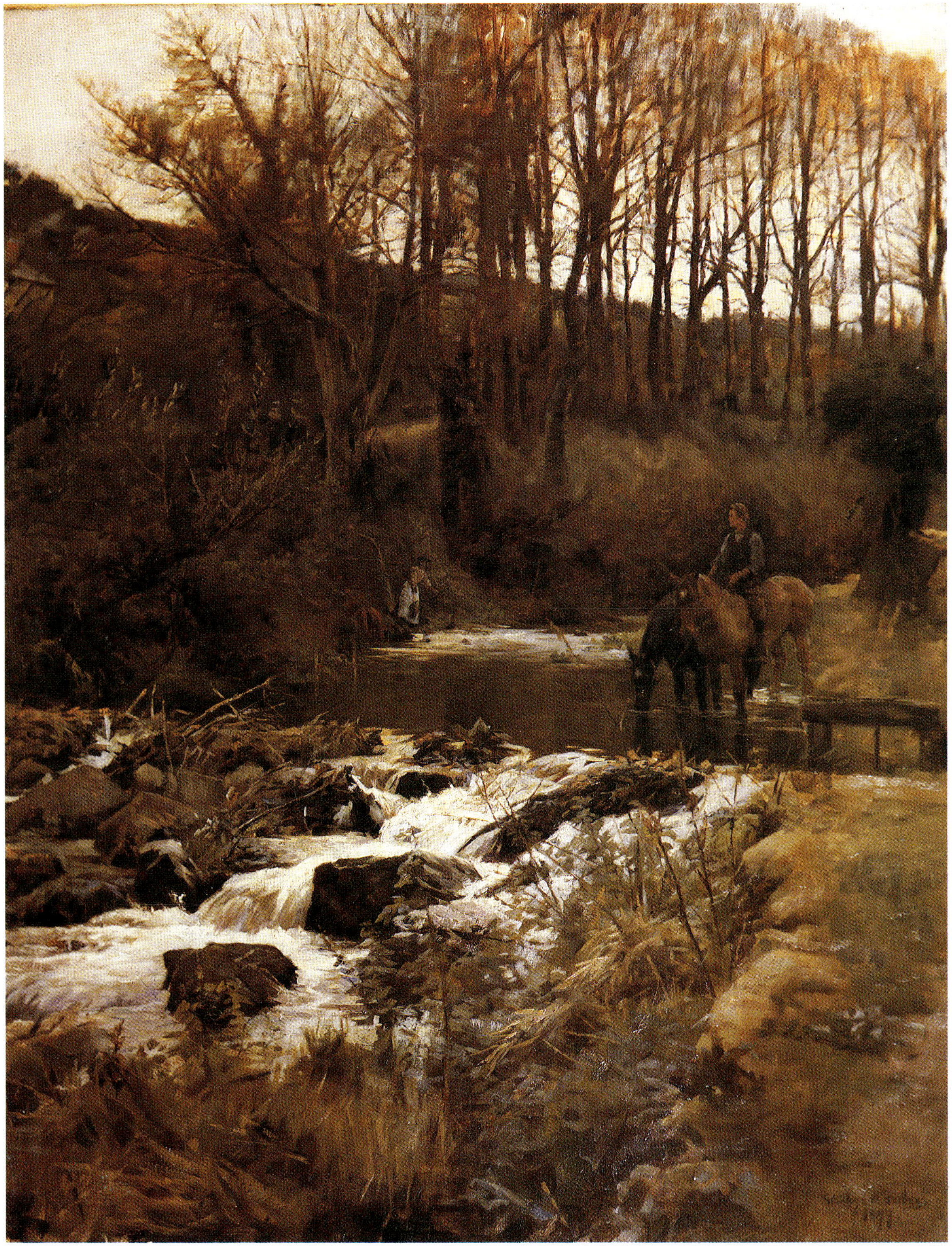

Sun Insurance Company for the Royal Exchange (see page 53). The painting still hangs in the Royal Exchange alongside a series of wall-paintings by artists such as Lord Leighton, Solomon J. Solomon and others. Painted on canvas, it was then applied to and incorporated with the wall by a process known as 'Maroflâge'. The painting was based on an entry in Pepys' diary of 1666:

> So I down to the waterside, and there got a boat, and through bridge, and there was a lamentable fire . . . everybody endeavouring to remove their goods, and flinging into the river, or bringing them into lighters that lay off; poor people staying in their houses as long as till the very fire touched them, and then running into boats, or clambering from one pair of stairs by the waterside to another.

It was painted in his studio at Trewarveneth after an exhaustive study of architectural details, costume, etc., from prints and books in the British Museum. Forbes found the size and other difficulties of execution made this a particularly trying work and was glad to be able to relax with Elizabeth afterwards on a holiday in the Pyrenees.

Two paintings of 1898 have been invested with an element of a story – *October* and *The Letter*. *October* depicts the little church at Sancreed, a village about five miles inland from Penzance, whose churchyard contains the graves of several Newlyn artists. The Whitechapel exhibition of Cornish paintings of 1902 described the painting in the following terms in the catalogue:

> A Cornish village churchyard, Sancreed near Penzance. The churches of Cornwall, built strongly like its cliffs, often stand in groves of trees. They suggest therefore thoughts of strength and gentleness, of youth and old age, or resistance and growth.

ACROSS THE STREAM (1897)
Stanhope Alexander Forbes
Oil on canvas, 48 x 36in (122 x 91.5cm)
By courtesy of David Messum, London

The subject of receiving letters or news was a popular one with the Newlyn artists, for instance Tuke's *The Message* (see page 36), and Walter Langley's *Anxious News* (1883, private collection), while T. C. Gotch's *Goodbye* (*Art Journal* 1889) is an example of a doorway scene.

In *The Letter* Forbes makes maximum use of the combination of three different light sources – in particular the hidden light source which dramatically lights up the faces of the family in the doorway. From the intent expression on their faces, it would seem that the letter is from a near relation, perhaps a son or even father who is far away. Owing to the vagaries of the fishing industry and the closure of certain mines, it was usual at this time for Cornishmen to go far afield in search of work.

Forbes continued to find portraiture a useful addition to his income and it seems there can have been hardly a member of the local Bolitho family who did not invite Forbes to paint their portrait at some stage. Richard Bolitho of Ponsandine (1896) and T. Bedford Bolitho (1896, private collection) were both painted in very natural poses, the former perched on the edge of the studio table holding his riding crop; the latter sitting in a relaxed position in a chair. Both are extremely fine portraits and demonstrate Forbes' strong aptitude for characterisation.

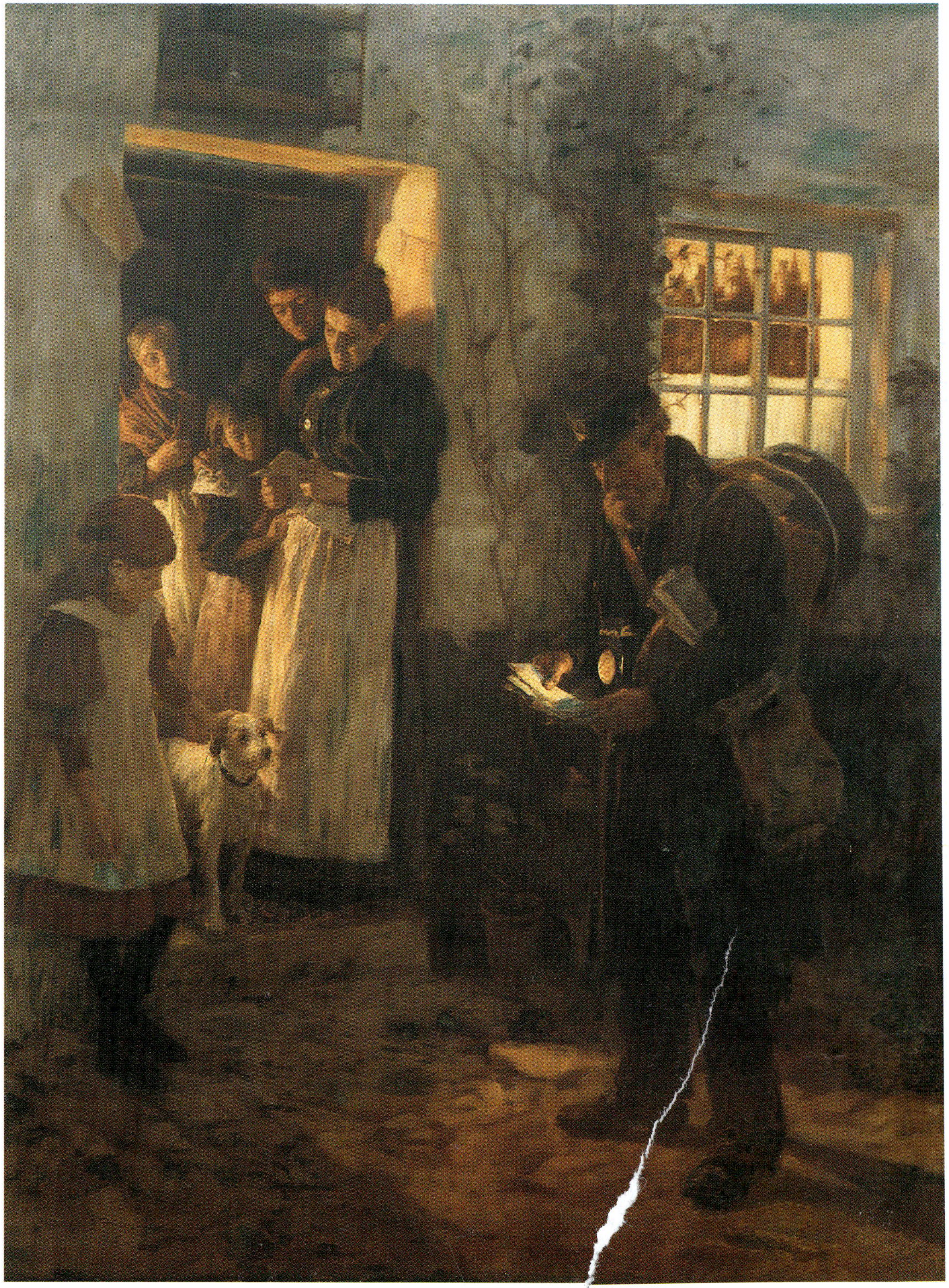

THE LETTER (1898)
Stanhope Alexander Forbes
Oil on canvas, 60 x 46in (152.5 x 117cm)
City of Plymouth Museums and Art Gallery

CHAPTER NINE

THE NEWLYN SCHOOL IN THE 1890s

Most members of the Newlyn School found they had to struggle quite hard to find their own particular niches within the Newlyn tradition. It was soon apparent that Forbes had cornered the market for 'village subjects' and that Victorian patrons on the whole preferred his straightforward paintings with a hint of a story to the more sensitive and painterly works of Garstin, Bramley, or Bourdillon. Thus while Garstin and Bourdillon increasingly moved away from their true métiers in a desperate search for sales, Forbes and Langley continued to prosper, and others, such as T. C. Gotch, found theirs by taking a completely different approach. Fred Hall was probably the only one of the group to actually develop stylistically to a looser form of 'English Impressionism', which was similar to the work of George Clausen.

Some artists felt they might achieve greater success away from Newlyn, and thus Bramley, Bourdillon, Tayler, Hall and Harris all left Newlyn for good during the 1890s. Ironically, these departures coincided with official recognition of the Newlyn artists in the completion of the Passmore Edwards Gallery in 1895. However, both Garstin and Forbes regretted the passing of the old style of private view, 'A granite picture gallery dumped down amongst us instead of producing a feeling of solidarity has seemingly led to a disintegration of the Newlyners.'

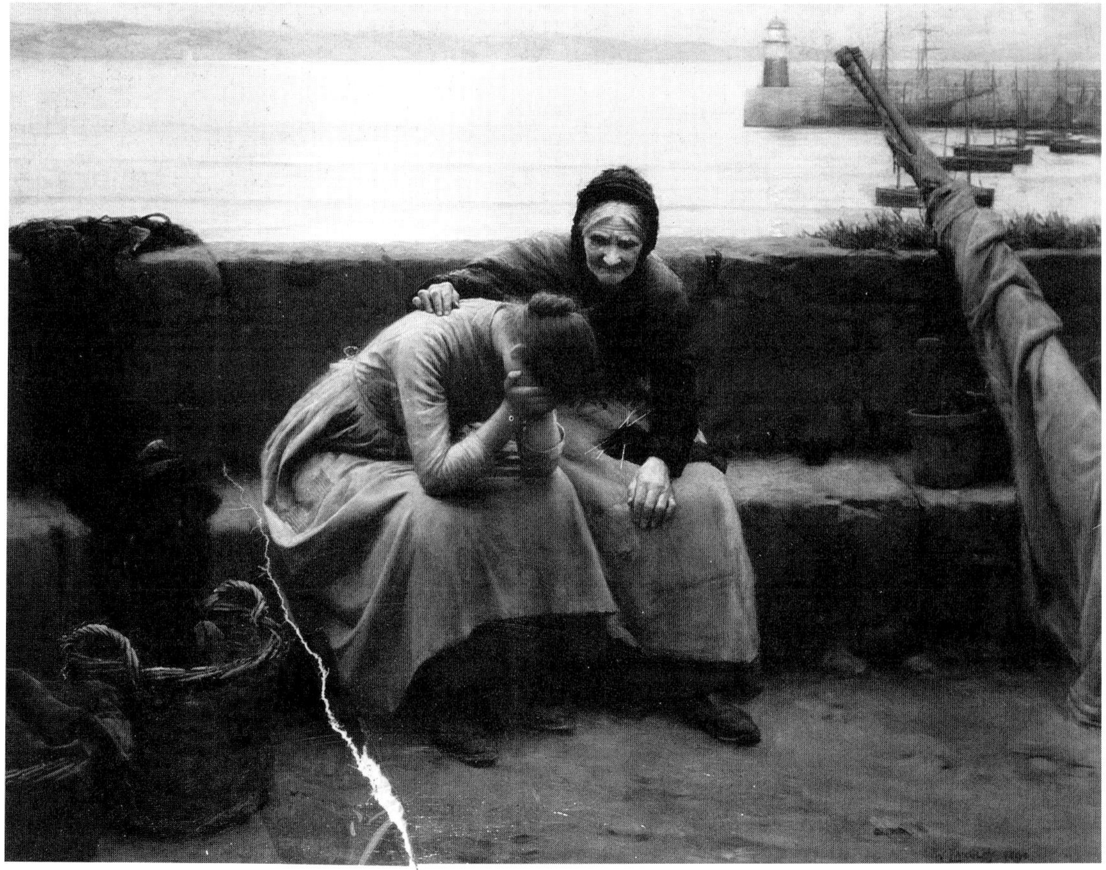

WALTER LANGLEY

The 1890s saw greater recognition of the work of Walter Langley. As early as 1884 Forbes had complained that 'Langley is only commencing in oil so he comes prying in here to see how my work gets done'. Little more is heard about Langley's oil paintings until he successfully exhibited *Sunshine and Shadow* (1892, private collection) at the Royal Academy of that year. Probably one of his most successful paintings, *Never Morning Wore to*

NEVER MORNING WORE TO EVENING BUT SOME HEART DID BREAK (1894)
Walter Langley
Oil on canvas, 48 x 60in (122 x 152.5cm)
City Museums and Art Gallery, Birmingham

Evening but some Heart did Break, demonstrated how much easier it was for an artist to achieve wider notice with oils than with watercolours. The subject matter is typical of Langley's personal preoccupation, showing a sorrowing girl being comforted by an elderly woman whose face is a moving portrayal of old age. The scene is a very simple one and the pathos is heightened by the contrast between the sorrowing figures in the foreground and the evening light on the calm sea in the background.

The *Moseley and King's Heath Journal* records that 'but for the fact that this painting has been sold to a private purchaser "from the easel", it would have been purchased by the Chantrey Bequest'. When Langley learnt this he tried to repurchase it at 50 per cent over the purchase price. The owner refused but sent Langley an additional cheque, in gratitude for which Langley sent a watercolour of the widowed mother in the painting.

The following year, Langley received the rare honour of being invited to provide a self-portrait for the Uffizzi Gallery's collection of paintings of great artists. Two years later, he sent a somewhat melancholy portrait of himself showing Newlyn harbour in the background. Together with his successes at the Paris exhibition where *Among the Missing* (*Moseley and King's Heath Journal*, July 1897, p.68) won a gold medal, and at Chicago where both *The Departure of the Fleet for the North* (*Art Journal*, 1889, p.97) and *Disaster* (see page 34) had won gold medals, Langley achieved further recognition when Tolstoy selected one of his paintings to be included in his essay 'What is Art?'. The painting, *In Faith and Hope the World will Disagree but all Mankind's Concern is Charity* (1897, private collection), was singled out in his essay as 'an admirable and true work of art'.

THOMAS COOPER GOTCH

A visit to Florence in the winter of 1891-2 completely transformed the work of Gotch. Straightforward depictions of village life such as *Sharing Fish* (1891) were replaced by extremely colourful and symbolic paintings, often based on the theme of childhood. Gotch's daughter, Phyllis, was the model for many of these extremely successful works, including *My Crown and Sceptre* (1891, Art Gallery of New South Wales), which was one of the most widely acclaimed paintings of that year. Phyllis is seated before a brocaded background, crowned with red berries, and holds a reed in her hand. *The Golden Dream* (1893, Harris Museum and Art Gallery, Preston) was an open air scene in which Gotch was said to have had the leaves and apples of an apple tree especially gilded.

Alleluia (1986), which was purchased by the Trustees of the Chantrey Bequest, shows thirteen richly clad children singing before a gilded background. Gotch recorded that this was begun in Alfred East's studio in London, then painted partly in the Malthouse, his Newlyn home, and partly in his studio. Lecturing many years later in 1939 to an audience in Penzance, Forbes described how 'Gotch was busy making angels of some of the fairest of your girls, clothing them in lovely silks and damasks'. A. L. Baldry in an article of 1898 described Gotch's work as representing the 'rarest phase of contemporary painting' which he called 'imaginative symbolism'. Baldry welcomed this as a relief from the skilful depiction of 'commonplace scenes of momentary importance and from the photographic representation of a saddening episode'.

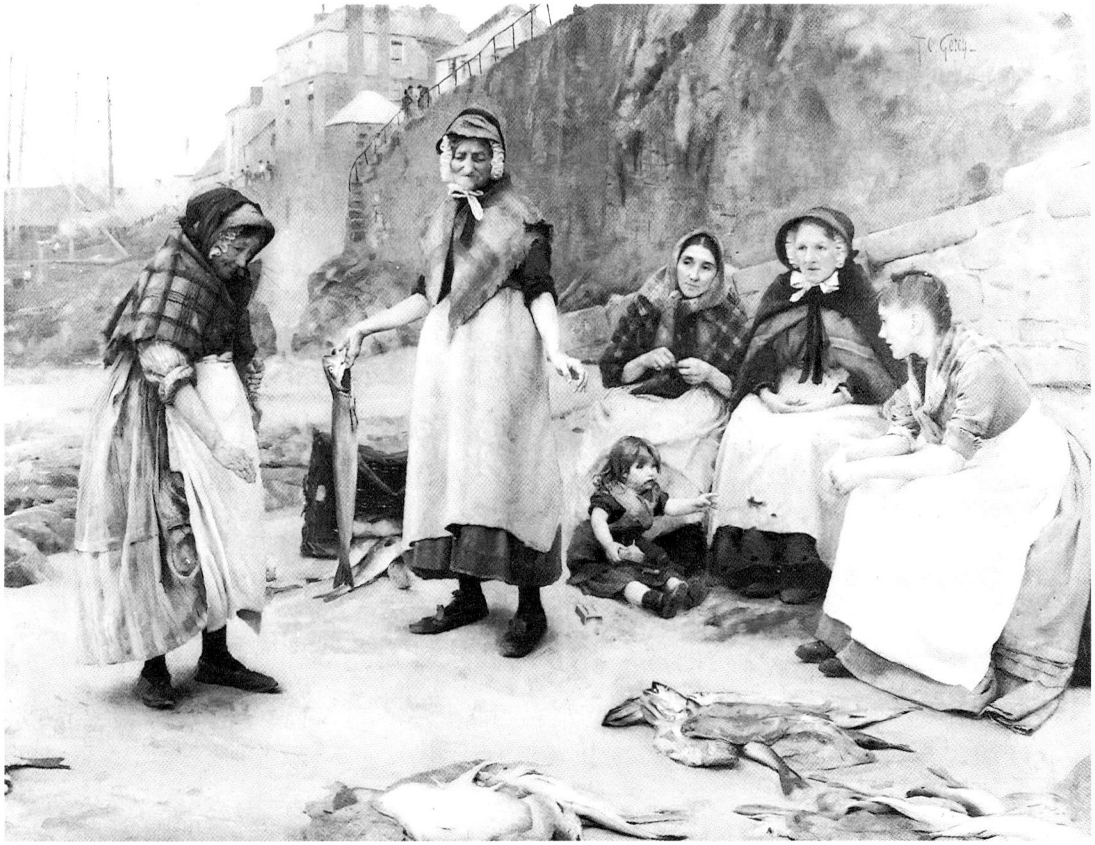

SHARING FISH (1891)
Thomas Cooper Gotch
Oil on canvas, 36 x 48in (91.5 x 122cm)
By courtesy of David Messum, London

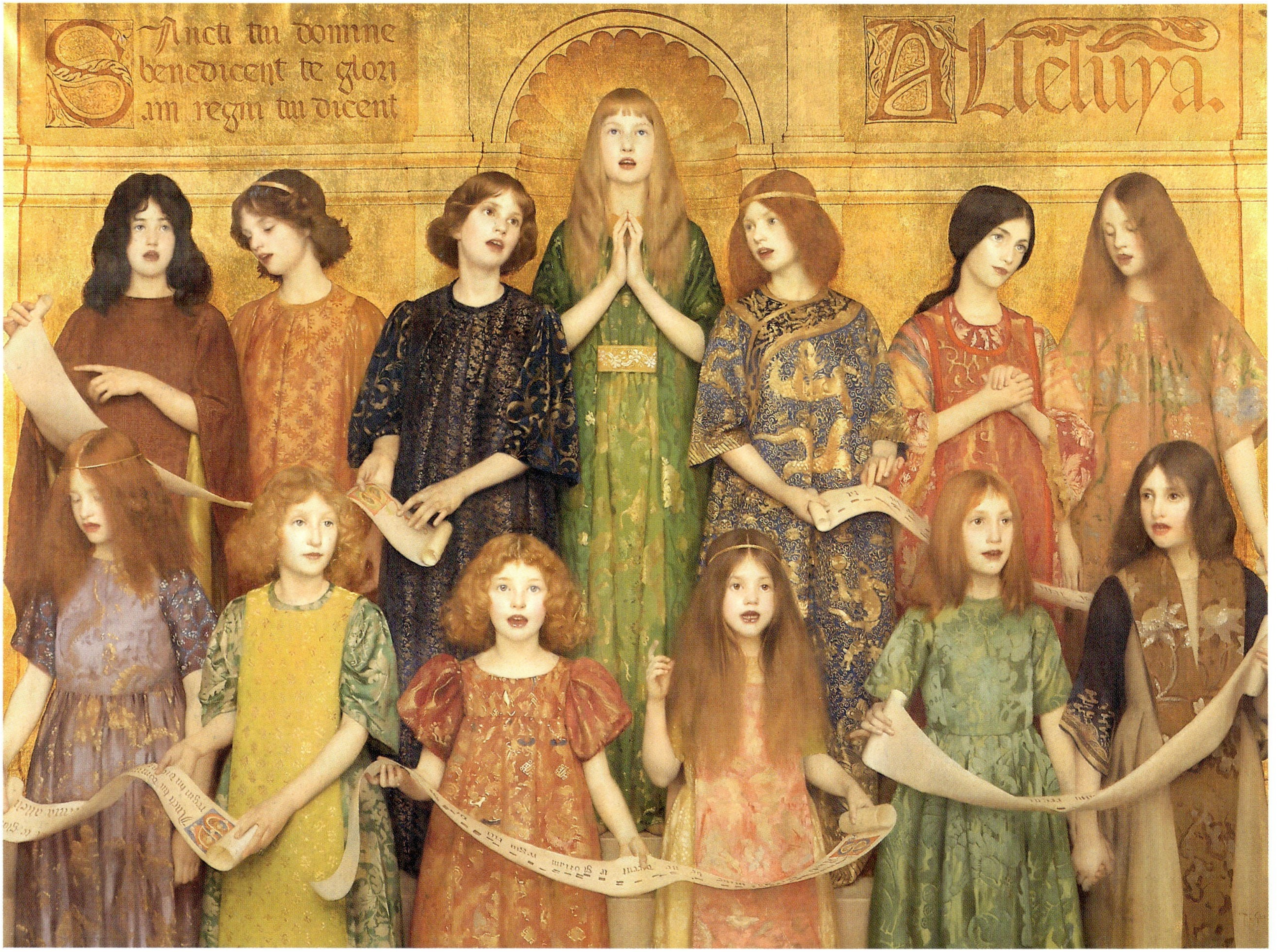

ALLELUIA (1896)
Thomas Cooper Gotch
Oil on canvas, 52¼ x 72½in (133 x 184cm)
Tate Gallery, London

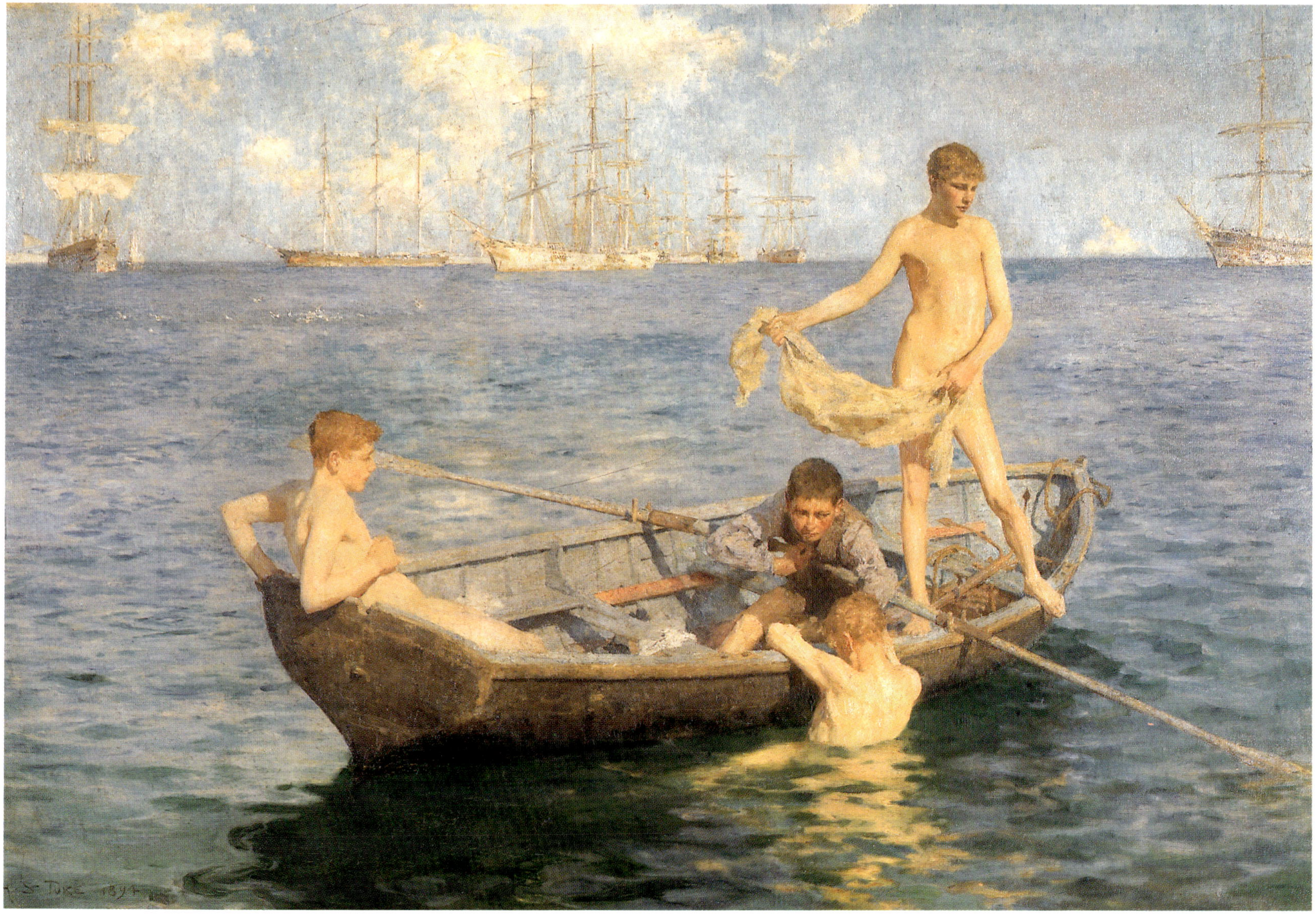

AUGUST BLUE (1893-4)
Henry Scott Tuke
Oil on canvas, 48 x 72in (122 x 183cm)
Tate Gallery, London

HENRY SCOTT TUKE

A five-month trip to Italy and Corfu in 1892 was to have a most dramatic impact on the work of Henry Scott Tuke. *August Blue* (1894), the first major painting to be completed on his return, demonstrates a lightening and brightening of tone and colour, the square brushwork and subdued tones of his earlier scenes having given way to a more fluid technique and the use of bright colours. The painting was purchased by the Chantrey Bequest, thus confirming Tuke in his change of subject matter and technique. *Ruby, Gold and Malachite* (1901, Guildhall Art Gallery, London) and *Noon-day Heat* (1903, Royal Cornwall Polytechnic Society, Falmouth), also feature the male nude out of doors and further explore Impressionist theories of light and colour.

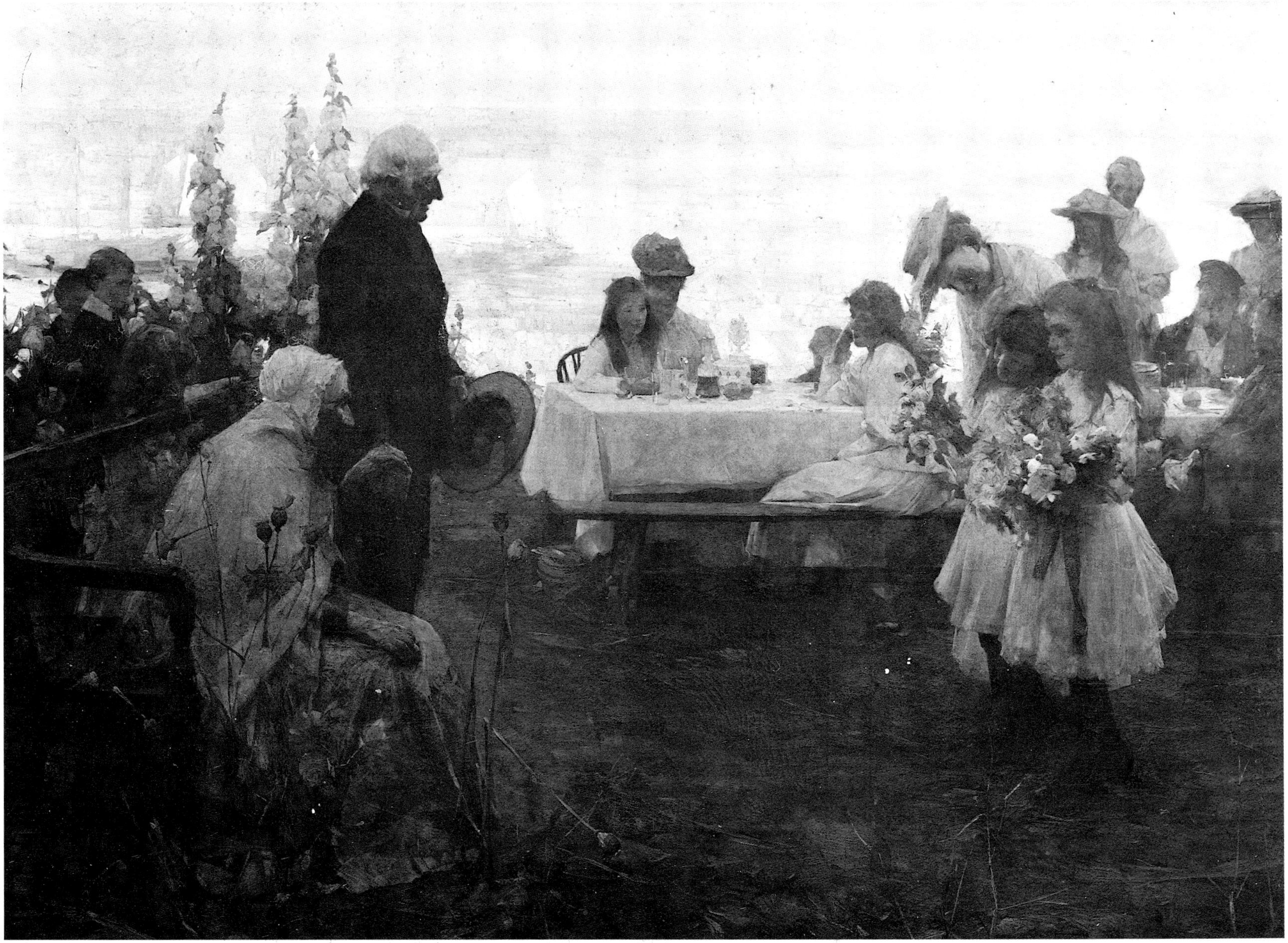

AFTER FIFTY YEARS (1893)
Frank Bramley
Oil on canvas, 67 x 94½in (170 x 240cm)
National Gallery of South Africa, Capetown

FRANK BRAMLEY

During the 1890s Frank Bramley's work became more decorative and his handling of paint much looser. *After Fifty Years* (1893), a major work of this period, shows the aftermath of an alfresco meal, celebrating a golden wedding, where the aged couple are surrounded by a profusion of hollyhocks and poppy seed heads. People are beginning to rise from the table to watch two shy young children, presumably grandchildren, or perhaps even great grandchildren, as they hesitate in the act of presenting bouquets to the old lady. In the background are boats in Newlyn harbour.

By the Light of the Fire (1894, Sotheby's, 23 May 1984[9]) is a much simpler composition, portraying a typical Newlyn interior with grandmother, mother and child 'glowing' in the firelight. Both *Evening* (1894,whereabouts unknown) showing a cart-horse being led home along a track, and *Autumn* (1894, whereabouts unknown), showing an old man asleep on a wooden seat surrounded by a profusion of sunflowers and poppies, reflect Bramley's extremely loose brushwork at this time and complete disappearance of his earlier painstaking square brushwork. The same year, Bramley was elected an Associate of the Royal Academy and left Newlyn with his wife Katherine Graham, eventually settling in her home county of Westmorland in 1900. *Grasmere Rushbearing* (1905, Grasmere) was a major work of these later years. It shows children and villagers carrying flowers and rushes; it still hangs in the village hall after its purchase by the local people. Other paintings of these years include middle-class interiors such as *A Truce* (1912, Royal Institution of Cornwall, Truro), and fashionable portraits such as that of *Helen Graham Chalmers and Her Mother* (1908, private collection). Bramley was elected a Royal Academician in 1911, and died in London in 1915 after a painful and crippling illness.

NORMAN GARSTIN

During the 1890s Garstin continued to paint works which explored his own special interests, as well as anecdotal subjects calculated to appeal to a wider audience. As already stated, he was a great admirer of the Japanese, whom he considered the 'most consummate masters of any period or land' and together with *The Rain It Raineth* (*see* page 39), *Mounts Bay and Tolcarne from Trewidden* (1898, Tate Gallery) is an especially important example of his appreciation of Japanese art. This

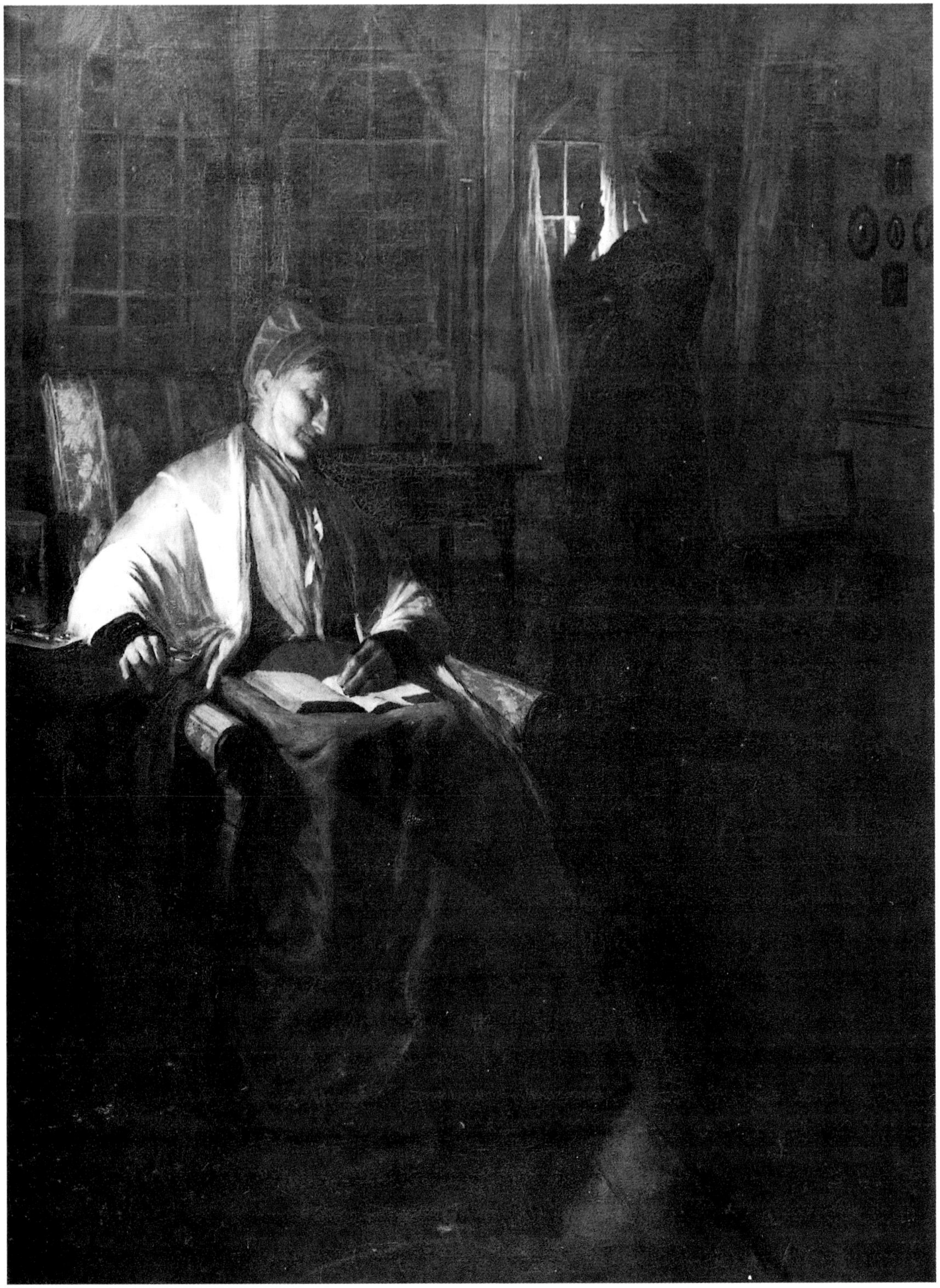

HER SIGNAL (1892)
Norman Garstin
Oil on canvas, 60¼ x 44¼in (158 x 113cm)
The Royal Cornwall Museum, Truro

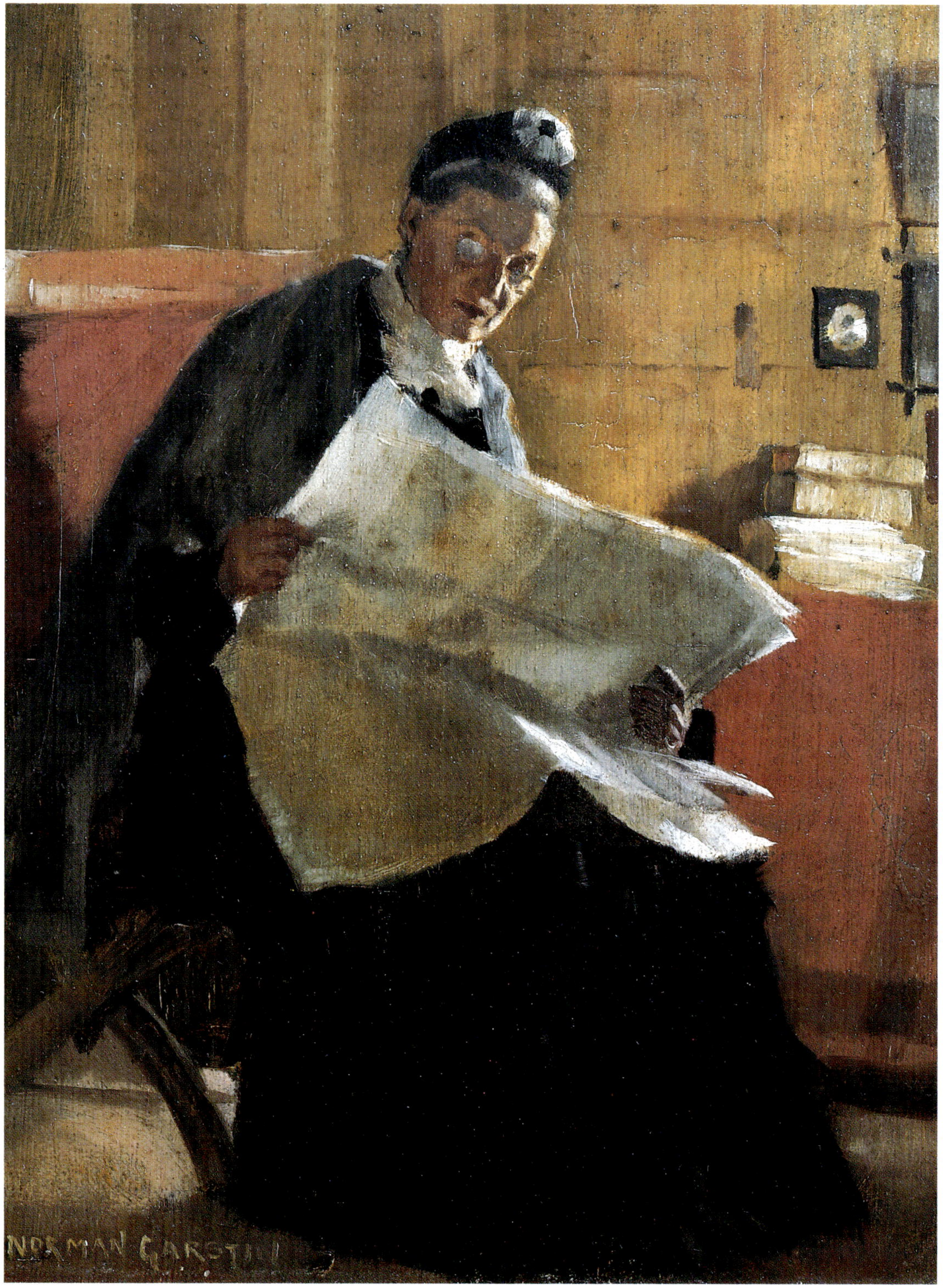

work shows his daughter Alethea with her mother, walking across a field with woodlands and the sea in the background.

A Woman Reading a Newspaper (1891) is an extremely fresh portrait of Ann Fitzgerald, the woman who acted as a mother to Garstin when he was a boy in Ireland. It reflects an understanding of the painting of Whistler and the Impressionists. In complete contrast is *Her Signal* (1892) which is mainly anecdotal in content although painted with a strong sense of depth and space. The Whitechapel catalogue for 1902 had inserted the following entry under this work, 'The older woman, the sands of whose life are almost run out, has fallen asleep, while the girl has seized the moment to show the signal to the young, perhaps forbidden, love outside.'

Garstin was to turn increasingly to scenes of upper class life such as *The Last Dance* (1895, whereabouts unknown) and to costume pieces such as *The Cotillon* (1892, whereabouts unknown) in his search for sales.

FRANK WRIGHT BOURDILLON

Bourdillon was likewise to turn to costume pieces during the 1890s. He developed a passion for Elizabethan history and several of his paintings were concerned with the exploits of Elizabethan heroes, such as *The Only Survivor* (1890, whereabouts unknown), *Aboard the Revenge* (1892, private collection), and *A Duel on Bideford Sands* (1889). Forbes wrote of him:

> A stranger entering a fish cellar at the time might have been surprised to find a fight in progress and two Elizabethan gentlemen with rapiers drawn engaged in fierce combat, for Frank Bourdillon was painting his clever picture, *A Duel on Bideford Sands*.

A WOMAN READING A NEWSPAPER (1891)
Norman Garstin
Oil on canvas, 10 x 8½in (25.5 x 21.5cm)
Tate Gallery, London

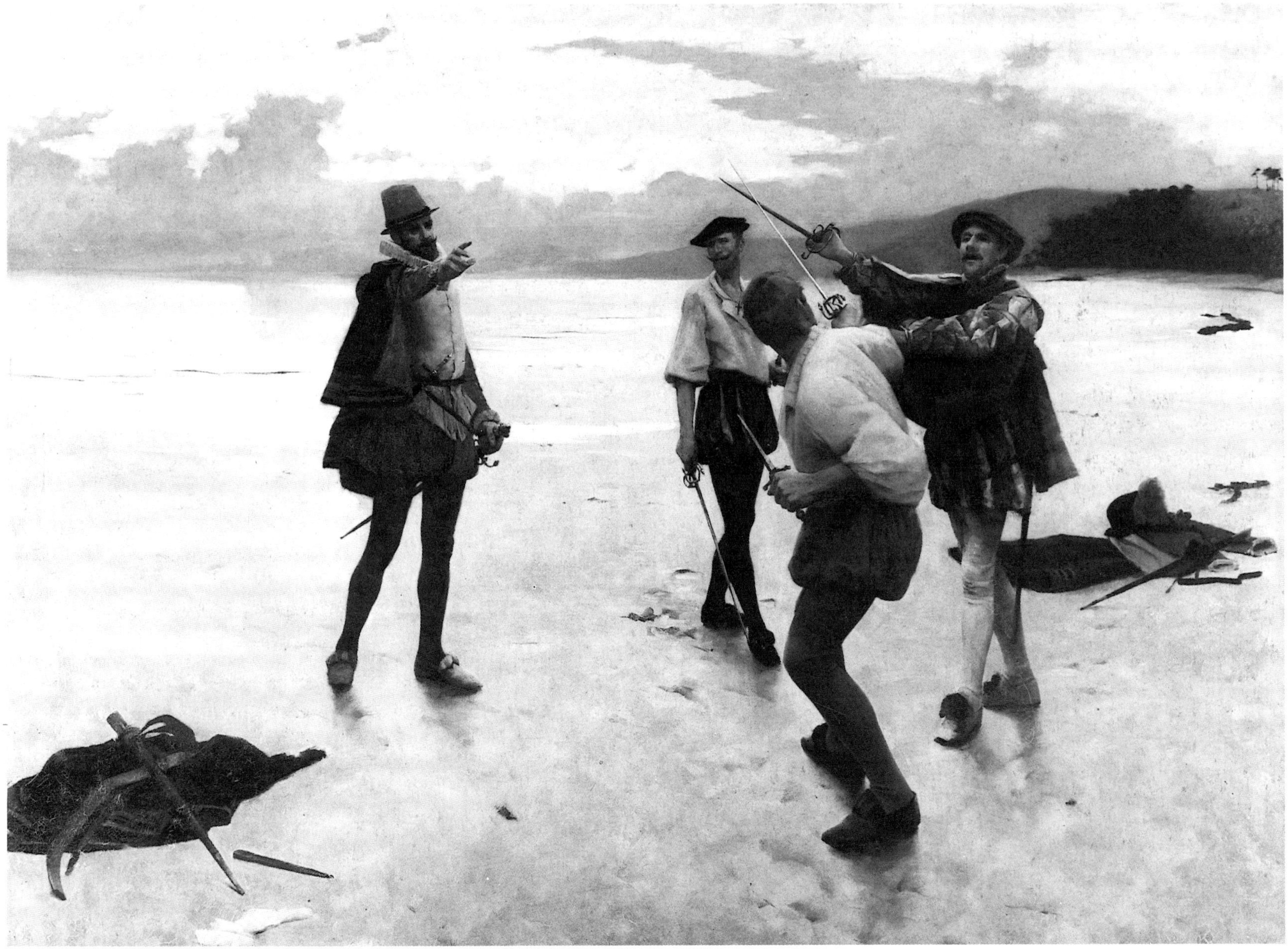

The background for this work was painted on the sands at Lelant, where Bourdillon went to stay for a couple of months.

Bourdillon came of an old Huguenot family and inherited strong religious beliefs. He became increasingly committed to these from 1892, when he gave up his mornings to Bible study and left Newlyn, probably in September of that year (the date of his last recorded Newlyn work), in order to become a missionary in India. There he married a fellow missionary but was later forced through ill-health to return to England, passing the remainder of his life as a curate in Ramsgate.

ON BIDEFORD SANDS (1889)
Frank Wright Bourdillon
Oil on canvas, 58½ x 72½in (147.8 x 184cm)
Art Gallery of New South Wales, Sydney
(Purchased 1890)

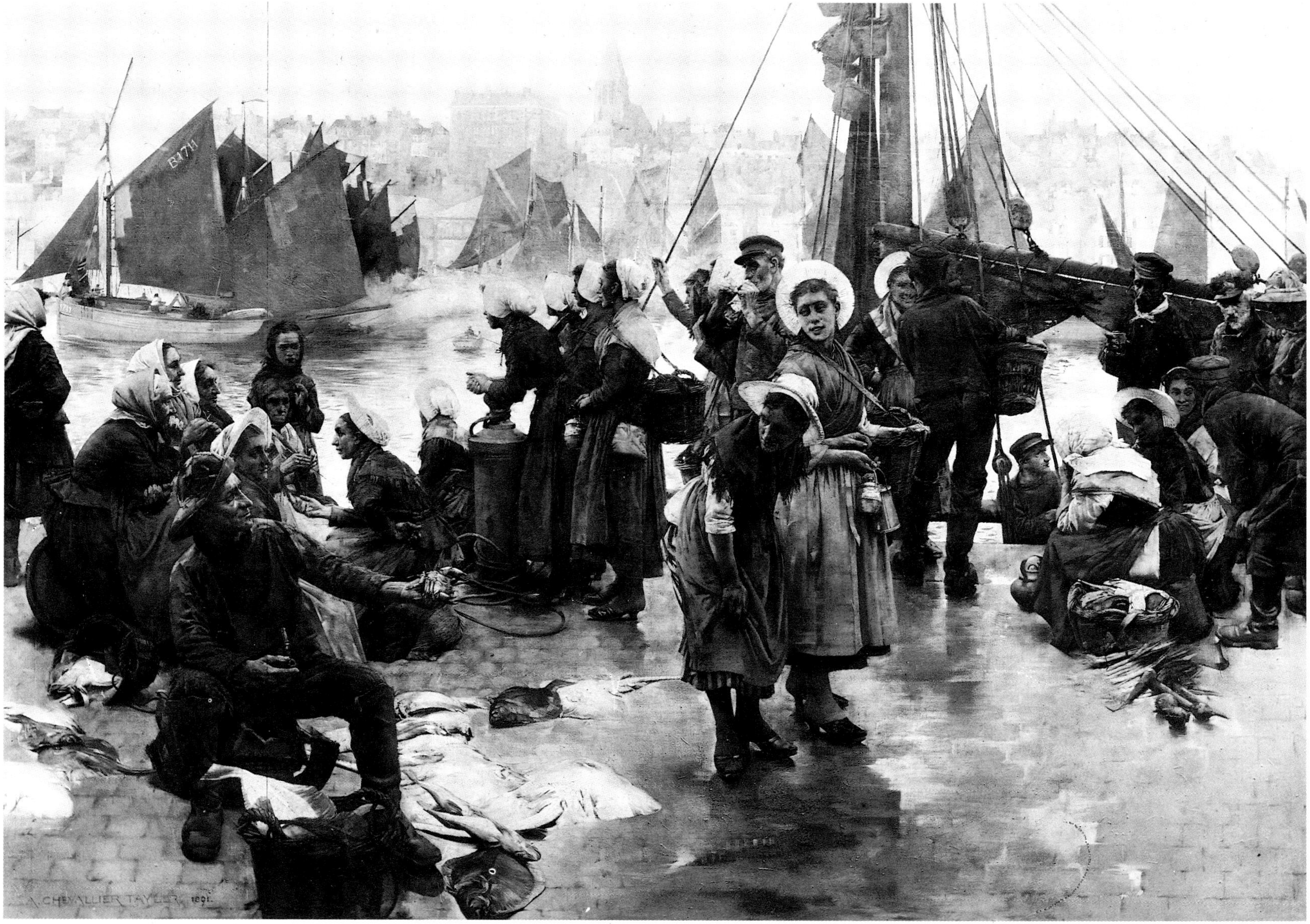

ALEXANDER CHEVALLIER TAYLER

During the 1890s Tayler moved away from typical Newlyn subjects to fashionable anecdotal paintings on the one hand, and specifically religious paintings on the other. *Departure of the Fishing Fleet, Boulogne* (1891) painted on the quayside at Boulogne, was an exception, and Bourdillon recorded that it was a commission. The painting seems curiously outdated and stylised when compared with Forbes' *Fish Sale*, painted seven years before.

Forbes had complained that Tayler's 'only weak point', in his opinion, was his inclination to go to church on Sundays, and it is probable that Tayler became a Roman Catholic in 1887. His religious works include *The Last Blessing* (1890), *Cantus Evangeli* (1897), and *Ecce Agnus Dei* (1900,

△ *DEPARTURE OF THE FISHING FLEET, BOULOGNE* (1891)
Alexander Chevallier Tayler
Oil on canvas, 52 1/4 x 76in (133 x 913cm)
Birmingham Museum and Art Gallery

THE DRINKING POOL (1898) ▷
Fred Hall
Oil on canvas, 29 x 63 1/4in (73.5 x 160.5cm)
Bradford Art Galleries and Museums

whereabouts of all three unknown). Other subjects of this period include fashionable scenes such as *A Summer Dinner Party* (1893, whereabouts unknown) and drawing-room scenes such as *Vanities* (1896, whereabouts unknown) and *Sisters* (1898, whereabouts unknown). All are a far cry from the early *plein air* ideals, but they served Tayler well for in 1904 he was made an Associate of the Royal Academy. Tayler, in fact, left Newlyn for London in 1895 when Garstin recorded that 'he has folded his sketching umbrella and silently stolen up to Kensington'.

FRED HALL

During the 1890s, Fred Hall spent increasingly more time away from Newlyn, at his Porlock studio in Somerset. He must have been greatly encouraged by the enormous success of an exhibition of his silhouette caricatures of members of the Devon and Somerset Staghounds, held at John Dunthorne's London Gallery in 1890. One reviewer wrote, 'Mr Hall has found his métier and he should stick to it.'

However, Hall's real métier lay in the mature landscapes for which he is now best remembered. Paintings such as *The End of the Day* (1891, whereabouts unknown), *The Plough* (1896, whereabouts unknown), and *The Drinking Pool* (1898) have the same scale and relationship of figures to the landscape as Forbes' *Drinking Place* (*see* page 83). The mood is, however, much mellower, and the figures and animals blend harmoniously into their backgrounds echoing the 'subtle evanescent tints' of the English impressionism of George Clausen and Henry La Thangue.

It is probable that Hall left Newlyn in 1897, and the following year he married the young and beautiful girl who inspired several of his best portraits. The couple settled near Newbury in 1911.

The work of the artists of the Newlyn School provides a major example of the influence of late-nineteenth century French painting on British art. During the height of their success in the 1880s and early 1890s, Newlyn works showed the characteristic traits of their French counterparts – including *plein air* realism, subdued tonality and the use of square-ended brushes. Their greatest achievement was to introduce a new degree of freshness and immediacy of observation into British painting as a whole. However, their success was to be short-lived and they were soon eclipsed by more advanced artists such as Walter Sickert and Philip Wilson Steer. During the 1890s, however, British artists as a whole became increasingly inward-looking and ignored the work of their French counterparts. This encouraged the more advanced ones, such as Sickert, to leave Britain for Dieppe in 1898. He returned to Britain in 1905, when French art was once more beginning to be taken seriously again. On the whole, the less progressive trend is reflected in the later work of the Newlyn artists.

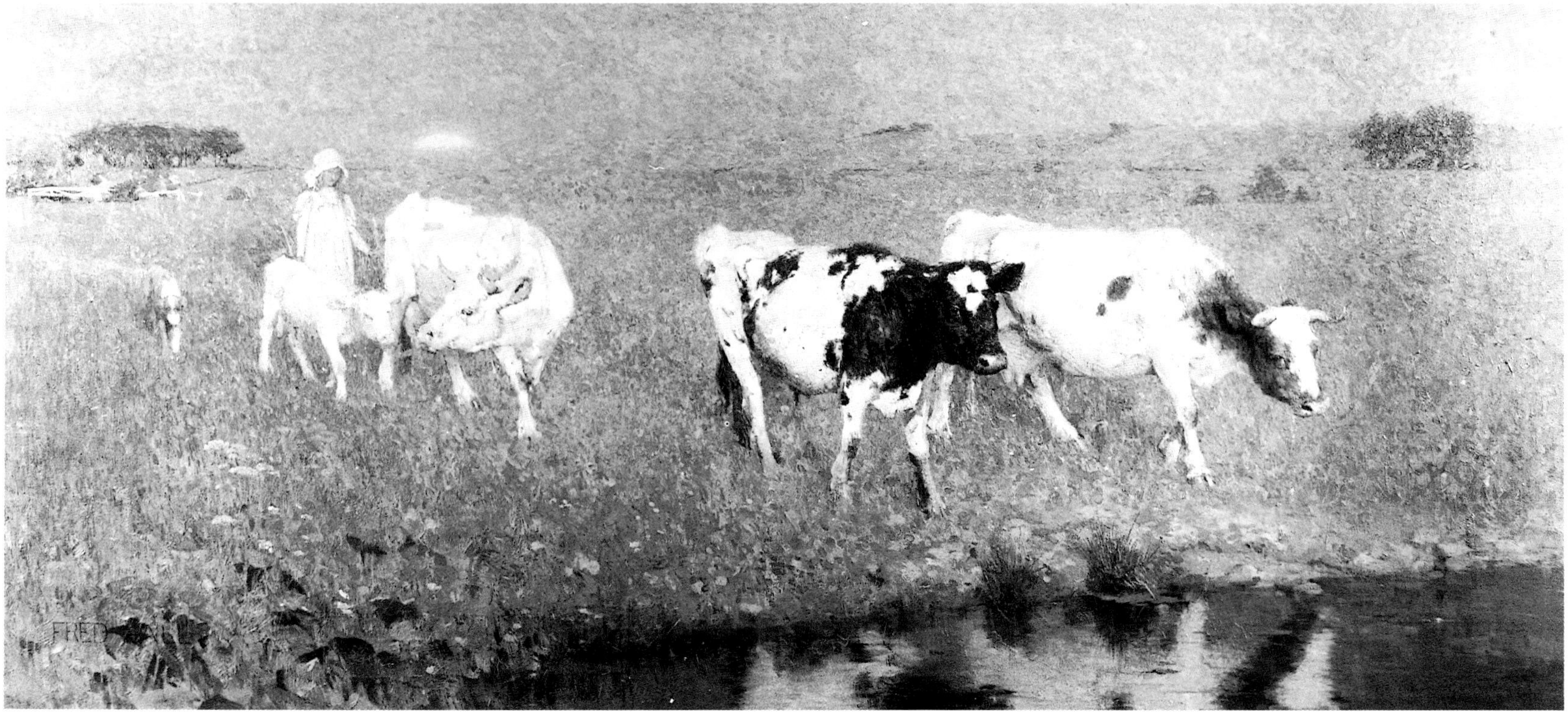

CHAPTER TEN

THE NEW GENERATION

The work of Forbes and the remaining Newlynites (Norman Garstin, T. C. Gotch, and Walter Langley) after 1900 has to be seen against the background of the 'new generation' of artists, many of whom came to Newlyn to study at the Forbes' School of Painting, started in 1899. The members of this new generation were more typical products of the twentieth century in their concentration on individual expression, though they all remained realists. The period up to World War I reflected the more fun-loving attitude of the Edwardian era, whose mood is perhaps best described by Laura Knight in her book *Oil Paint and Grease Paint*, 'At that time the very bright life beamed on us. We had never known the joys of youth before. We danced, played games and lived half the night as well as working hard all day.' C. E. Vulliamy, a one-time student at the Forbes' school, reflects a similar attitude in his book *Calico Pie*:

> How trivial, how brightly frivolous were my days! How void of discretion and responsibility! We were careless then; we knew a happiness and a freedom which, perhaps, the world is never to know again. The illusions of peaceful continuity persisted, even as we danced upon the final egg-shell crust of civilisation, and we laughed at those who were muttering already of 'Kaiser Bill' and his infamous designs.

S. B. P. Mais wrote of the second generation of Newlyn artists in the *Cornish Riviera*, first published in 1928:

> Not that the Newlyn artists of today are engaged in imitating their predecessors, Stanhope Forbes and Henry Tuke, who spent most of their time painting fishermen and bathing boys. The younger generation headed by Harold and Gertrude Harvey, Harold and Laura Knight, Dod and Ernest Procter, Gladys Hynes, show a certain affinity with the Primitives. They are a most sincere band of pioneers who strive to express man's deepest feelings in a new way, both in regard to combination of colour and subject matter. They have fought an amazingly successful fight against the pretty-pretty and the conventionally beautiful. Their Madonnas are sturdy Cornish girls . . .
>
> At first sight their work seems to bear no relation to the place they work in . . . But look a little deeper and you will see that they owe their almost fantastically beautiful colours to the colour you may yourselves see any day of the week on the cliffs or moors of this intensely light district. Their pictures make you remember the ancient saints who once made pilgrimages here, make you look more than casually at the farmgirls and fishermen and realise that frocks do not make a figure any more than paint makes a face. Best of all you will at last see how amazing are the effects of light and shade in this strange land that is almost an island.

The first of the new generation to arrive was S. J. 'Lamorna' Birch (nicknamed 'Lamorna' by Stanhope Forbes to distinguish him from another artist called John Birch), who came to Cornwall from the Midlands in 1889. Instead of settling in Newlyn, Birch lived near the village of Lamorna in order to concentrate on painting the landscape. Harold Harvey was a native of the area, who may perhaps have been inspired to take up painting by seeing the work of the previous generation. Similarly Alethea Garstin, as the daughter of Norman Garstin, was encouraged to paint from an early age. The majority of this generation arrived after the founding of the School of Painting in 1899, although they did not all study there. Charles Simpson came to Cornwall in 1905, attracted by the landscape and the work of the early artists. Ernest Procter and Dod Shaw came to Newlyn in 1906 to study at the Forbes' School, while the Knights arrived in late 1906 from the fishing village of Staithes in Yorkshire.

In contrast to some of the more soulful and sentimental scenes of the previous generation, the subject matter of this generation reflected the more joyful and ebullient aspects of the Edwardian era. Straightforward depictions of the local fisherfolk in their natural settings gave way to exuberantly colourful representations of a variety of subjects often lacking any commitment at all to *plein air* realism. The Penzance-born Harold Harvey was to follow closest in the steps of the previous generation in his concentration on local subjects and models, but others, such as Laura Knight, imported models from London, while Munnings employed his groom as a model. As time went on, the depiction of local inhabitants was replaced by that of well-dressed figures in sophisticated middle-class interiors. This is particularly evident in the work of Harold Knight, and later of Harold Harvey. Several of the group were attracted by the colourful and exotic aspects of fairgrounds, horse-racing and gypsy life. While Laura Knight, Ernest Procter, Harold Harvey and Lamorna Birch all delighted in the atmosphere of the local fairs, Sir Alfred Munnings was inspired by the world of horse-racing (*St Buryan Races*

1930, Walker Art Gallery, Liverpool, shows the start of the local races at St Buryan).

The village of Lamorna became an artistic centre at this time, not only for the landscape artists such as Birch, Robert Hughes and Charles Naper, but it also provided a temporary residence for Munnings, the Knights and the Simpsons, all of whom were attracted by its beautiful scenery. Lamorna is situated about five miles west of Penzance and comprises a group of houses along a wooded valley, through which a stream flows into the sea. The cove itself is particularly attractive and was often a centre for picnics and outings. Village life centred on the *Wink*, the local inn whose genial landlord, Mr Jory, appears to have been a great character. Mr Jory's wife, to whom he reputedly never spoke, ran a rival institution in the local temperance hotel (now the Lamorna Cove Hotel), and the artists patronised both places.

Lamorna and its surrounding countryside is especially beautiful in the spring, as described by Bernard Walke, the legendary parish priest of the Church of St Hilary near Penzance, in his book *Twenty Years at St Hilary*:

> Here in the valley the tops of the ash trees are tinged with green, primroses and daffodils are in bloom and the blackthorn is opening its buds. Such a flowering of blackthorn from the head of the valley to where the stream flows out into the sea, is not to be found in any other spot in Cornwall.

The School of Painting provided a solid grounding in drawing and painting, and students were initially required to paint with absolute fidelity to nature before developing their own individual styles. The emphasis was on the study of the human figure. Vulliamy described how the school was situated in the area of Newlyn known as 'The Meadows' and consisted of three huts. The smallest of these contained plaster casts for beginners to copy, drawing with charcoal and crumbling bread. In the largest of the huts, known as the head-room, students drew or painted from the living model, presumably clothed, and the third hut was known as the life-room. The 'head' models were usually local people, fishermen, old women and young girls anxious to earn a few pounds. The nude models were usually imported from London and were often Italian. They were regarded with great suspicion by the locals and often had great difficulty in obtaining lodgings.

Forbes enjoyed teaching and being in contact with younger artists, and very soon became known as the 'Professor'. He was sometimes assisted by Elizabeth and by J. Sherwood Hunter, but the character of the school depended largely on his personality and a former student, Ruth Simpson (née Alison) recalled her pleasure when he returned from a period away. He was seen as an authoritarian figure and was known to be extremely tough on his students at the regular Saturday morning 'Crit'. Ruth remembered how she actually shook with fright when he approached her work on one occasion and, perhaps aware of this, he was extremely kind and told her that her work was 'well drawn and done very tenderly and carefully', though another time he 'slanged' her work.

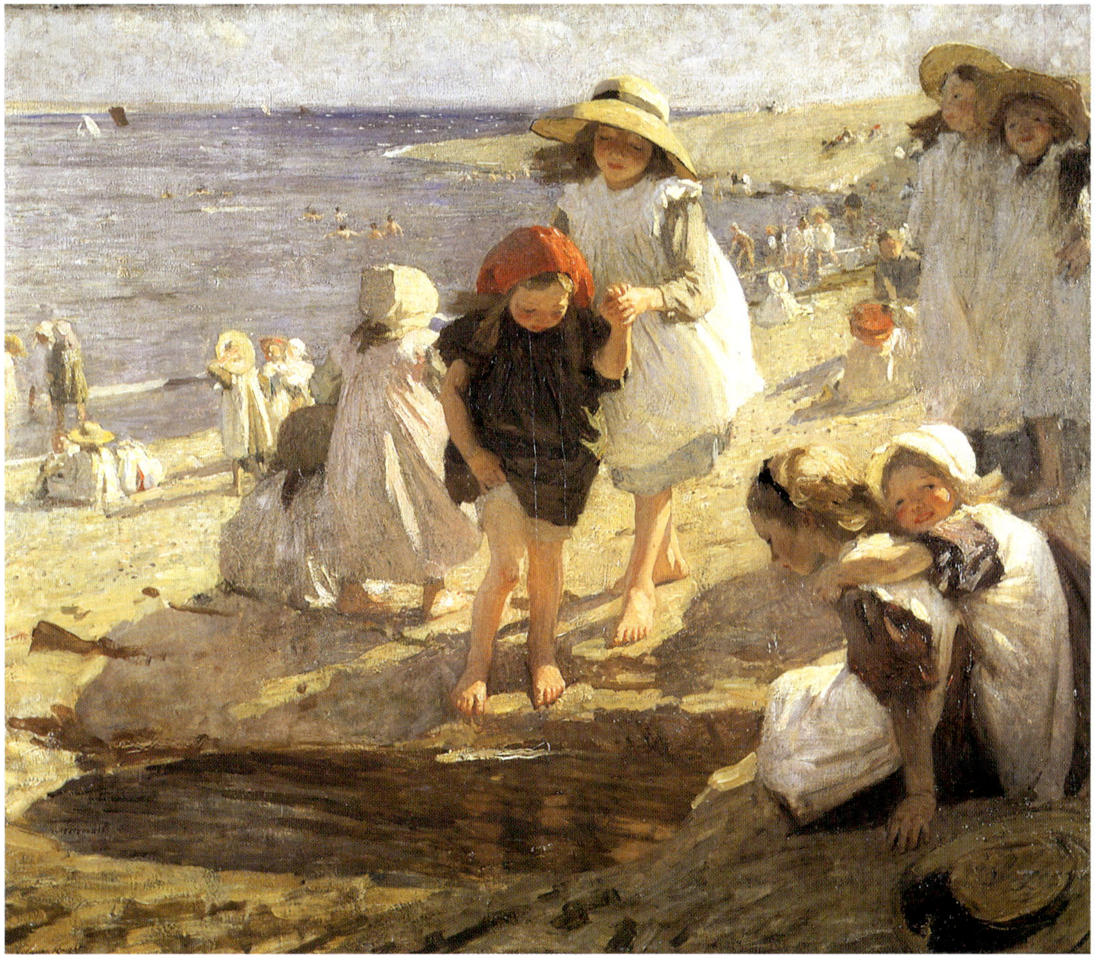

THE BEACH (1909)
Laura Knight
Oil on canvas, 50¼ x 60¼in (127.5 x 153cm)
Laing Art Gallery, Newcastle upon Tyne
(Tyne and Wear Museums)

The school attracted a wide variety of students, many of whom intended to become serious artists. These included Dod Shaw, Ernest Procter, Gladys Hynes, Eleanor Weymouth, Robert Hughes, Ruth and Rose Alison, Kathleen Earle, Frank Heath and his future wife Jessica, Midge Bruford, Christine Vivian, Jill and Geoffrey Garnier and Joey Carter-Wood. Several of these artists subsequently married each other. There were also a number of eccentrics satirised by Vulliamy in his book, as well as elderly students who viewed the school more in the light of an evening class. Ruth Simpson described the younger men at the school as being 'horribly artistic with bow ties, etc'.

For the young, the school also provided a centre for the enjoyment of a particularly free and varied social life. Parties and dances were frequent events in Newlyn before World War I. Among the most popular occasions were those organised by the students themselves and held in the school studios or in the homes of the older established artists such as the Forbes and the Gotches. A former student, who later became a well-known novelist, Winifred Tennyson Jesse, described one such party held at the Gotches in her diary:

> 26 March 1908: The day of Phil's (Phyllis Gotch) Gypsy Beano. You looked from the pink-lit glow out into the dark garden, where a fat Chinese lantern hung against the sky. The men all looked frightful ragamuffins, with teeth blacked out . . . then all became a scene of wild confusion, each person stamping and jumping and yelling. Every now and then came a crash of broken glasses, swept down by the stampede. Little Mrs Knight was the wildest of the wild, her hair streaming and ragged skirts awhirl; even Harold unbent and was dancing and kicking with a broomstick.

Laura Knight recalled a 'Dickens Christmas' which lasted for several days, with long country walks during the day and parties at night. She was eventually found asleep at four o'clock in the morning under the grand piano with 'A. J.' (Alfred Munnings) 'roaring out songs and vamping over-head'.

More sober entertainment consisted of concerts and play readings. Concerts were sometimes held at the Faugan, the home of the Forbes, while Charles Simpson founded a Beethoven Society together with C. E. Vulliamy 'to which none but really serious musical people were admitted'. Vulliamy described how he was gradually seduced away from regular attendance at the school by the further delights of fishing and shooting, picnics and outings. Tennyson Jesse recalled:

> 7 September 1908: Dod and Cicely came over from Lamorna, and A. J. was round early, agog for us all to go out for the day in a wagonette . . . Then through Penzance, lustily singing, we drove, and at Gurnard's Head had lunch at the Inn, the discussion waxing so heated that the landlady was overheard to remark to some minion: 'Must be all mad, I should think!'

Newlyn itself had changed greatly since the arrival of the first artists. The harbour had been transformed by the additon of two new piers – the South Pier, built in 1884 and the North Pier, built in 1894. Norman Garstin wrote:

> The Newlyn of today and that of the first artist settlers twenty-five years ago are two quite different places. When Mr Stanhope Forbes painted his *Fish Sale* there was no harbour, today there is a spacious one, which, large as it is, is crowded with fishing boats, steamers, sailing vessels and craft of all descriptions. All this has brought a life and animation that no one would have dreamt of a quarter of a century ago.

The sight of artists painting in the village was no longer a novelty and the local people had grown accustomed to supplementing their incomes by modelling. Forbes himself was a familiar and much loved character in village life, frequently watched by crowds as he painted. He recorded he was more encouraged by hearing 'The old pictur's coming along a bit better today, Mr Forbes', from a child who had been watching him at work in Mousehole, than by a good press notice.

Sir Alfred Munnings

Although based in Norfolk, Sir Alfred Munnings was a frequent visitor to Cornwall from 1908. As he wrote in his autobiography *An Artist's Life*, 'For years we had known of the famous Newlyn School and were curious to see this country which attracted artists.' At first he stayed in Newlyn, later moving to Lamorna where he rented a studio and stable at the Lamorna mill. He brought his horses and his dog with him and employed a local lad, Ned Osborne, to act as model-cum-groom. Munnings took immediate charge of the social round in Newlyn and boasted later in life that he had organised 'more parties, picnics, outings and Christmas festivities than anyone in the country'.

He was probably happiest when painting animals in the landscape and he produced a series of paintings of the local hunt at Zennor. Of *Going to the Meet of the Western Foxhounds* he wrote: 'Yet another picture of Ned on his grey was bought by the Newcastle Art Gallery. In this he is riding towards you silhouetted up against the sky, and the leading hounds are coming out of the picture'.

Laura Knight

Laura Knight (1877–1972) was well into her thirties by the time she came to Newlyn in 1906. The years spent in Cornwall were especially important for her because it was there that she developed her mature style and began to taste the fruits of success. It was also an extremely happy time for both Laura and Harold after the difficulties of the preceding years, and they found themselves in an idyllic world of sun, sea and companionship. Laura recalled 'Student life in surroundings such as we had never dreamed of; a carefree life of sunlit pleasure and leisurely study. I felt old and experienced with these youngsters who really knew so much more than I of fun and social graces.' She formed close and sometimes lifelong friendships with many of her fellow artists, and her joy in her new friends and lifestyle is reflected in her work of the period. Painted with increasingly bright

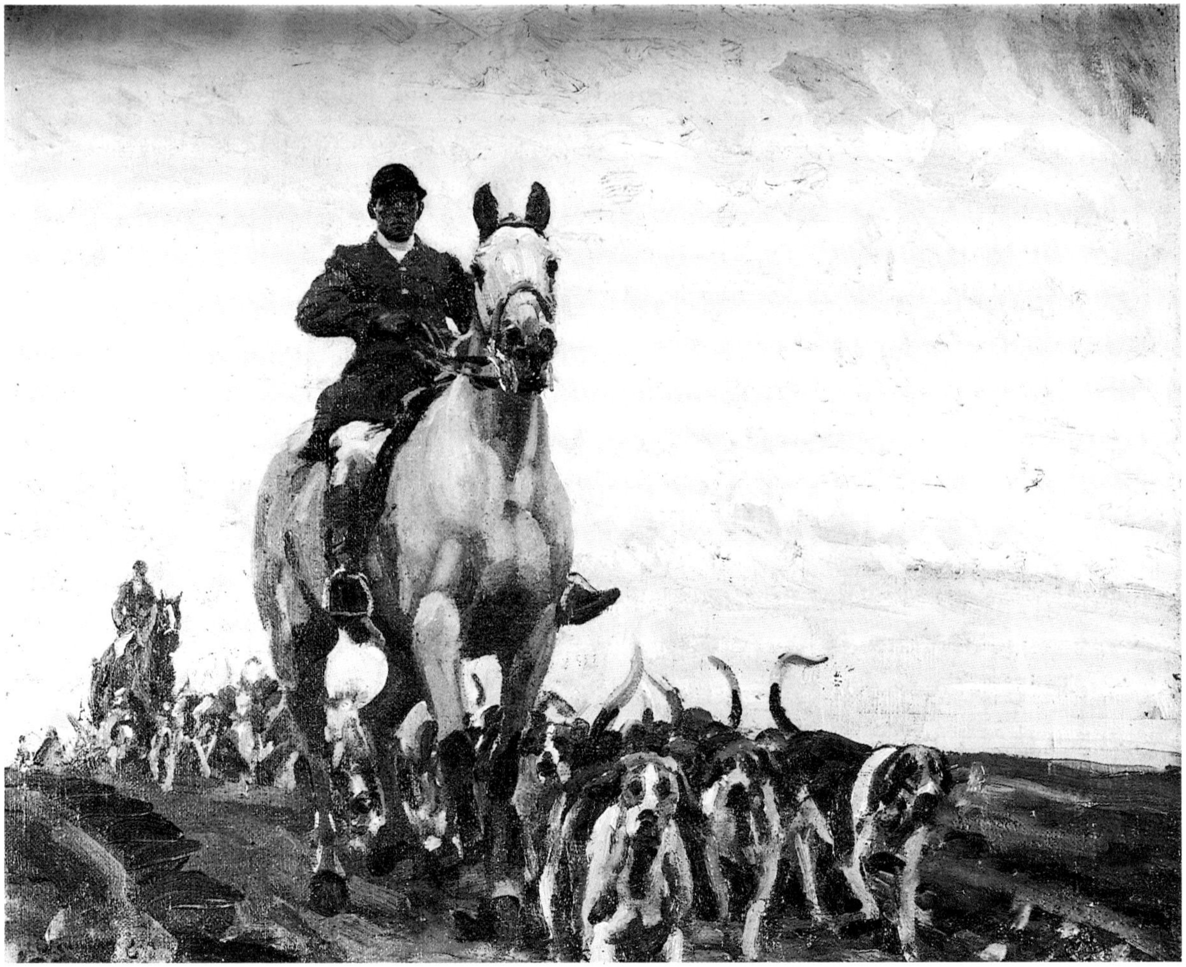

colour, Laura's works express, perhaps more than any of the other artists of this generation, the carefree delights of the Edwardian era.

The Beach (1908), her first Newlyn painting, was an immediate success and is an expression of her delight in her new-found surroundings: 'An ebullient vitality made me want to paint the whole world and say how glorious it was to be young and strong and able to splash with paint on canvas any old thing that one saw.' The serious commitment to realism of her Staithes paintings has given way to a more frivolous enjoyment of a lighter kind. Two further paintings, *Flying a Kite* (South African National Gallery, Cape Town) and *The Boys* (Johannesburg Art Gallery), both of 1910, reveal her free and dramatic handling of paint.

The success of these works gave Laura confidence to experiment further, and women posing on the clifftops soon became a favourite subject. Her models serve as focal points in these works and as colour contrasts to the rich blues and blue-greens of the sea. *On the Cliffs* (1917, Richard Green, London) reveals a particularly dramatic use of dark purple shadow on the cliff face, contrasting with the light falling on parts of the figures and sea beyond. The critic C. E. Vulliamy considered that in the years immediately preceding World War I, Laura Knight was by far the most conspicuous of the painters then living in Cornwall:

Her facility and energy were overpowering. She placed her nude and lovely models in the open air, down on the rocks at Lamorna. She spread upon her enormous canvases white and yellow dollops of creamy sunshine with a palette knife. I sometimes think that the superb exuberance of her style may have tended in those days to obscure the gentler merit of the work which Harold Knight was producing at the same time . . .

GOING TO THE MEET OF THE WESTERN FOXHOUNDS (c. 1913)
Sir Alfred Munnings

Oil on canvas, 20¼ x 24¼in (52 x 62cm)
Laing Art Gallery, Newcastle upon Tyne

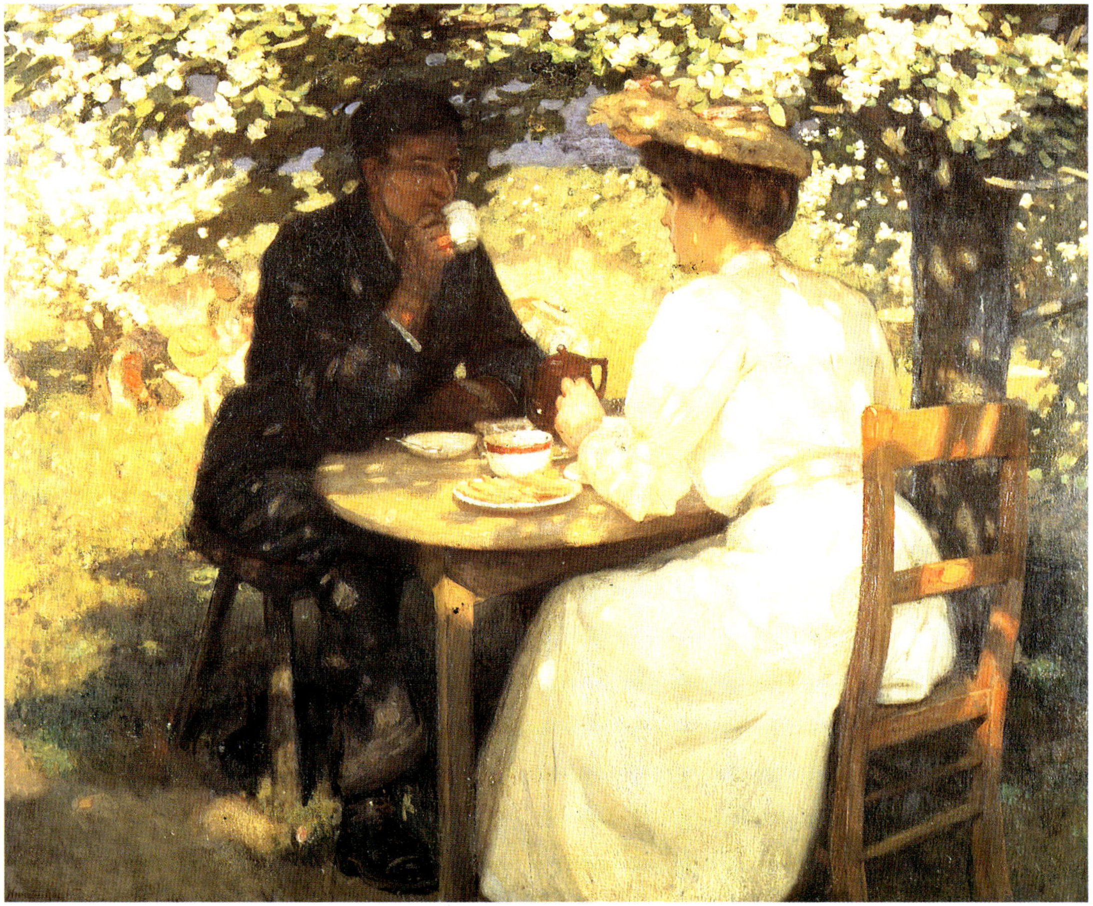

In the Spring (1908-9)
Harold Knight
Oil on canvas, 52 x 62¼in (132 x 158cm)
Laing Art Gallery, Newcastle upon Tyne
(Tyne and Wear Museums)

Other important works of these years include the very striking, *Self-Portrait with Nude* (1913, National Portrait Gallery, London), *Penzance Fair* (1914, private collection) and *Spring* (1916, Tate Gallery, London), all of which were painted with characteristic vigour and enjoyment. In addition, she painted some extremely sensitive watercolours while in Cornwall, of which *Wind and Sun* (*c.*1913, Pyms Gallery, London) and *Two girls in a Garden* (1914, Doncaster Museum and Art Gallery) are particularly fine examples.

Harold Knight

The work of Harold Knight (1874–1961) also flourished during the years he spent in Cornwall. By the time he came to Newlyn in 1906, he had been exhibiting at the Royal Academy since 1896 and had already achieved some success with his work. *A Cup of Tea* (1905) had been purchased by the Queensland Art Gallery, Australia, and *The Girl and the Letter* (1906) by the Harris Museum and Art Gallery, Preston, UK.

Harold's *In the Spring* (1908) was exhibited at the Royal Academy the same year as Laura's *The Beach*, and the two works were purchased by the Laing Art Gallery, Newcastle. Harold's painting is a particularly delightful work in which he has enjoyed painting the dappled effects of light and shade under the blossom tree. Increasingly during these years, Knight was to concentrate on portraiture, which he always considered his forte as well as providing a steady source of income. He painted several very fine portraits of Florence, Munnings' first wife, and often included his fellow artists in group portraits such as *The Sonnet* (1911, whereabouts unknown) and *The Council: Portrait Group* (1916, private collection). The latter was painted at the Lamorna Inn, which was a favourite meeting place. It includes Lamorna Birch gesturing towards Robert Hughes in the foreground. In the background are two villagers, Captain Joe Ladner and Robert Matthews, and to the far right 'Old Jory', the landlord of the inn.

After the war, the Knights settled in London, which was a convenient base for Harold's portrait commissions. Following his wartime experiences as a conscientious objector shunned by artist friends and the local people alike and forced to work on the land, Harold was probably relieved to go, but Laura was extremely sad to leave Cornwall and admitted later in life to 'shedding many tears at being enclosed in bricks and mortar'. The Knights did, however, keep studios at Sennen Cove to which they returned during the summers of the 1920s, and Laura continued to exhibit paintings of Cornwall at the Royal Academy during the early 1920s. *Lamorna Cove* (1920, whereabouts unknown), *Summer* (1921, whereabouts unknown) and *Autumn Sunlight, Sennen Cove* (1922, City Museum and Art Gallery, Birmingham) are particularly colourful examples. She also painted some delightful interiors in Cornwall at this time which come close to the work of Dod Procter (see *A Cottage Bedroom* 1929, Sothebys, and *Susie and the Washbasin* 1929, Harris Museum and Art Gallery, Preston). By then, her major interests lay elsewhere, with Diaghilev's Ballets Russes, the theatre and the circus. During the 1920s Harold Knight concentrated almost exclusively on painting portraits and women in interiors, and *In the Studio* (1921, private collection) is probably one of the finest interiors he painted in this period.

CHAPTER ELEVEN

POST-WAR DEVELOPMENTS

'In August 1914, much of the work and all of the play were suddenly at an end,' wrote Munnings in his autobiography. World War I broke up the easy-going pattern of life among the artists in Newlyn. Birch and Munnings went off to enlist, and Ernest Procter joined the Friends Ambulance Unit serving in France, leaving his wife Dod to cope on her own in Newlyn. Harold Knight meanwhile had a particularly difficult time as a conscientious objector in Cornwall. Some suffered losses in the war. Arthur Newton lost two sons and Forbes lost his only son, Alec, a few years after the death of his wife.

After the war, Munnings and the Knights left Cornwall for good. Of the remaining artists, the Procters, Harold Harvey and Alethea Garstin were probably the most interesting. At Lamorna, Birch continued to reap success, while the other artists such as the Hughes, Charles Naper and Frank Heath continued to paint and exhibit in a more modest way.

HAROLD HARVEY

Harold Harvey (1874–1941) was one of the most delightful artists of the new generation. His lifelong commitment to depicting the people and countryside of West Cornwall was an important feature of his work and one that probably arose from his being a native of the area. His best work expresses a true joy in the countryside and a real understanding of the movements and gestures of the men, women and children he so often depicted. Wallace Nicholls, writing in *Studio* in 1942, described him as one of the 'truest and sincerest of British painters'.

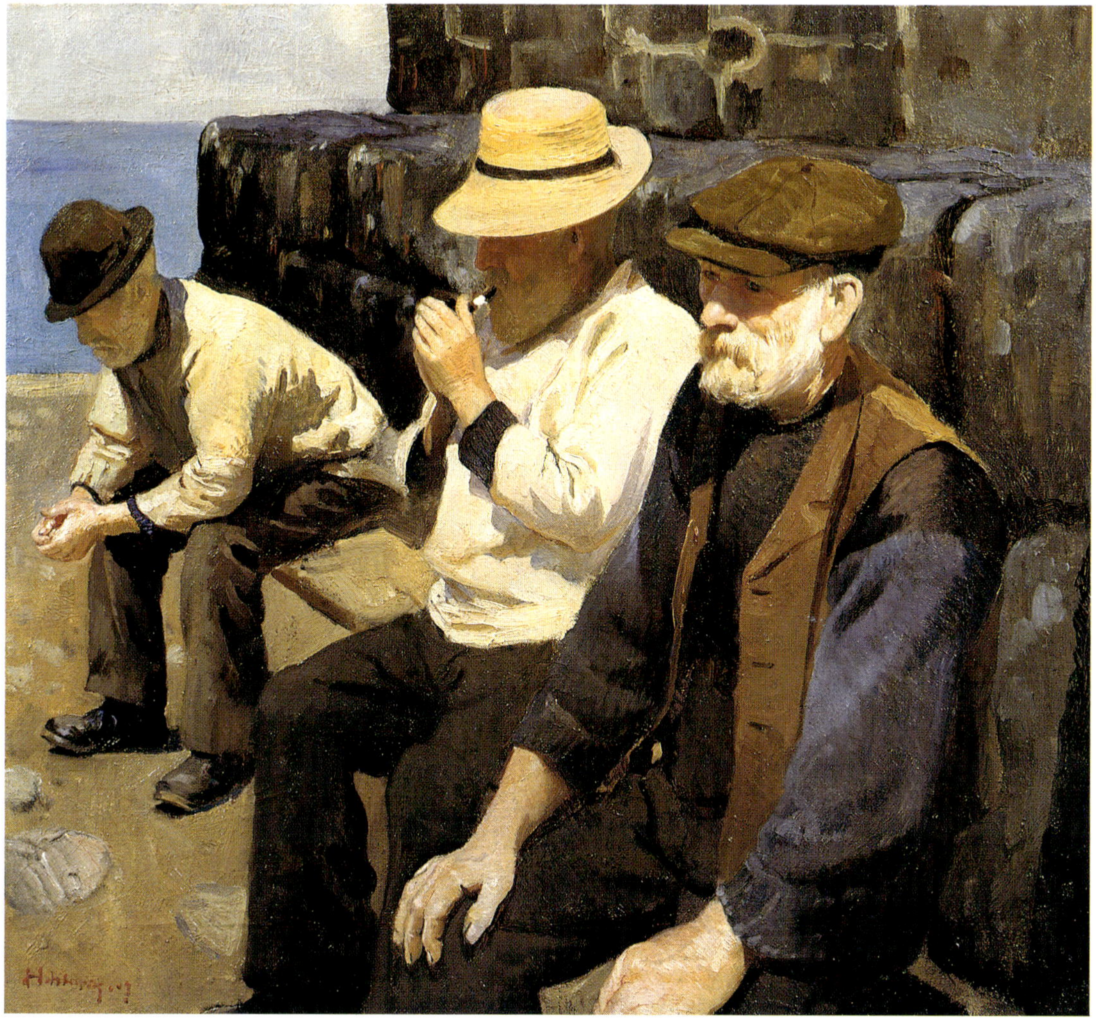

THREE FISHERMEN (1909)
Harold Harvey
Oil on canvas, 18 x 20in (45.5 x 51cm)
By courtesy of the Richard Green Gallery, London

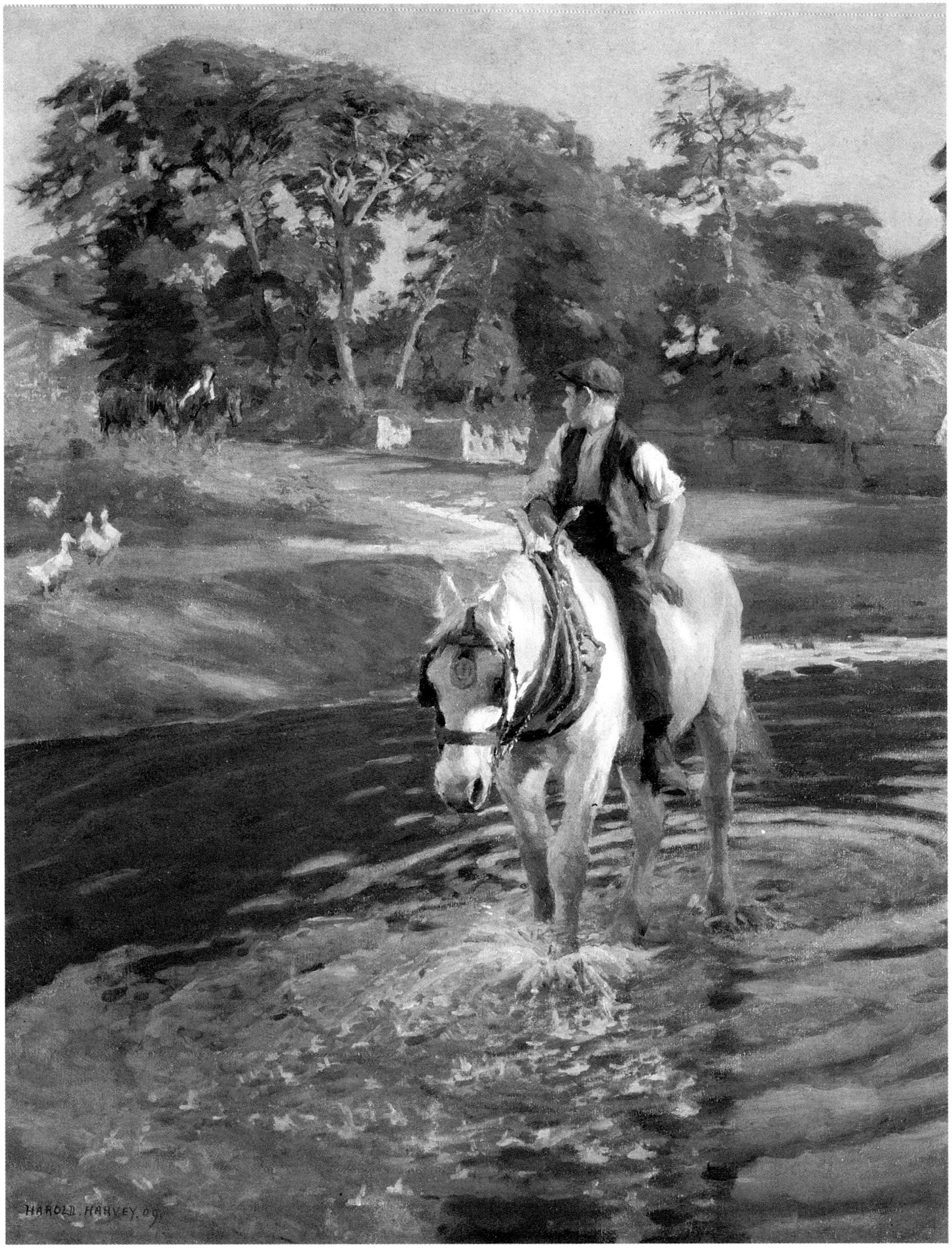

During the 1900s, Harvey painted many evocative studies of figures in the Cornish countryside, following on the Forbes tradition; these include *Sailing in Newlyn Harbour* (1906, Whitford and Hughes, London), and *Maytime* (1912, private collection). *The Close of a Summer's Day* (1909) is typical of much of his work of this period and expresses his deep understanding of country life. His evocative treatment of the contrasting light and shade in the field and the ripples and splashes in the pool fully realises the complex effects of fading sun. In contrast, *Woman Reading* (1917, Richard Green, London) shows a subtle and pale-coloured corner of a livingroom with a model, possibly his wife Gertrude, reading. Although a simply-conceived work, it is a particularly harmonious one.

From 1914–15, Harvey's work became gradually more stylised with a greater concentration on form and outline rather than the painterly values of his earlier works. He also began to paint more sophisticated interiors. Gertrude modelled for some interesting studies in the bedroom of their Newlyn home, in which the themes of light and reflections have fascinated the artist: *Reflections* (1916, Cyfartha Castle Museum, Merthyr Tydfil) and *At the Dressing Table* (1920, Cyfartha Castle Museum, Merthyr Tydfil). During the 1920s, he continued to paint interiors, of which *The Critics* (1922) and *My Kitchen* (1923, Oldham Art Gallery) are particularly fine examples. They show his love of painting figures with simple, colourful objects in the background. They were probably inspired by the contemporary concern with seventeenth-century Dutch interiors, an influence which can also be seen in the work of Harold Knight, who was interested in the visual problems of Vermeer and Pieter de Hooch. The use of chequered floors in the paintings is typical of Dutch seventeenth-century interiors. Other works of the 1920s suggest the heavy sculptural

The Close of a Summer's Day (1909)
Harold Harvey
Oil on canvas, 50 x 40in (127 x 101.5cm)
Private collection

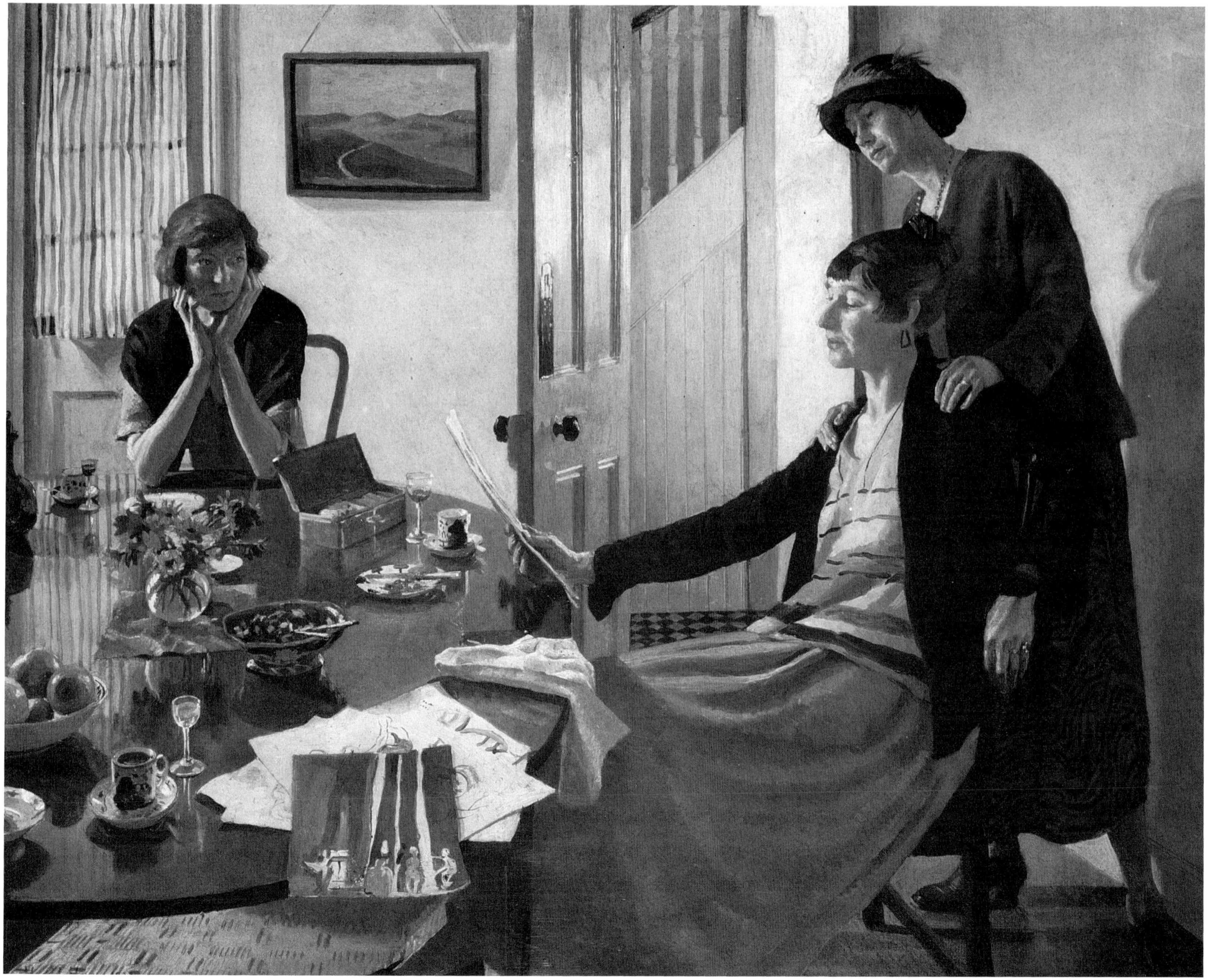

THE CRITICS (1922)
Harold Harvey

Oil on canvas, 23¾ x 29¾in (60 x 75.5cm)
City Museums and Art Gallery, Birmingham

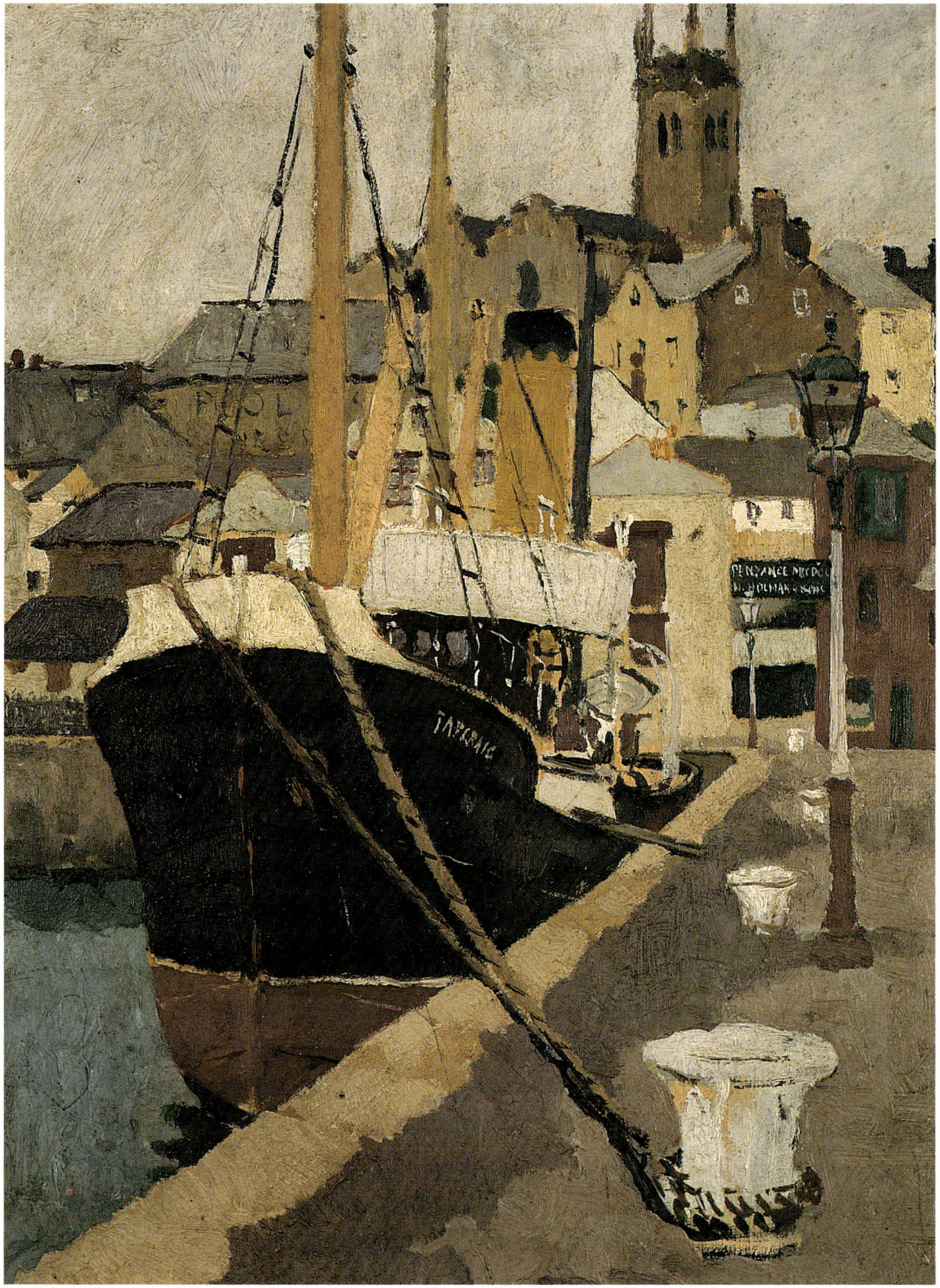

style employed by Dod Procter at this time, for example *Anemones* (1926, private collection), where the figures appear monumental and the background is 'telescoped'.

Harvey was a religious man and became a Roman Catholic later in life. Along with several Newlyn artists he painted some panels for the Church of St Hilary, near Penzance, whose parish priest, Father Bernard Walke, was a very colourful character and a great lover of the arts. Harvey also painted several religiously-inspired works, all of which are set in local backgrounds. *The Madonna of the Bridges* (private collection) is a neo-Renaissance composition showing a Madonna and Child with Newlyn Coombe in the background, and *The Flight* (1926, whereabouts unknown) takes place on a wild Cornish moor.

Harvey was a regular exhibitor at the Royal Academy, and also held several one-person exhibitions of his work in London. However, like Alethea Garstin he never achieved the recognition which was his due. Unlike the Procters, he rarely visited London, preferring to stay in Cornwall and lead a simple yet satisfying life painting, fishing and bird-watching.

ALETHEA GARSTIN

The work of Alethea Garstin (1894–1978) is in marked contrast to the other artists of this generation. Her freedom, lightness of touch and lively compositions show a much wider knowledge of twentieth-century European painting than many of this generation, with the exception of Dod Procter. Her father's statement 'I am always fond of the experiments young men make' could equally well be applied to her. She was in sympathy with the work of the St Ives artists and, in particular, with the old retired fisherman turned artist, Alfred Wallis, one of whose paintings

PENZANCE HARBOUR AND ST MARY'S (n.d.)
Alethea Garstin
Oil on panel, 13½ x 10¾in (34 x 27.5cm)
Private collection

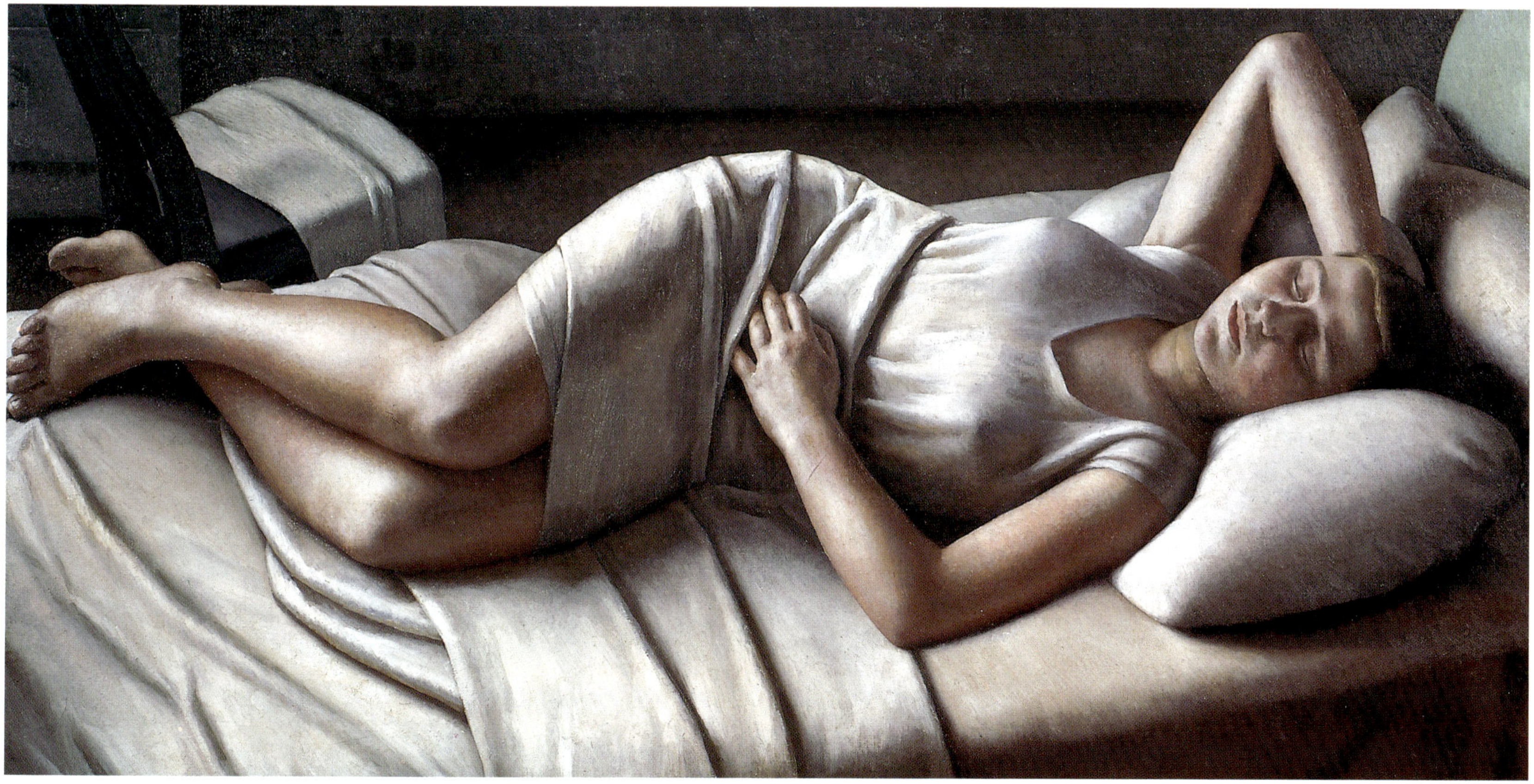

appears in the background of Alethea's *Molly by Gaslight* (date unknown, Penwith Gallery, St Ives).

Alethea's father Norman was her main source of tuition, although she spent a brief period studying life drawing at Heatherly's School in London, and she began exhibiting at the Royal Academy in 1912. Her favourite subjects include domestic animals, horses, and street scenes, which she painted both in this country and abroad. She loved travelling and painting abroad, and visited Belgium, France, Morocco, Kenya, Tanzania, Australia, Grenada, and St Lucia, sometimes in company with Dod Procter, who was a close friend. In 1928, she met the painter Edward Wolfe, and briefly adopted his Fauve colouration. Later she returned to a more restrained palette under the influence of her friend Morland Lewis, who had himself been a pupil of Walter Sickert.

Alethea's paintings, which are usually quite small, were at variance with the large-scale productions of her contemporaries. The small scale possibly encouraged the element of humour inherited from her father with which she invested many of her works (for instance, *Romeo and Juliet*, date unknown, private collection, showing a cock and hen). The fact that she usually painted *en plein air* from her red Morris tourer also encouraged the production of smaller works.

Alethea was a charming though reticent person who did not push herself or her work. Although she exhibited widely in this country and abroad, her paintings are concentrated in a few hands and are appreciated by the discerning who knew her well rather than being rewarded by much public acclaim.

MORNING (1926)
Dod Procter
Oil on canvas, 30 x 60in (76 x 152.5cm)
Tate Gallery, London

DOD PROCTER

The human figure was always of prime importance for Dod Procter (1892–1972), who was one of the most widely acclaimed artists of the second generation. Like her future husband Ernest, she came to Newlyn in 1906 to study at the school, where she was also an outstanding student. Tennyson Jesse described her at the time as 'much the cleverest student not only as regards drawing and painting, where she was streets ahead of anyone except Ernest Procter, but also in the management of her life'.

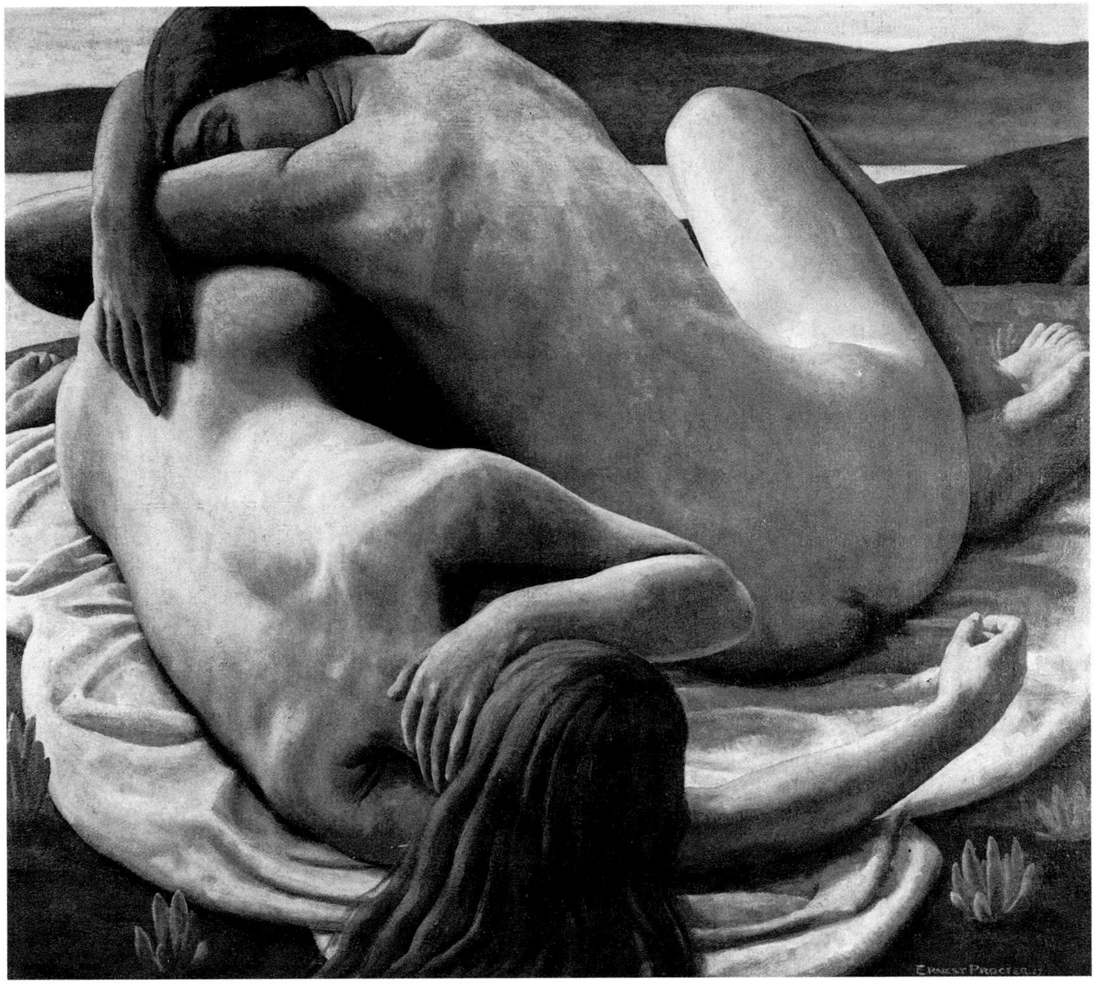

THE DAY'S END (1927)
Ernest Procter
Oil on canvas, 36 x 42in (91.5 x 106.5cm)
Leicestershire Museum, Leicester

She lived with her mother, brother and several other female artists in a house in the centre of Newlyn known as 'The Myrtage'. After her marriage in 1912, she and Ernest went to live in Dunton House, Newlyn, where their son Bill was born the following year. They later moved to a house called North Corner, which remained their home for the rest of their lives.

While studying in Paris, Dod was able to see works by the Impressionists and Post-Impressionists and was particularly impressed by Seurat and Cézanne's use of light and Renoir's depiction of the female figure. Her early work shows an appreciation of the work of Stanhope Forbes (for instance, *Steps at Oakhill Cottage*, 1910, private collection), but she soon discovered her own more characteristic style which she was to employ throughout the 1920s. She achieved major success with a series of paintings of women, painted in hard sculptural outlines which have a strong sense of monumentality, a technique probably absorbed from Picasso – including *Lilian* (1923, Manchester City Art Gallery), *Clara* (1927, Stoke-on-Trent Art Gallery), and *A Baby* (1927, private collection). Her masterpiece was *Morning* (1926), which was bought by the *Daily Mail* for the nation when still on show at the Newlyn Art Gallery. The model was 16-year-old Cissie Barnes, daughter of a fish merchant, who posed every day for five weeks. The work was acclaimed 'Painting of the Year' at the Royal Academy and caused a great stir in the art world; it was even caricatured in *Punch* (11 May 1927). Another painting of Cissie Barnes, *The Model* (1925, private collection), was praised by the critic, Frank Rutter, who told Dod that she had most definitely 'arrived'.

About the same time that Dod was elected an Associate of the Royal Academy in 1934, her sculptural style gave way to a much softer, more impressionistic approach where the outlines of her subjects become increasingly blurred and the contrasts are less pronounced, for example *In the Rock Garden* (1937, private collection). She became increasingly interested in the texture of her paint surface, using the paint very sparingly and with a lighter touch, sometimes applying it in small brightly coloured dabs (such as *Jeanne's Door*, 1948, Phillips: 17 June 1986 [58]). She travelled widely during her life, to the Canary Islands, Basutoland in South Africa, and Tanzania, and her portrayals of the native children are some of the most delightful of all her works. She died in Newlyn in 1972 after a long and active life.

ERNEST PROCTER

Ernest Procter (1886–1935) came to Newlyn in 1906 to study at Forbes' School and soon became one of the best students. He formed a close friendship with a fellow student, Dod Shaw, and the two later studied at the Atelier Colarrossi in Paris *c.* 1910–11 and married the following year.

While serving with the Friends Ambulance Unit in France during World War I, Procter made some lively sketches of the camp where he was based. These interesting records are now in the Imperial War Museum. All his work, including landscapes, for example *The Cornish Farmstead* (*c.*1922, Whitford & Hughes, London), are characterised by a strong sense of design. Indeed, in 1934, the year before his death, he was appointed Director of Studies in Design and Craft at the Glasgow School of Art.

In 1920, he and Dod were commissioned to decorate the Kokine Palace in Rangoon and, working together with Burmese, Indian and Chinese plasterers, guilders and carvers he undoubtedly absorbed some eastern concepts of design.

He painted a series of allegorical works, including *The Four Elements* (1928, Whitford & Hughes), *Aphrodite* (1930, Sotheby's 1984), and *The Day's End* (1927). These are highly symbolic and derive from a mixture of early Italian, classical and oriental sources. He also invented a 'new art form' which consisted of painted glass decorations which he called 'Diaphenicons'. Like Harold Harvey, Procter was interested in church decoration and designed and painted a screen for St Mary's Church, Penzance, showing angels with trumpets, and the rooftops of Penzance in the distance. He was also involved with Bernard Walke's church at St Hilary where he painted a subtle *Visitation* (1933), and a *Deposition* (1935). More ordinary subjects such as *The Merry-Go-Round* (*c.* 1924, private collection) and *All the Fun of the Fair* (1926-7, Worthing Art Gallery) show a high degree of stylisation.

Procter's work was exhibited widely and his talent recognised. His painting, *The Family* (1934-5) was purchased by the Laing Art Gallery, Newcastle, and *The Zodiac* (1935), another allegorical work, was bought for the Tate Gallery. A reviewer of his memorial exhibition at the Leicester Galleries in 1935 praised not only his astonishing range of work but also the feeling behind it: 'All the work is characterised by a poetic feeling and much of it has a peculiar joyousness due to his appreciation of light and sunshine.'

Samuel John 'Lamorna' Birch

Samuel John 'Lamorna' Birch (1869–1955) was an early arrival, first visiting Cornwall from Manchester in 1889 though not settling until later. His overriding interest in painting the landscape encouraged him to go and live near Lamorna where he was immediately captivated by the beautiful valley and stream which remained important inspirations throughout his life. In 1902 he married Emily Houghton Vivian (known as 'Mouse') and they settled at Flagstaff Cottage in Lamorna.

Birch was almost entirely self-taught as a painter and a deep love of nature pervades all his work. He was especially interested in painting light effects on water, whether rivers, streams or the sea, as well as capturing the ever changing colours of the sky. *Storm over Sheffield* (1910, private collection) shows his delight in painting the changing effects of stormy skies. He was a first-class draughtsman and his drawings, with a hint of watercolour or wash, are especially sensitive. His pure watercolours are also very fine and featured in two major articles in *Studio* magazine. His talents were recognised by his peers and he was elected an Associate of the Royal Society of Painters in Watercolours in 1912, becoming a full member two years later.

During the 1920s Birch painted some extremely large oils, of which *Tregiffian Cliff* (1922) is a particularly fine example. The vast sense of scale of this work gives it a special grandeur. *Morning Fills the Bowl* (1926, Royal Institution of Cornwall, Truro) and *Kerris Quarry* (1926,

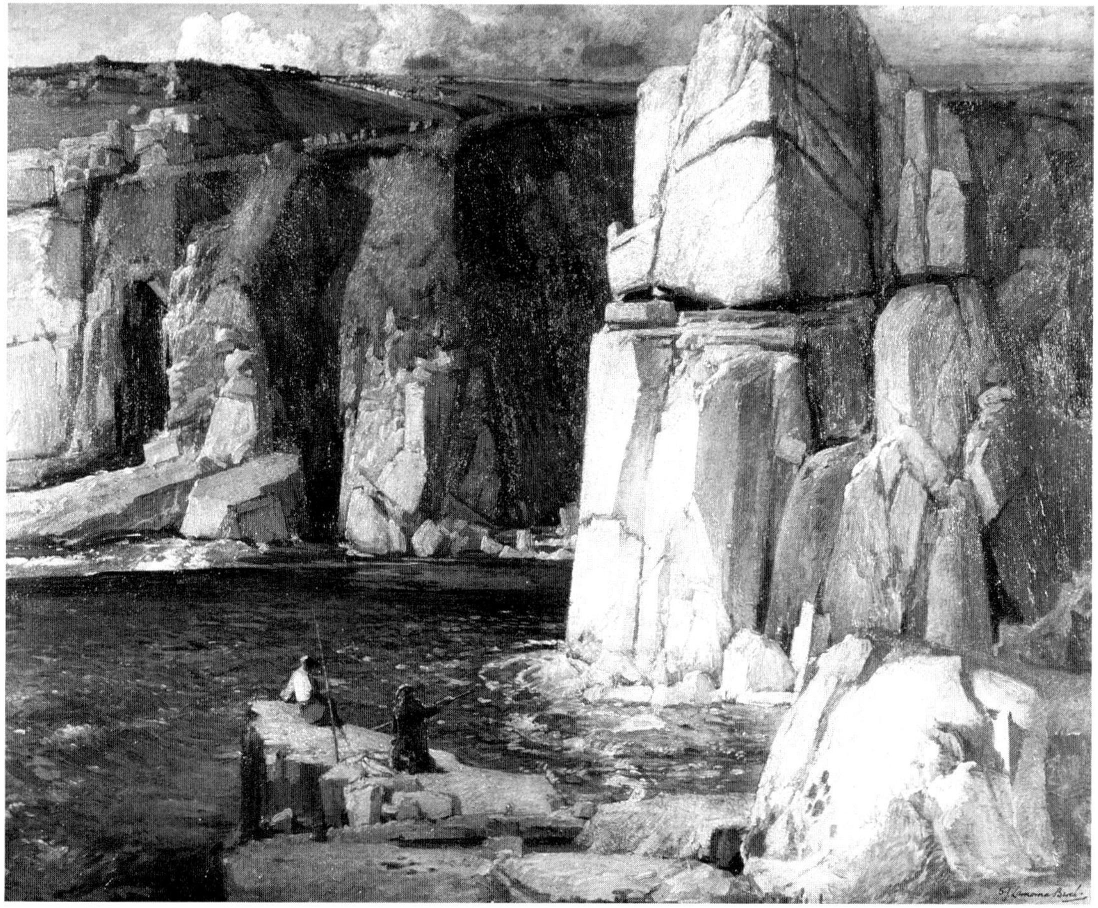

Tregiffian Cliff near Lamorna (c. 1922)
S. J. Lamorna Birch

Oil on canvas, 47½ x 59½in (120.5 x 151.5cm)
City of Bristol Museum and Art Gallery

Penzance Charter Trustees) are two further examples of his large oils at this time in which the colour is extremely bright. Birch travelled widely in Britain and also visited New Zealand and Australia. He was an extremely prolific artist who exhibited widely both at the Royal Academy and elsewhere.

CHARLES SIMPSON

Like Lamorna Birch, Charles Simpson (1885–1971) was a nature lover. He came to Newlyn in 1905 and had his first large oil, *Autumn Ploughing*, hung at the Royal Academy in 1906. After a brief period studying at Julian's *Atelier* in 1910, he was able to hold his first one-man show in London.

In 1913 he married Ruth Alison and they set up house in Newlyn, where their daughter Leonora was born. In 1916 they moved to St Ives and ran a painting school at the Piazza Studios. Simpson painted large bird and landscape subjects, and also some sensitive paintings of young girls on the beach at St Ives, one of which, *The Sand Castle* (1919), features his wife and daughter.

The Simpsons lived in London from 1924 to 1931, where Charles held an exhibition of sketches of the rodeo. Further commissions included writing and illustrating books on hunting, and a series of articles for *Country Life*. He returned to Cornwall in 1930 to concentrate on painting the landscape he loved – these works include *The Stream at Clapper Mill, Lamorna* (1945, Newport Art Gallery), and *Wheeling Gulls and Glittering Water* (1944, whereabouts unknown). Many of these paintings, such as the earlier *Duck Shooting: the Punt-Gunner* (1924, Russell Cotes Art Gallery, Bournemouth), include wild birds. *The Herring-Season* (1924, Laing Art Gallery, Newcastle) is closer to the large exhibition paintings celebrating the Cornish fishing industry initiated many years previously with Stanhope Forbes' *Fish Sale*.

The landscape around Lamorna absorbed several other artists besides Birch and Simpson. Eleanor (1882–1959) and Robert Hughes (1873–1953), who met while studying at Forbes' School, built themselves a house in Lamorna at Chyangwheal in 1912. Robert devoted much of his life to painting the landscape and the coastline nearby and his work demonstrates a strong sense of the abstract shapes and qualities of the rock and cliffs. The quality of his designs are highlighted by the rich dramatic colouring of the paint. Eleanor was a talented watercolourist and draughtswoman who had a very sensitive feeling for trees and buildings (see *Farm Buildings, Lamorna*, Newlyn Art Gallery). She exhibited widely and was elected to the Royal Institute of Painters in Watercolour in 1933.

Another artist couple who lived near Lamorna were Charles and Ella Naper. Charles (1882–1968), who had an architectural training, painted some exquisitely detailed works showing the rock formations near Land's End as well as other landscapes. When not posing as a model for her fellow artists, Ella (1886–1972) made very fine pottery and jewellery.

Frank (1873–1936) and Jessica Heath also lived at Lamorna, at a house called Menwinnion (now a hotel). They had three daughters, Aileen, Nancy and Gabrielle, who feature in a number of Frank's paintings, including *A Summer Afternoon* (Richard Green, London).

Newlyn was visited briefly in the 1920s by two avant-garde artists, Frank Dobson (1886–1963) and Cedric Morris (1889–1982). For both it was a starting point before achieving success elsewhere. Dobson became a leading sculptor with an international reputation and Morris achieved great prominence as an artist. He also ran a painting school in Suffolk with his friend Lett Haines, where he created an internationally famous garden.

Although the work of this generation did not create such an impact on British painting as that of their predecessors, it is nonetheless an important reflection of current trends in British and European art. Most of the group were in contact with the major artistic developments of their time and many had studied in France and seen the work of the Impressionists and Post-Impressionists. This is particularly evident in the work of Dod Procter, which shows the influence of, among others, Picasso, Renoir and Seurat, and also in the work of Alethea Garstin, who had a deep understanding of French Post-Impressionism. The brighter palettes, so typical of all the artists, is another reflection of this influence, while the stylisation and realism in the work of the Procters and Harold Harvey belongs to the British tradition of such varied artists as Gerald Brockhurst, Meredith Framptom, Algernon Newton, Glynn Philpot and Stanley Spencer. Visits from artists such as Cedric Morris and Frank Dobson further strengthened links with the avant-garde.

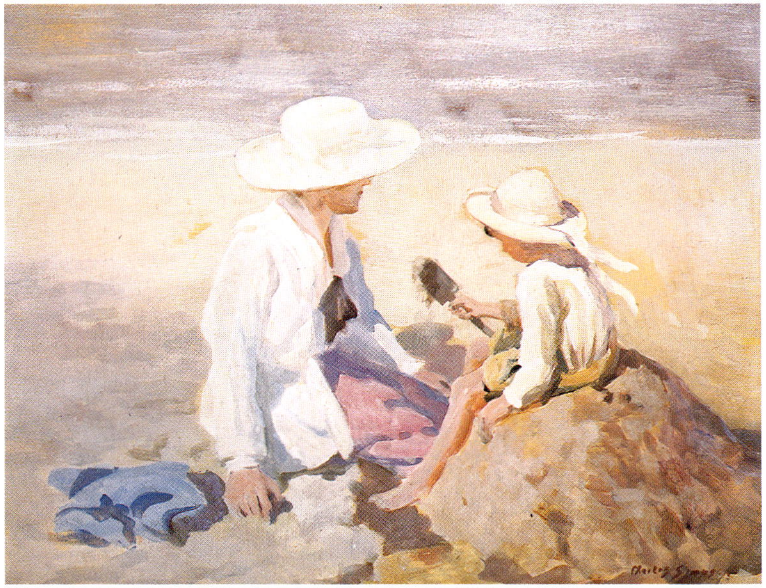

THE SAND CASTLE (c. 1919)
Charles Simpson
Tempera on board, 29 x 21in (73.5 x 53.5cm)
Private collection

CHAPTER TWELVE

FORBES' LATER YEARS

It is significant that Forbes still held a central place in Newlyn in the early years of the twentieth century, not only in his position as 'Professor' of the School of Painting but also as a much respected artist who was a prolific and regular exhibitor at the Royal Academy, and whose paintings could be found in many major municipal art galleries. He continued to paint scenes of village and country life in the early twentieth century and possibly, in sympathy with the artistic climate of the period as reflected in the paintings of the new generation, his muted tones gave way to a much greater emphasis on colour, while his square brushwork became increasingly looser.

During the early 1900s Forbes was enormously prolific and painted a number of works based on sea and harbour subjects. These include *Goodbye – Off to Skibbereen* (1901), *Chadding in Mounts Bay* (1902, Worcester Museum and Art Gallery), *The Seine Boat* (1904), *Whiffing* (1905), *Newlyn* (1906) and *Gala Day in Newlyn* (1907) (*see* front jacket illustration). On the whole, these concentrate on a few figures seen from quite close range, and the observation of individual features is especially good. *Chadding in Mounts Bay* is painted in brilliant sunlight and is an especially delightful work. A sketch for this (Sothebys 12 November 1986 [38a]), shows the boat with only two boys – the central one who has just caught a fish, and the boy to the left of him dangling his line in the water.

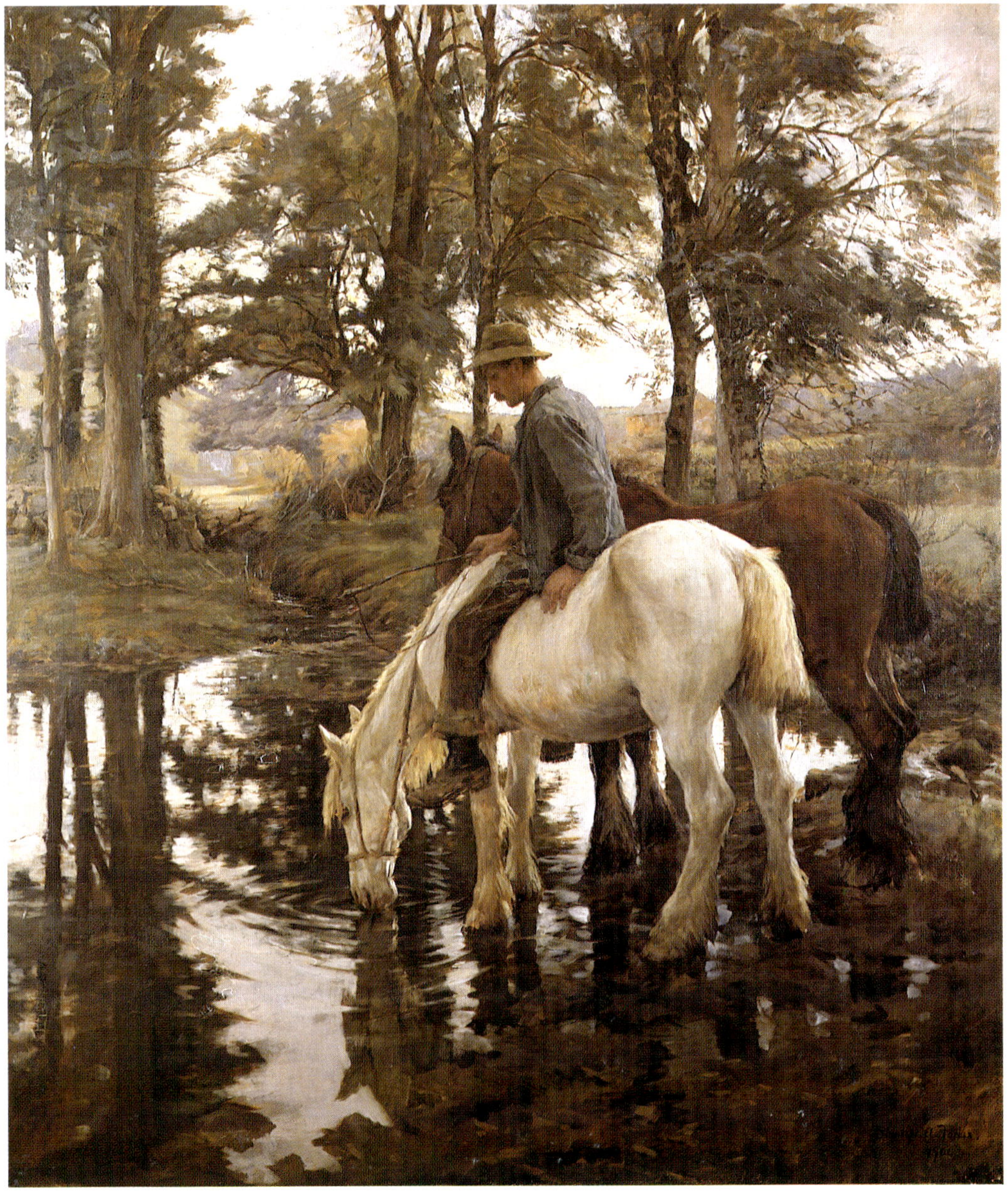

THE DRINKING PLACE (1900)
Stanhope Alexander Forbes
Oil on canvas, 70 x 60½in (178 x 154cm)
The Bridgeman Art Library/Oldham Art Gallery

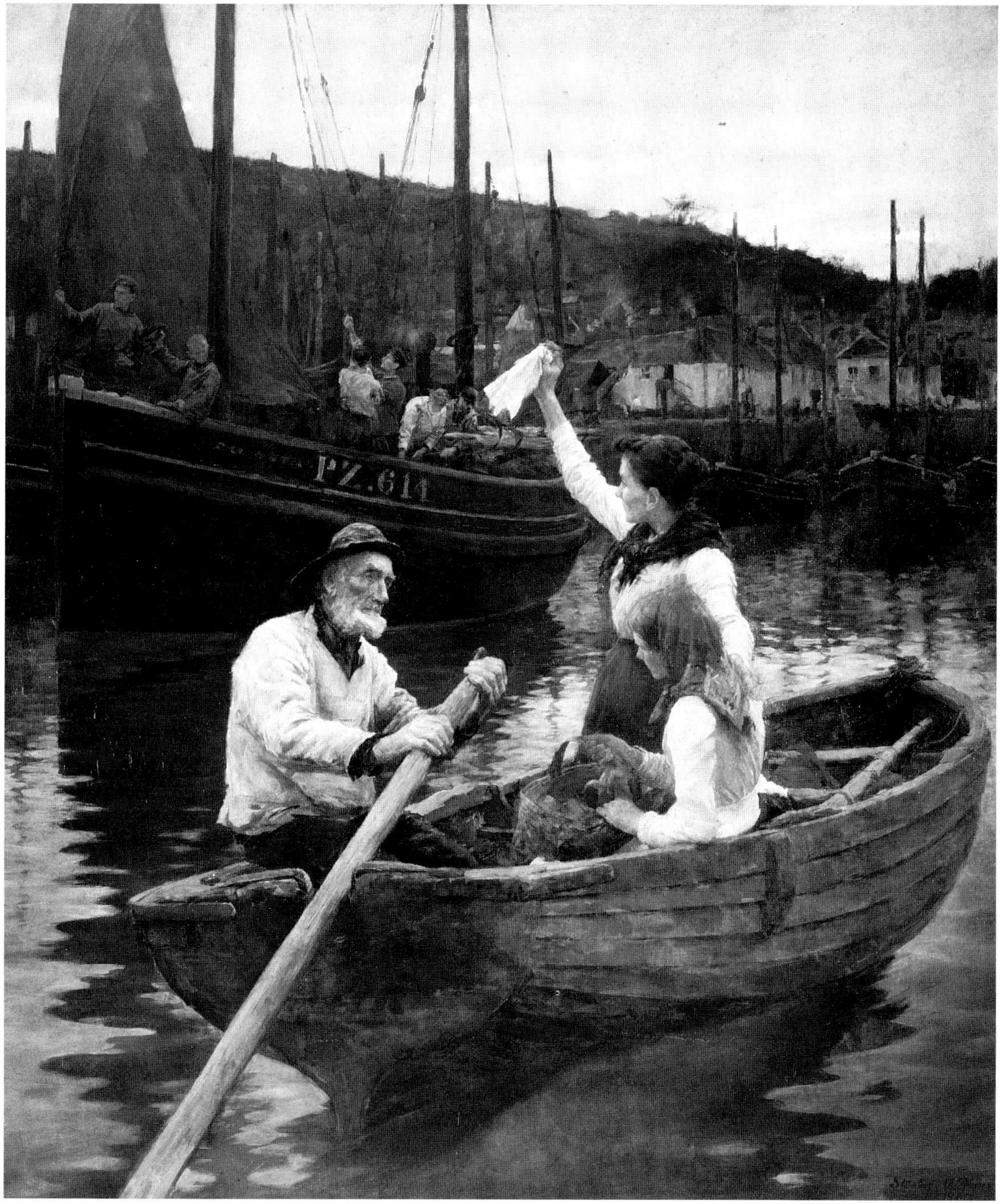

GOODBYE – *OFF TO SKIBBEREEN* (1901)
Stanhope Alexander Forbes
Oil on canvas, 66 x 58in (167.5 x 147cm)
By courtesy of David Messum, London

The inclusion of the other children, and particularly of the girls in their delightful hats, foreshadows Laura Knight's delight in painting children on the beach at Newlyn.

The Seine Boat and *Off to Skibbereen* recall *Off to the Fishing Ground* of 1886 (*see* page 23) but are happier compositions. The figures appear more relaxed and less posed, and the crowded seine boat is painted from a more straightforward angle, recalling that of the punt in *The Lighthouse*. *Off to the Fishing Grounds* was painted on a grey day and the models look cold and tense as a result, whereas the warm sunshine plays on the healthy weather-beaten faces of the men in the crowded seine boat. The bearded old man, known as 'Uncle William', occurs in both *The Seine Boat* and *Off to Skibbereen*, where he wields the oar like a punt at the back of the boat, with an impassive gaze. The two women are waving to their husbands/brothers setting off in the larger boat for the fishing grounds of Skibbereen off the coast of Ireland. Forbes was presumably able to overcome his fear of sea-sickness since he would almost undoubtedly have painted these works from a boat.

Forbes' painting, *Newlyn*, bears strong similarities to a painting entitled *Whiffing* (whereabouts unknown) of the previous year. One could almost be the other in reverse, except that where *Newlyn* shows an older fisherman with two boys preparing their lines and a view of the harbour in the background, in *Whiffing* the older man dangles his line into the water, watched with great interest by a boy and a girl, and a sail behind blocks out any further view.

The Annual Gala which was the subject of *Gala Day at Newlyn* 1907 (Hartlepool Art Gallery), took place in Newlyn harbour on a Whit Monday. It consisted of a procession of villagers and children who carried a banner designed by J. D. Mackenzie and Frank Bramley, through the streets of Newlyn, accompanied by the Newlyn brass band. The procession finished up in the grounds of Trereife House, owned by one of the local landowners, the Le Grice family, where a fête was held.

The foreground figures in shadow in the *Gala*

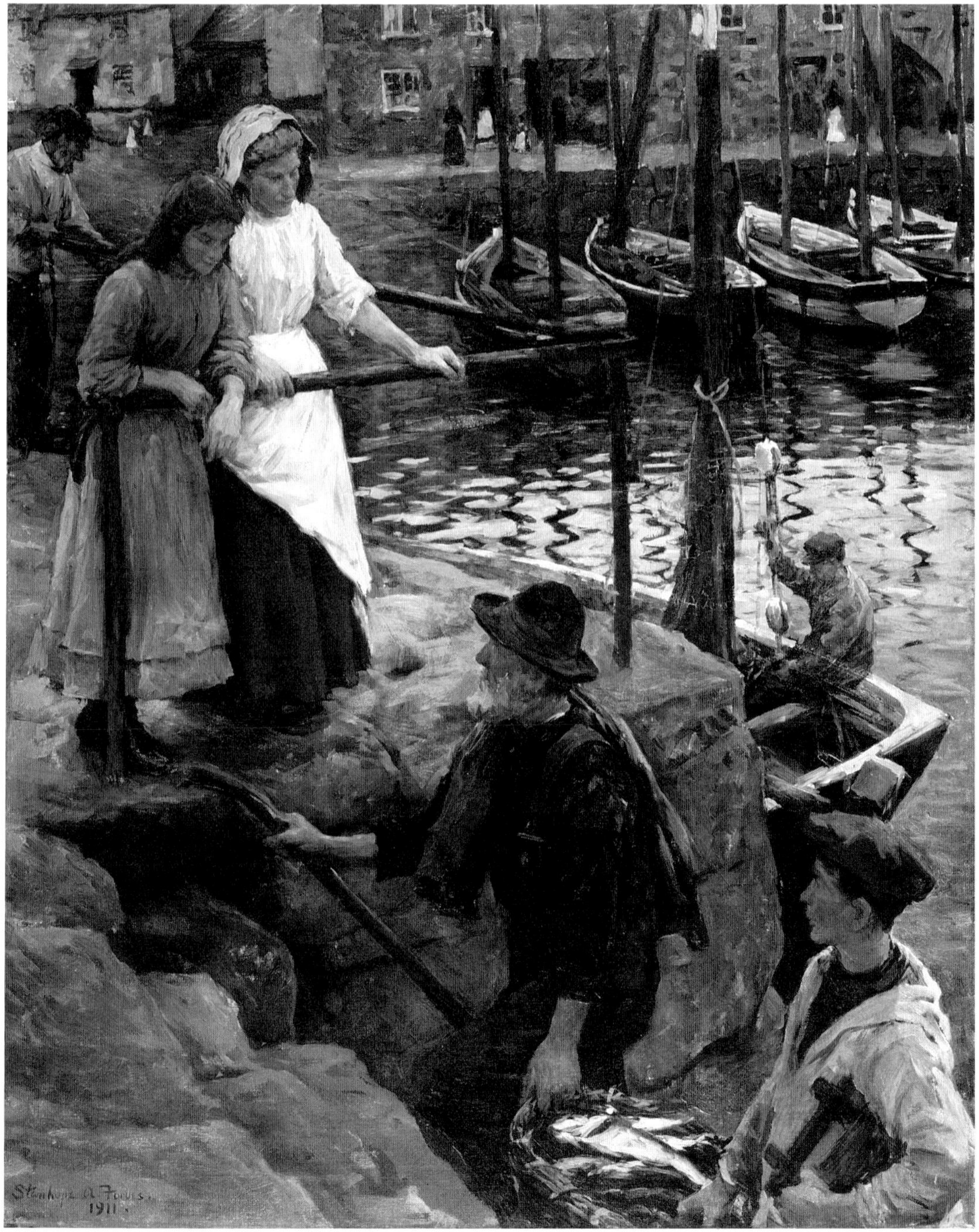

The Old Pier Steps (1911)
Stanhope Alexander Forbes
Oil on canvas, 51¾ x 42in (131.5 x 106.5cm)
Bradford Art Galleries and Museums

Day lead the eye into this work where in the middle ground the light catches the procession of children and villagers and also the boats in the harbour beyond. Apart from being a delightfully bright and colourful painting, this work demonstrates Forbes' deep concern with local history and custom.

Forbes painted a number of harbour scenes in Mousehole during the early 1900s. These include: *Home Along* 1905 (City of Bristol Museum and Art Gallery), *Evening in the Village* 1906 (Royal Academy Pictures 1906), *At Their Moorings* 1907 (Ferens Art Gallery, Hull), *A Safe Anchorage* 1909 (whereabouts unknown), *The Old Pier Steps* 1911 and *Fitting out, Mousehole Harbour* 1919 (Bradford Art Galleries & Museum). With the exception of *Home Along* and *The Old Pier Steps* where the grouping of figures is more intimate, the concentration on the figure gives way in these works to a much wider panorama and the human interest becomes secondary.

Forbes painted a number of extremely successful interiors at this time, including *Against Regatta Day* (1906, Royal Institution of Cornwall, Truro), which is a very happy composition showing an old woman and a young woman mending a sail, watched by a group of fishermen and others. *The Village Industry* (1908, Royal Academy Pictures 1908) shows J. D. Mackenzie instructing some village lads in copperwork. The light falls on the figures at work while the mastery of detail of the equipment recalls that shown in *Forging the Anchor* (*see* page 55), though the figures appear more relaxed and less 'heroic'. *The Young Apprentice* (1908) shows Johnny Payne Cotton, aged 15 years, beating copper repoussé work, watched by Mackenzie.

In 1901, Forbes painted a simple homely interior in a Cornish cottage entitled *22 January 1901*. It was intended to appear as a family group, though some of the models had been used many times before by Forbes. Others were members of the Hitchen family, who lived in Primrose Cottage, now no longer in existence.

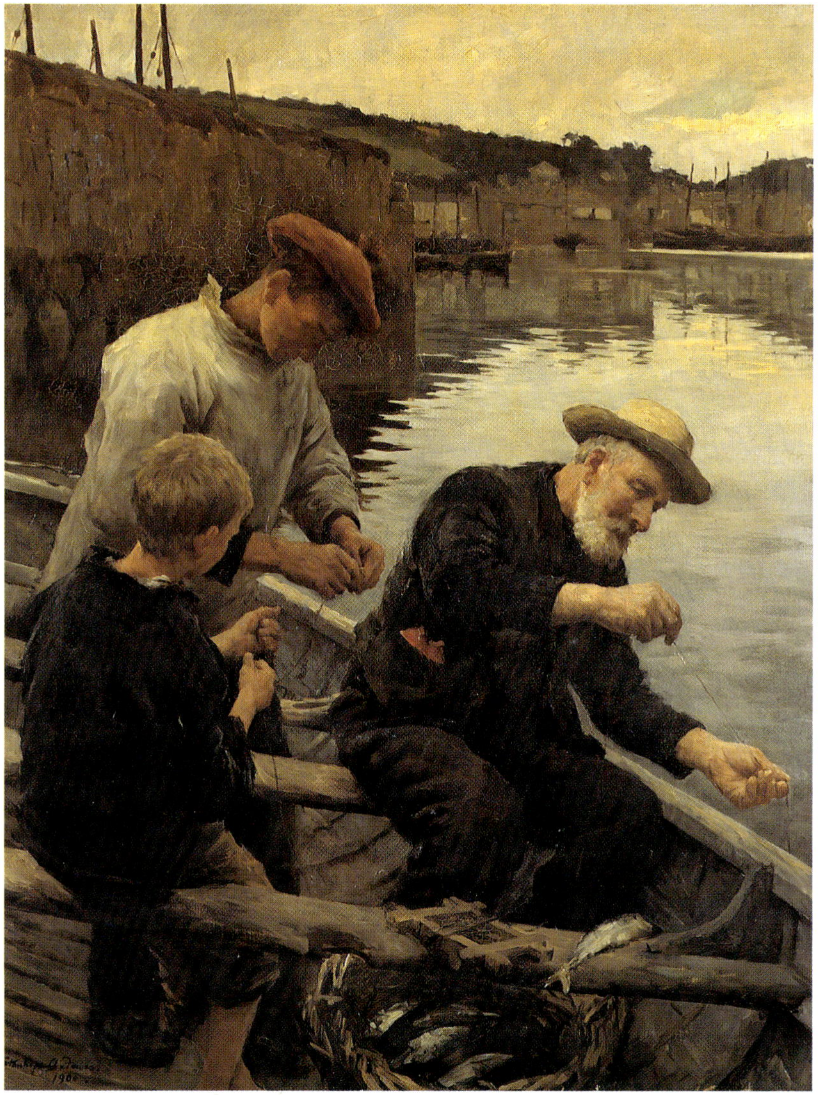

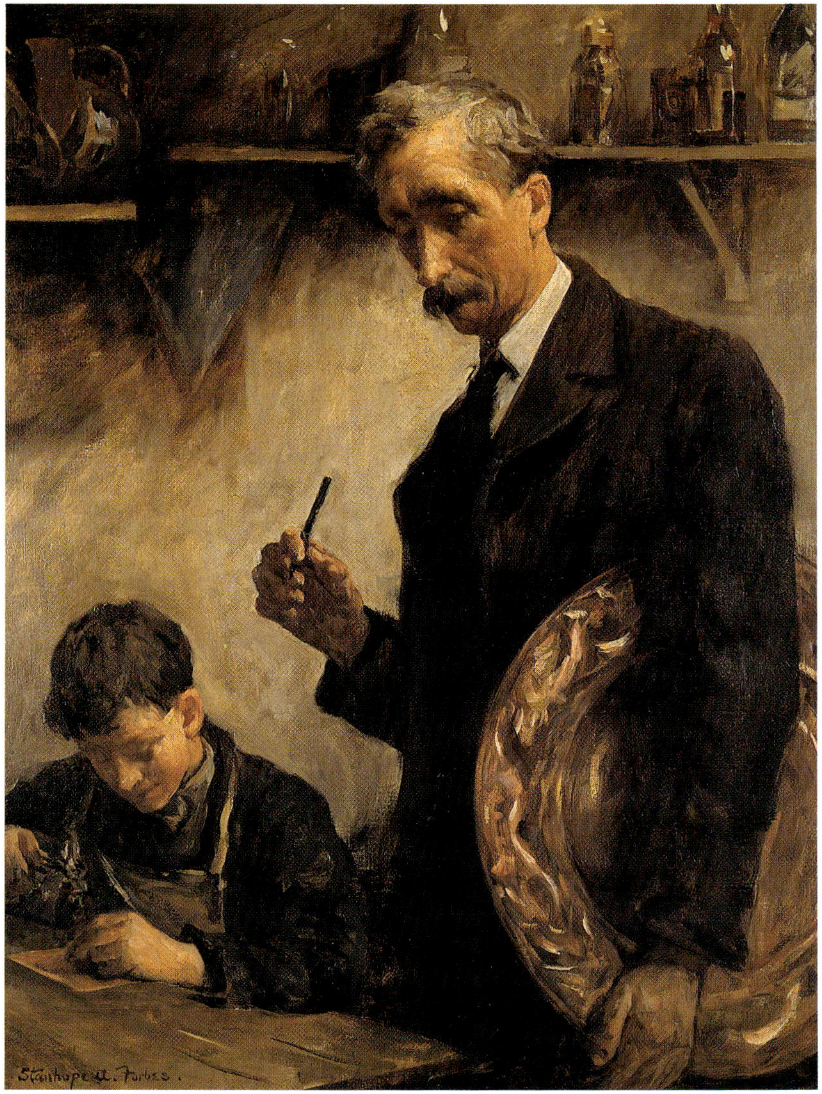

(Above) *NEWLYN* (1909)
Stanhope Alexander Forbes
Oil on canvas, 48½ x 38¼in (123 x 97cm)
Ferens Art Gallery, Hull City Museums and Art Galleries

(Right) *THE YOUNG APPRENTICE* (1908)
Stanhope Alexander Forbes
Oil on canvas, 29¾ x 24in (75 x 61cm)
Penzance Town Council, Penzance and District Museum and Art Gallery

The main light source in this painting comes from the window and falls on the table and gently highlights the features of the three seated figures. Nineteen years later, Forbes painted a similar scene of a family in a Cornish cottage called *The Saffron Cake* (1920, *see* page 90). This was painted at night and the light sources are artificial ones. A lamp to the left of the old lady's head makes her appear as if in silhouette while the shadows cast by the other three figures add dramatic contrast.

Forbes continued his interest in the dramatic effects of artificial light sources in two outdoor night scenes, *Round the Camp Fire* 1903 (Laing Art Gallery, Newcastle) and *Snared* 1907, (whereabouts unknown). The first shows a gypsy family sitting in the glow of a fire in the left foreground with darkness all around them. In *Snared* the light from a lantern highlights the main features of a group of poachers with their dog and prey while the rest of the painting merges into semi-darkness.

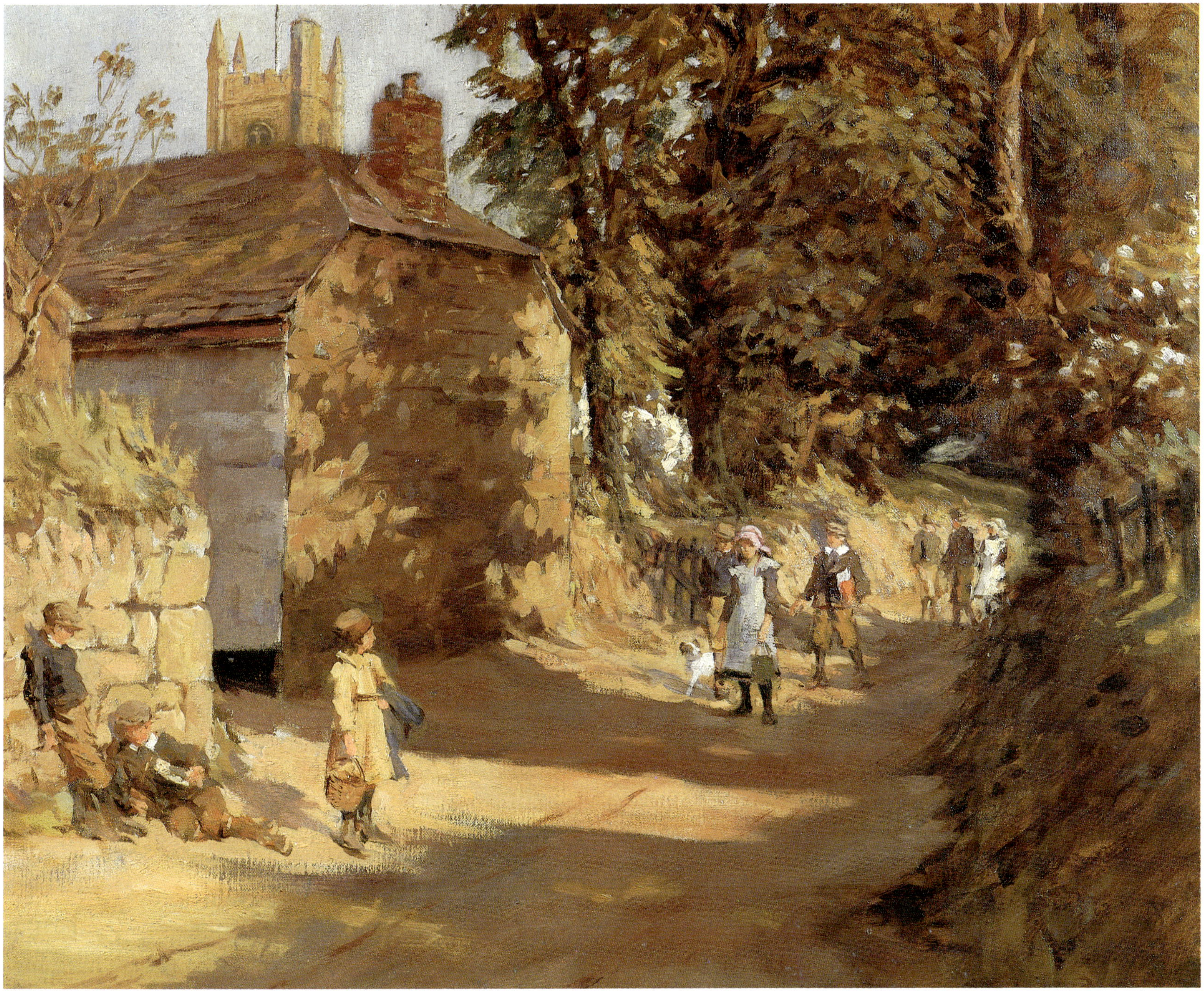

GOING TO SCHOOL, PAUL (1917)
Stanhope Alexander Forbes
Oil on canvas, 20 x 24in (51 x 61cm)
By courtesy of the Richard Green Gallery, London

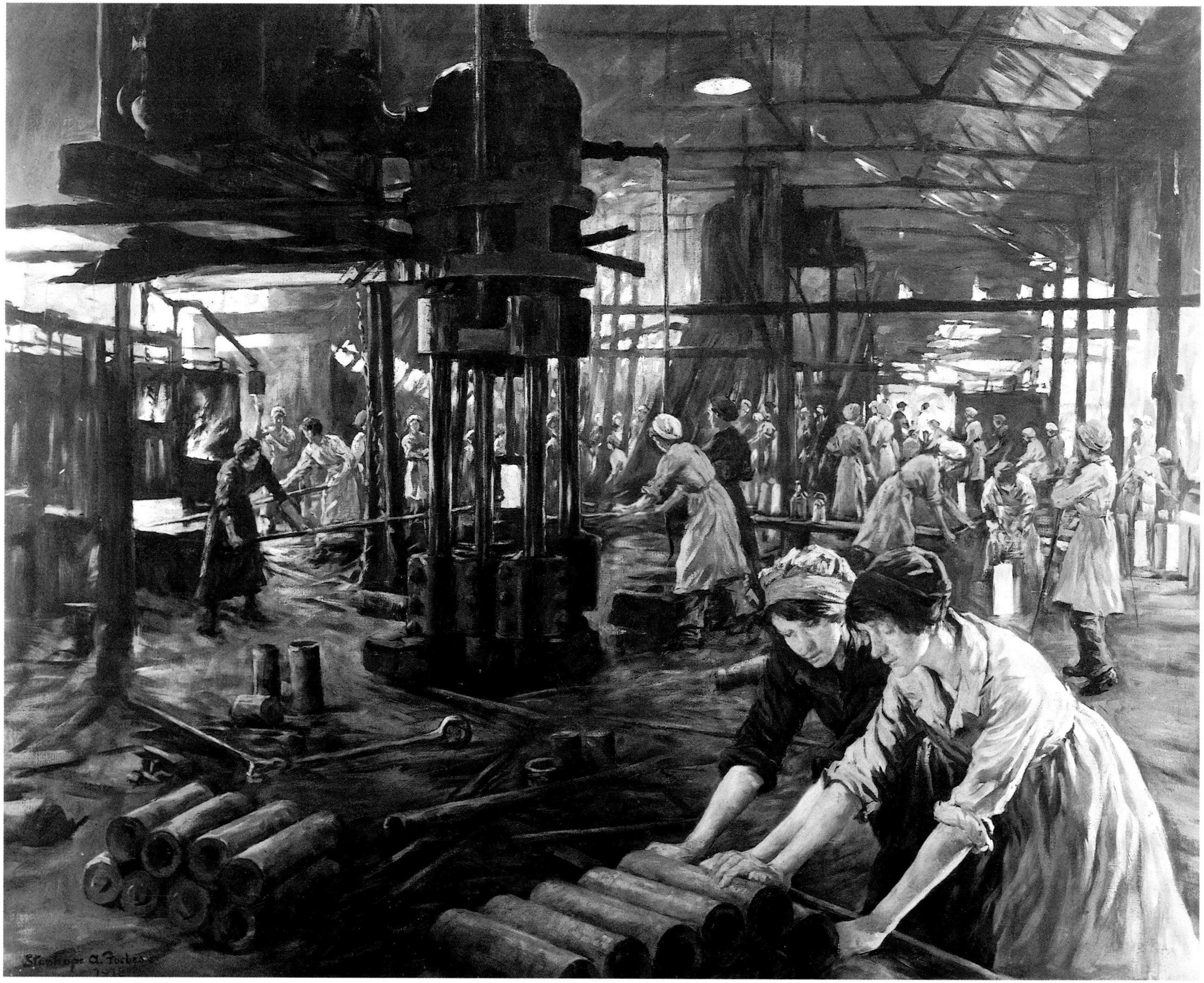

THE MUNITION GIRLS (1918)
Stanhope Alexander Forbes

Oil on canvas, 40¾ x 50in (103 x 127cm)
Trustees of the Science Museum, London

Forbes' works became increasingly variable from about 1911 onwards and this may be accounted for by personal tragedies in his life, first of the death of Elizabeth in 1912 and later, that of his son, Alec, in World War I. Some of these works appear deliberately illustrative, such as *The Drinking Trough* (1912, location unknown) and in others such as *The Fleet in Sight* (1911, Royal Academy Pictures), and his Royal Academy Diploma work (Forbes was made a full Royal Academician in 1910), *The Harbour Window* (1911, Royal Academy) the paintwork is slick and the figures more generalised. Some interiors of this period, such as *The Morning Room* (1913, Royal Academy pictures), *Through the Looking Glass* (1914, Royal Academy Pictures), and an undated woman in interior (Phillips, 15 November 1988 [13]), bear similarities to the women in interiors painted by Harold Knight and Harold Harvey at about the same time (for example Harold Knight, *Portrait of Florence*, 1909/10, private collection; Harold Harvey, *Reflections*, 1916 Cyfartha Castle Museum, Merthyr Tydfil).

Like Laura Knight after him, Forbes' style of painting was ideally suited to the depiction of war-time subjects, among which *The Steelworkers* (1915, Institution of Civil Engineers), *The Munition Girls* (1919, Science Museum) and *WRNS Naval Ratings Sail-Making* (1919, Imperial War Museum) are some of the finest examples. *The Munition Girls* was commissioned by George Baker of John Baker & Co., Kilnhurst Steel Works, Rotherham. It is a record of an industrial process; red-hot steel billets are re-heated in an intermediate furnace on the left and, still glowing, are moved by hand to a steam hydraulic press for forging. The process is repeated at other work stations in the background. At the turn of the century John Baker & Co. had specialised in producing forge tyres and axles for railway wagons and in 1915, in common with many other steel makers, the firm had to prepare for armament manufacture and, in particular, to meet the demand for shells on the western front.

The women in the painting were all daughters of local miners or steelworkers, with the exception of the two in the foreground who were painted from models in Forbes' studio (*see* opposite). The painting was commissioned as 'a memento for our women workers, and each of them received a framed copy of it'. The call to the front meant that there were very few skilled male operatives left, and women had to leave their traditional tasks, such as file cutting, in order to operate equipment previously the prerogative of men. The picture caused an uproar when exhibited at the Royal Academy because the public were shocked to see women in factory dress making weapons. Forbes, writing to Mrs John Baker at the beginning of World War II in 1940, expressed a very different view: 'It was indeed an unforgettable sight to see those fine women carrying on their work so splendidly and the opportunity which Mr Baker gave me to record this wonderful service is one for which I can never be sufficiently grateful.'

The painting itself is extremely complex with a great sense of depth and space, in which Forbes has created the impression of a vast factory teeming with women workers, and the closer view of the two girls in the foreground leads the eye into the painting. It appears that Forbes could always rise to the occasion and create a work worthy of posterity. The painting was purchased by the Science Museum in 1983 and unveiled the following year, when several of the original factory workers, then in their eighties, were present. *The Steel-workers* is another extremely dramatic work where the concentration is on a group of figures in the foreground manipulating an incredibly long bar of molten steel. As with the previous painting, there is a tremendous sense of depth and space in this work. In contrast, *WRNS Naval Ratings Sail-Making*, painted on board HMS *Essex* at Devonport, is a more intimate scene in which three girls are shown at work sewing a sail in the foreground. Behind them is a trestle table and two sailors, one of whom is instructing another girl in her work.

During the 1920s Forbes painted several views of Penzance. These include *The Market Place* (1922, Royal Academy Pictures) with its busy stalls, *The Abbey Slip* (1921, private collection) showing the inner harbour with St Mary's Church and buildings in the background, and several views of the main street called Market Jew Street. The name derives from the Cornish *Margas Yow*, meaning Thursday market, which was the original name for the settlement at Penzance and has survived in the name of its main street. Forbes painted one view of Penzance (1924, Royal Academy Pictures) looking up Market Jew Street towards the market and Lloyd's Bank at the top, and two views looking down the street, *Market Jew: Thursday* (1923) and *Market Jew: Nocturne* (1923, David Messum Fine Paintings). The former is probably one of the finest of Forbes' views of the main street in Penzance, with the light falling on the buildings and pavement to the left and a wonderful array of horses and carts. The latter is a particularly atmospheric rendering.

Forbes also painted the main streets of *Penryn* (1931) and *Coinage Hall Street, Helston* (1935, both Royal Academy Pictures). In contrast to previous paintings, these works show a mainly topographic interest where people, cars, horses and carts are generally of secondary importance to the surrounding architecture which in many cases appears to dwarf them, and while being of great interest to the local historian, they have less to offer as works of art. On the other hand, whether one likes the finished results or not, one has to admire Forbes' skill in accurately portraying the architecture of these towns and the correct scale in which the figures are related to it.

Through his family connections with the Great Western Railway, Forbes received commissions to design railway posters. *The Terminus* (1925, Royal Academy Pictures) shows a train at Penzance station with a busy platform full of passengers. A sketch for this painting shows that Forbes' handling of paint could be extremely free at times in contrast to the tightness of the finished work. *The Sidings* (1925, David Messum Fine Paintings), showing a steam engine in the distance, may well be a sketch for a larger work of this subject.

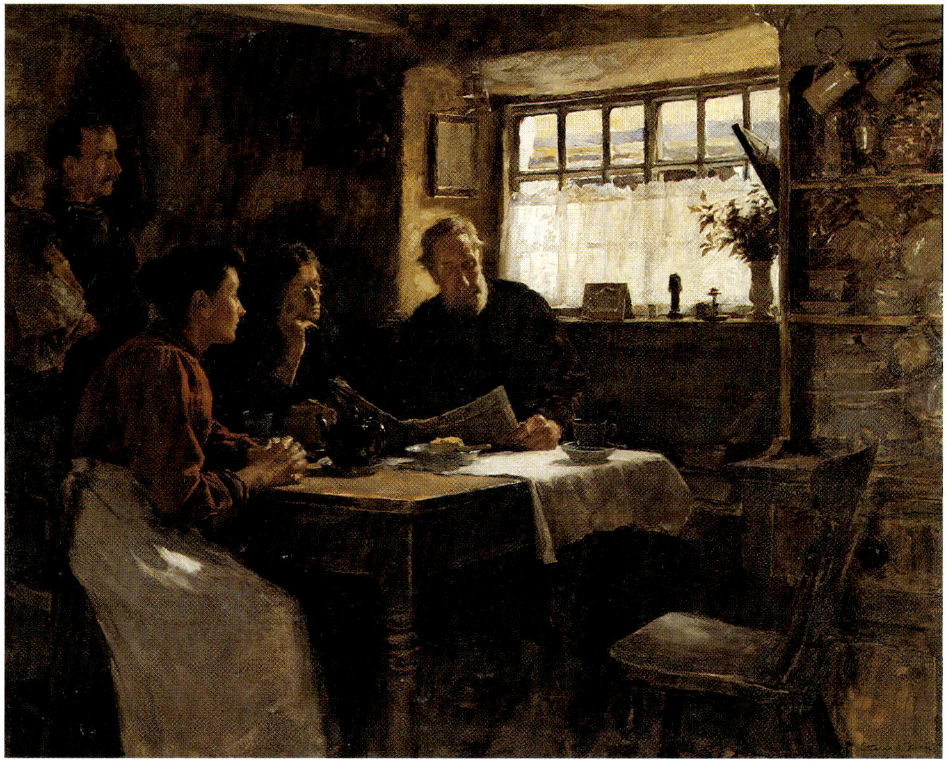

'22 January 1901' (Reading the News of the Queen's Death in a Cornish Cottage) (1901)
Stanhope Alexander Forbes
Oil on canvas, 38 x 49in (96.5 x 125cm)
Royal Albert Memorial Museum, Exeter

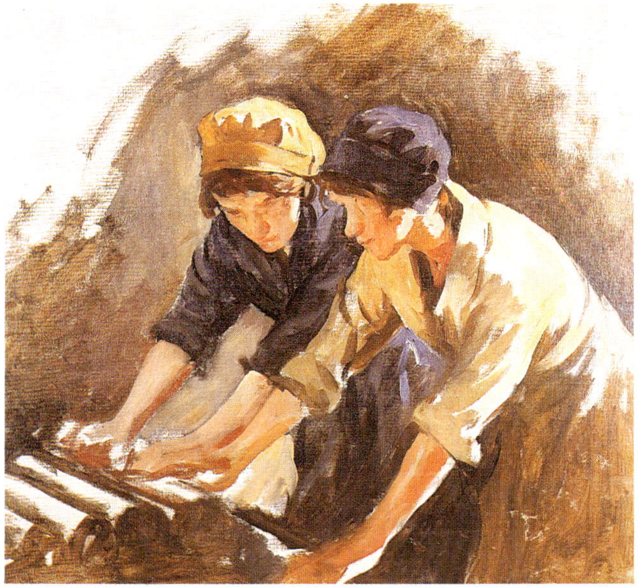

Study for the Munition Girls (1918)
Stanhope Alexander Forbes
Oil on canvas, 20¾ x 23¼in (53 x 59cm)
Private collection

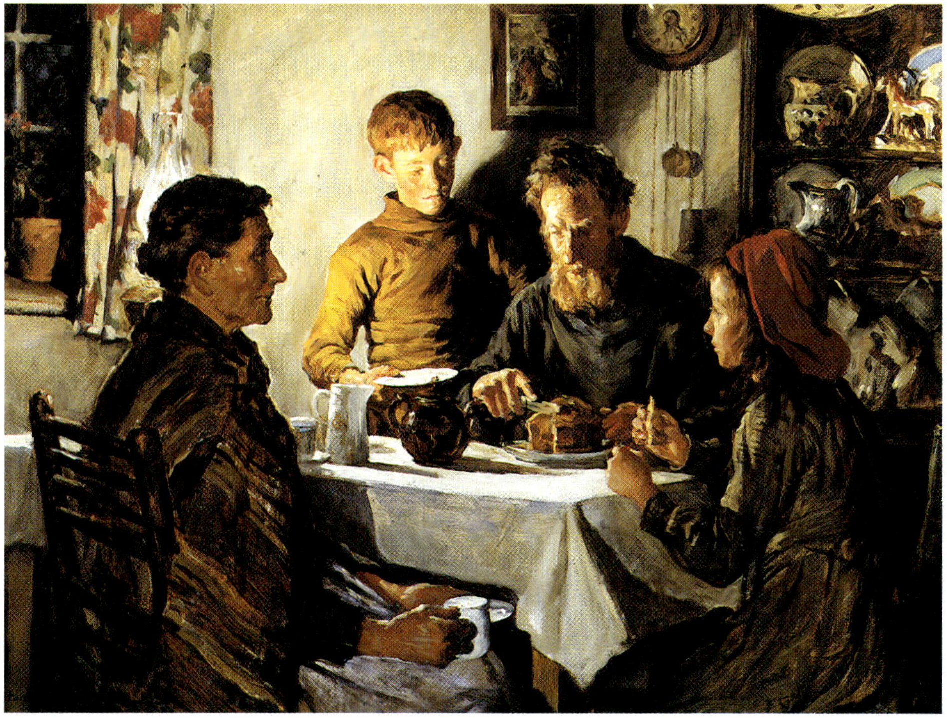

The Saffron Cake (1920)
Stanhope Alexander Forbes
Oil on canvas, 30 x 40in (76 x 101.5cm)
Private collection, by courtesy of Pyms Gallery, London

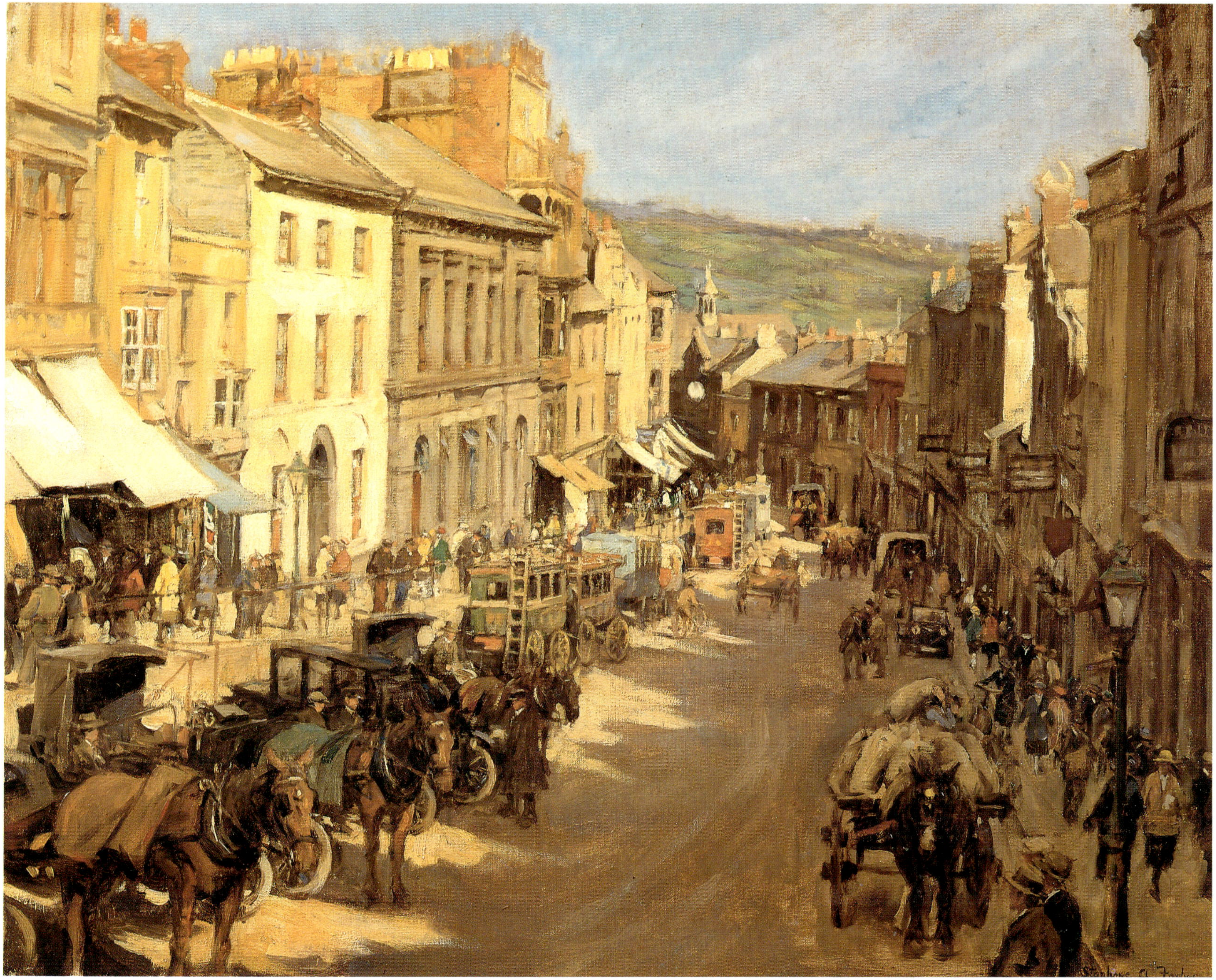

MARKET JEW: THURSDAY (1923)
Stanhope Alexander Forbes
Oil on canvas, 30 x 24in (76 x 61cm)
By courtesy of David Messum, London

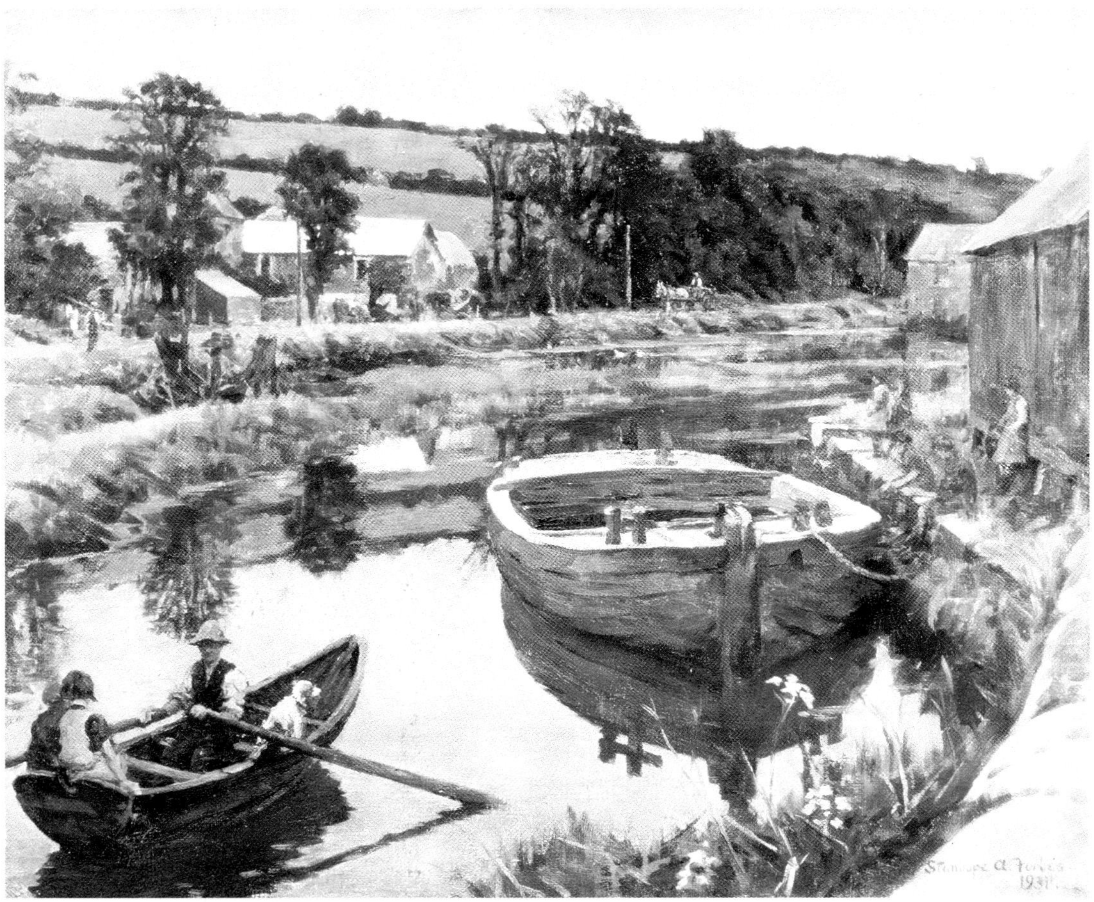

BOATS AT MOUSEHOLE (1931)
Stanhope Alexander Forbes
Oil on canvas, 23½ x 29¼in (59.5 x 75.5cm)
Christie's

Paintings of the countryside suffered a similar fate to townscapes, generally becoming more like landscapes with some figures added, not as previously where the people were seen as an essential element in the landscape. Examples include *Bridge at Gweek* (1932), *The Village Rendezvous* (1938), *Boats at Mousehole* (1931), and *The Blue Window* (1926). Forbes probably found it difficult to find models when away from centres such as Newlyn and Mousehole. Yet despite the generalisation of the figures in these later works, Forbes continues to express his deep love of and reverence for the Cornish countryside and its ways of life. Although as works of art they may appear less satisfying, they still convey the mood and atmosphere of this strange land known as West Cornwall.

Some of the more successful of his later scenes were those painted of children in the countryside around Hayle. These include *The Viaduct* (1934, private collection), *Hayle Pool* (1930, Royal Academy Pictures) and *The Water Rat* (1932, Royal Academy Pictures). *The Viaduct*, showing four children sitting along the banks of a stream and waving at a train passing way overhead on the railway viaduct, is probably the most successful of these. The curving stream with its lovely reflections and overhanging tree leads the eye into the painting, and everything is dwarfed by the size of the viaduct. One wonders if Forbes was expressing his fear of modern life – nature being tamed by man and, in the process, man being increasingly reduced to a small cog in the machine.

It should also be noted that Forbes never gave up portraiture, and portraits remain among his Royal Academy submissions to within a few years of his death. Several of these portraits were obviously important commissions which may well have come through his family connections. For example, in 1920 he painted Sir James Ball, Chief Engineer, L.B. & S.C. Railway, in 1925 Basil Mott CB, President of the Institution of Civil Engineers and in 1937 Major Douglas V. B. Cooper, OBE (whereabouts unknown).

Stanhope Forbes combined the best in the Victorian tradition of solid academic drawing and well-planned compositions with a softer, semi-impressionistic technique of painting which he had learnt in France. The combination served him well during the 1880s when he was briefly at the spearhead of the *avant garde* and was the most successful of his Newlyn contemporaries. He ran his own School of Painting which imparted these values to a whole new generation of artists, providing them with a solid base from which to experiment and develop their own styles.

His deep love for and commitment to the Cornish village of Newlyn and its people gave meaning and purpose to his life and work. In an unsettled and changing world he felt at home in Newlyn which provided a secure haven of old-fashioned and simple values as well as a reasonable income from the sales of his paintings. His passionate love for the way of life, the people with their joys and sorrows, the events and tasks of their everyday lives, is expressed in all his best paintings. Langley sympathised with and understood the sorrows and hardships of the Newlyners because of the similarities of his own experience. Forbes saw the way of life in Newlyn as something of lasting value in an increasingly troubled world. It was something that he felt with an almost religious zeal needed to be preserved and recorded for posterity. Though he may at times have glossed over sufferings and hardships, he spared himself no pains in order to produce paintings that conveyed the atmosphere and reality of what he saw. The lengths to which he went have already been discussed. His paintings are so popular today because they show a world where human values and endeavour, in the face of the forces of nature and of poverty, shine out. It is their very wholesomeness which feeds the nostalgia of our own difficult times.

Forbes was the artist *par excellence* of Newlyn. Though his contemporaries produced some superb individual works, to Forbes alone fell the major task of providing a wealth of good and varied paintings of every aspect of life in and around Newlyn. Nor has anyone since then produced such a vast quantity of work devoted to such a small area.

Forbes inherited the best of a conventional upper middle-class upbringing – guts, grit, determination, hard work and discipline. On the other hand it was the very rigidity of these values which had once stood him in such good stead, that prevented him from developing stylistically. By the 1900s Forbes had become the upholder of what was seen as a superseded academic tradition. He became increasingly intolerant of most forms of modern art and on one occasion was recorded as saying, 'And who is this fellow, Matisse?' This may have reflected his fear of change, and his underlying nervous temperament as described in his letters of the 1880s probably prevented his exploring too far beyond the known. Like Laura Knight after him, he had found a ready market for his work, he never tired of painting local subjects, and he saw no need to change. He believed in honest hard work and good solid draughtsmanship, but any exploration of deep inner feeling in his work would have been too painful for him.

Forbes undoubtedly produced his best works in the 1880s though he was still doing good work in the early 1900s. Somehow after about 1912, with notable exceptions, his paintings become increasingly repetitious and, at times, slick. I have suggested that this growing superficiality may be the result of an inability to come to terms with personal loss and a basic inability to change and grow. Beside the work of the Camden Town artists of the early 1900s, Forbes' paintings of those years appear almost illustrative, and they lack depth and subtlety. With a thorough knowledge of French Post-Impressionist painting, the Camden Town artists express a whole new world of freedom, spontaneity, subtle mood and unusual colour – from which Forbes with his more limited ideas was excluded.

Nevertheless, despite a so-called delicate constitution, Forbes possessed a wiriness which enabled him to outlive all his fellows of the first generation by a wide margin. By any standard, his output was phenomenal and he was exhibiting to within a few years of his death at the age of 90 in 1947. A letter from George Clausen towards the end of Forbes' life implies an increasing sense of isolation and aloneness and a harking back to his early successes, notably the *Fish Sale*. One senses that in Clausen's eyes this still remained his greatest work and its underlying magic lingers on, fascinating people as much today as over 100 years ago when it was first painted.

THE BLUE WINDOW (1926)
Stanhope Alexander Forbes
Oil on canvas, 19½ x 23½in (49.5 x 59.5cm)
Christie's

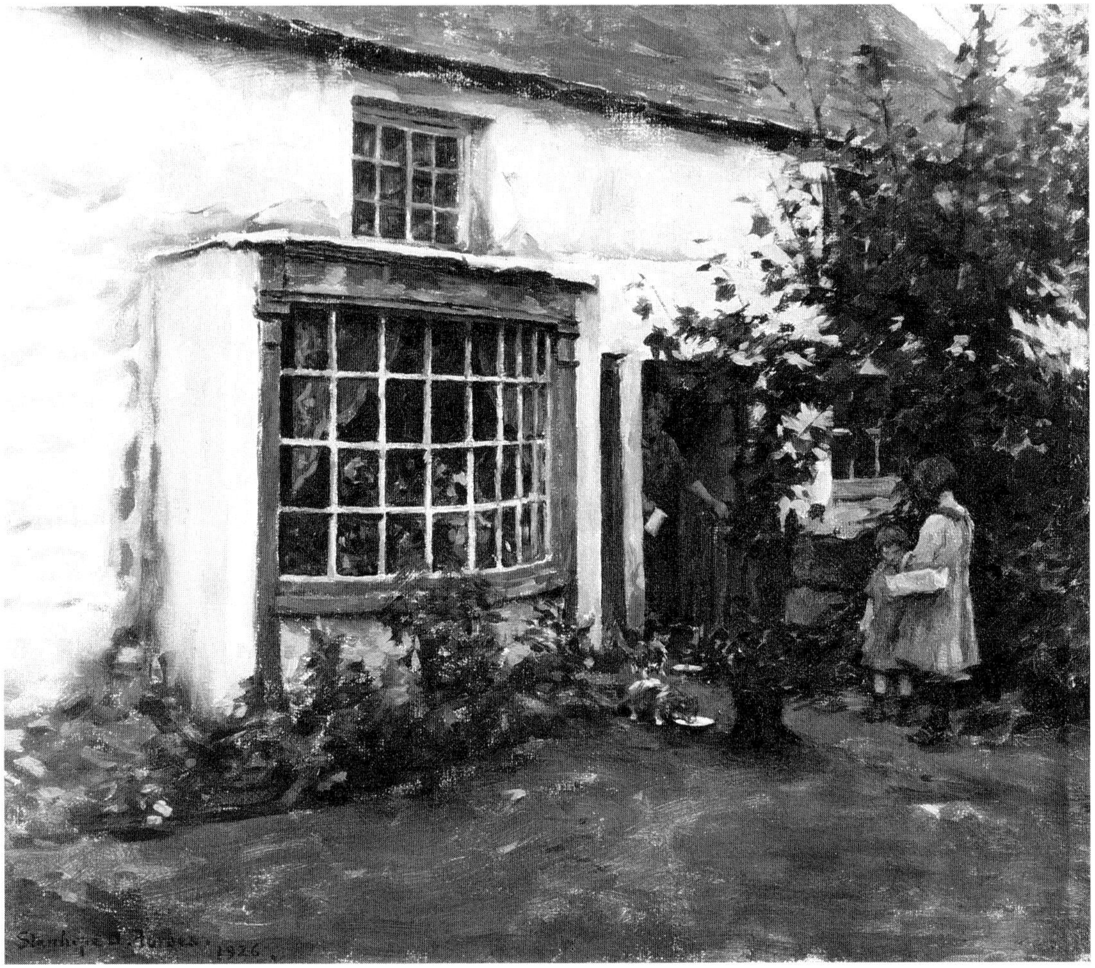

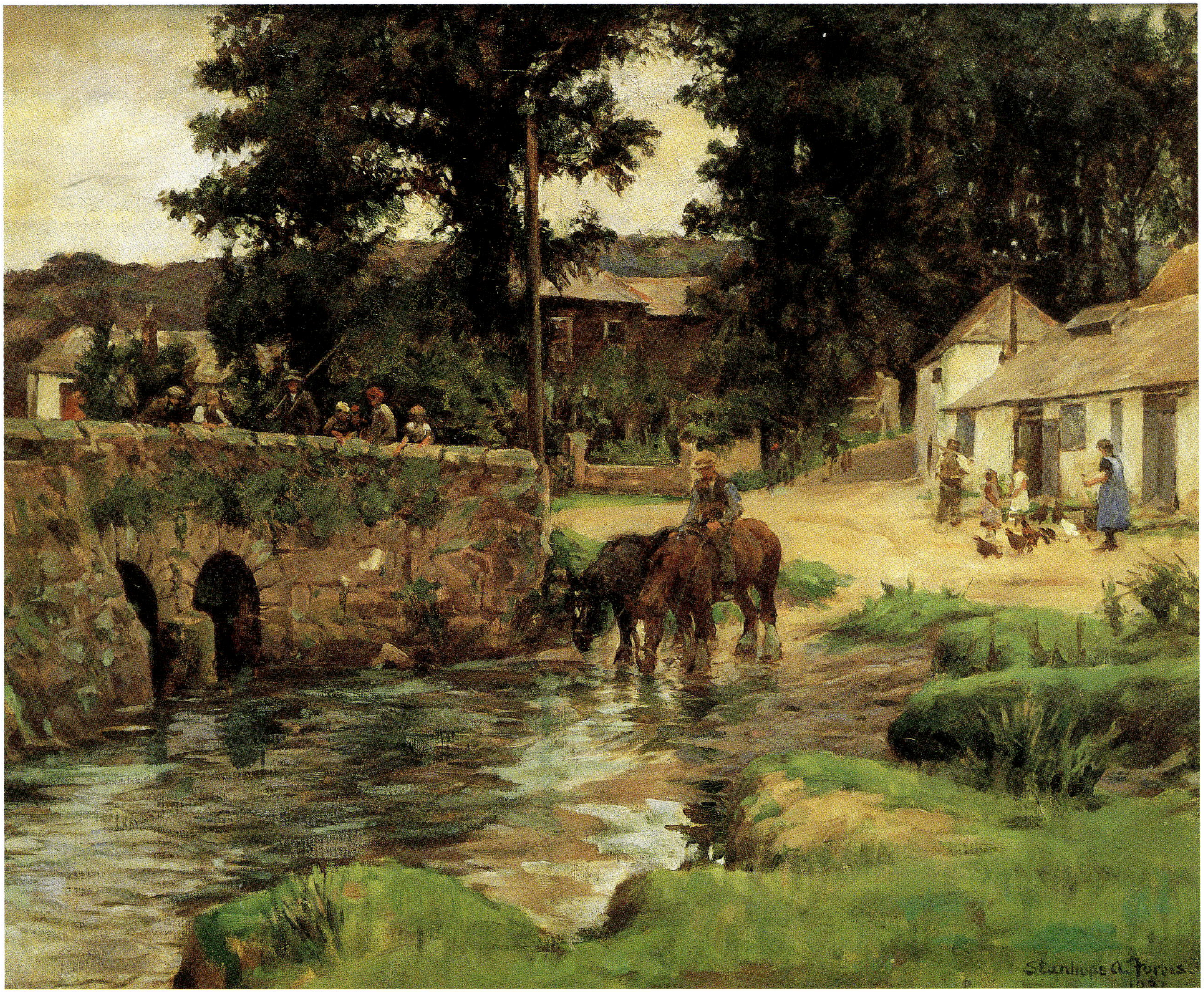

BRIDGE AT GWEEK (1932)
Stanhope Alexander Forbes

Oil on canvas, 24 x 30in (61 x 76cm)
Christie's

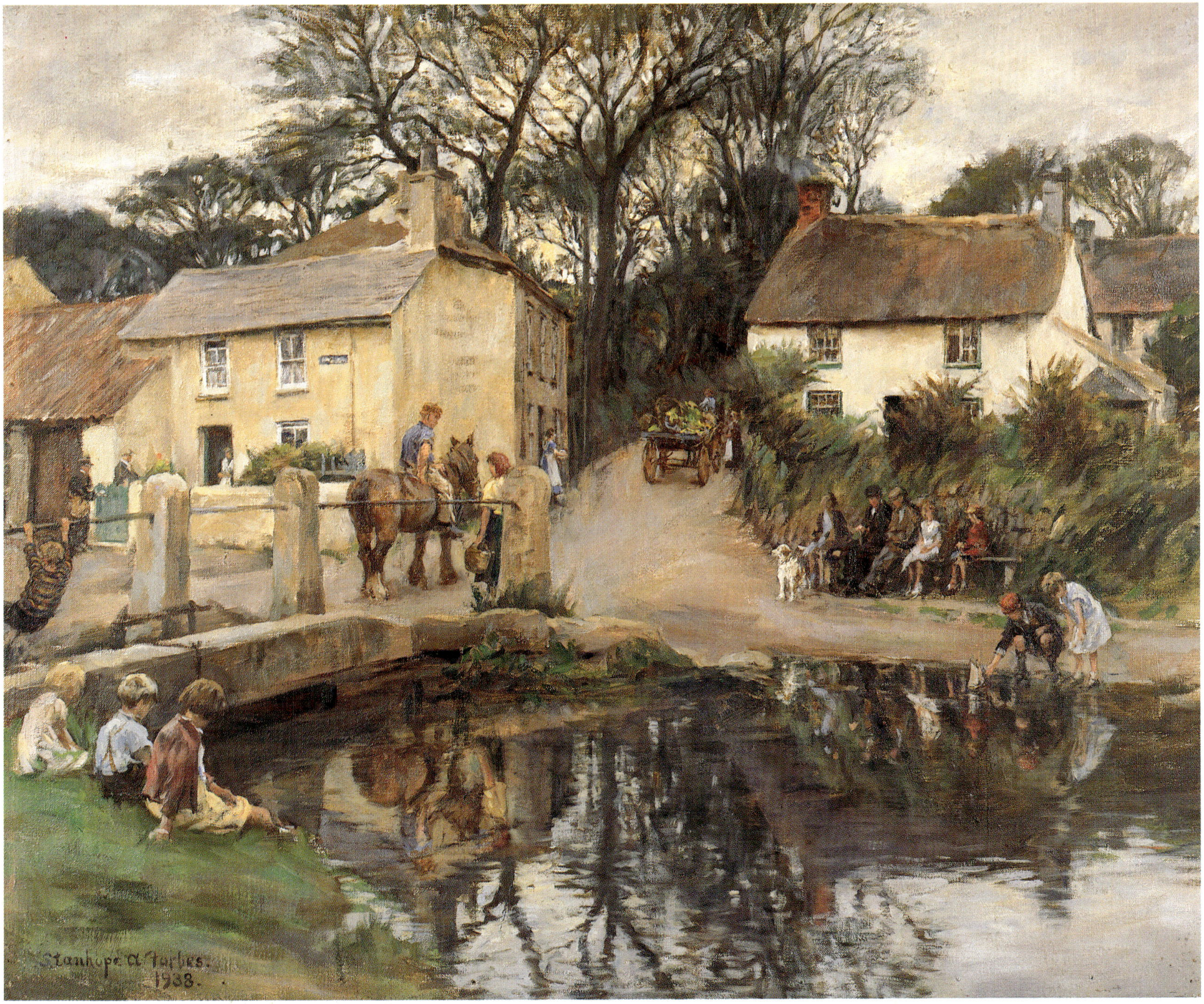

VILLAGE RENDEZVOUS (1938)
Stanhope Alexander Forbes

Oil on canvas, 24½ x 30¾in (78 x 62.5cm)
Plymouth Museum and Art Gallery

INDEX

Numbers in **Bold** indicate illustrations